THE
NOVELS OF
VIRGINIA WOOLF

THE
NOVELS OF
Virginia
Woolf
FACT AND
VISION

Alice van Buren
Kelley

The
University of
Chicago
Press
Chicago
and
London

ALICE VAN BUREN KELLEY received her Ph.D. from the City University of New York in 1972. She is an assistant professor in English literature at the University of Pennsylvania. (1973)

The University of Chicago Press, Chicago 60637
The University of Chicago Press, Ltd., London
© 1971, 1973, by The University of Chicago
All rights reserved. Published 1973
Printed in the United States of America
International Standard Book Number: 0–226–42985–7
Library of Congress Catalog Card Number: 73-77134

TO
R. I. K.

Contents

Introduction

VIRGINIA WOOLF wrote in her diary while working on *The Years,* "What has happened of course is that after abstaining from the novel of fact all these years—since 1919—and *N & D* [*Night and Day*] is dead—I find myself infinitely delighting in facts for a change, and in possession of quantities beyond counting: though I feel now and then the tug to vision, but resist it."[1] It is surprising, given the wide range of criticism of the writings of Virginia Woolf and the number of times that she herself uses the terms "fact" and "vision," that this dichotomy has been so little explored.[2] To follow the trail of these elusive terms and to extract their definitions from her novels is to discover one of the central themes of her work and to find an answer to many of the questions that she asks about life.

The recognition of a dualism in life was certainly not new when Virginia Woolf began to write her novels. Philosophers and theologians from the Orphics to Plato, from Descartes to Spinoza and on into Virginia Woolf's own day had discussed questions of soul and body, mind and matter, reality and appearance, and had devised careful systems around these divisions. But Virginia Woolf herself was no philosopher. She approached the world with the flexibility of the artist and used others' theories as she used her own keen observations of the London scene or a country landscape to support the themes of her art. In other words, she was not intent on proposing a system, but was concerned primarily with describing the universe as she experienced it, with embodying her understanding of life in her novels. Probably the one thinker whose ideas seeped into her novels most frequently was G. E. Moore, the man whose work influenced many of the so-called Bloomsbury group.

Although Moore's theories do not by any means explain the whole of Virginia Woolf's concept of life, they do seem to have introduced her to several useful and ready-made tools for her work. In the first place, Moore's *Principia Ethica* contained the suggestion that the Absolute Good "exists" in a realm divorced from time and space and is not a member of the class of either natural objects or mental facts.[3] Albeit Virginia Woolf never refers to this "self-evident" good, her concept of infinite and eternal vision does resemble Moore's Ideal in that it is not bounded by the finite. Then, too, Moore argues that the material is a necessary constituent of the Ideal[4] and that "if it is said that what exists in time can be only a manifestation of the true reality, it must at least be allowed that the manifestation is another true reality—a good which we really can cause to exist."[5] Virginia Woolf's theory that fact is necessary to vision and that human effort can create a sense of infinite order within the concrete, chaotic world goes hand in hand with Moore's. Third, Moore may well have been instrumental in Virginia Woolf's choosing love, art, and natural beauty as keys to her vision when he wrote: "By far the most valuable things, which we know or can imagine, are states of consciousness, which may be roughly described as the pleasures of human intercourse and the enjoyment of beautiful objects. No one, probably, who has asked himself the question, has ever doubted that personal affection and the appreciation of what is beautiful in Art or Nature, are good in themselves."[6] In spite of the similarities of several of her approaches to Moore's theories, it would be a mistake to overemphasize the influence of philosophy per se on Virginia Woolf's writings; for in order to appreciate the achievement of her art, one must be able to see in it the personal struggle of the artist with the unruly world around her.

Virginia Woolf, as all her writings indicate, was extremely sensitive to the plight of modern man in a seemingly fragmented and unordered world. She saw that the solid foundation of belief that supported earlier authors was no longer available to the modern novelist; that universally accepted "relations of human beings towards each other and towards the universe"[7] no longer existed. Thus life had to be approached afresh, reexamined in a search for a new basis for belief. Once the set laws that used to apply were gone, the paradoxes began to emerge:

> Now is life very solid or very shifting? I am haunted by the two contradictions. This has gone on for ever; will last for ever; goes down to the bottom of the world—this moment I stand on. Also it is transitory, flying, diaphanous. I shall pass like a cloud on the waves. Perhaps it may be that though we change, one flying after another, so quick, so quick, yet we are somehow successive and continuous we human beings, and show the light through. But what is the light?[8]

This search for the light of a deep reality led Virginia Woolf to confront many such paradoxes; for the answer could be found in any number of dissimilar places. "It overwhelms one walking home beneath the stars and makes the silent world more real than the world of speech—and then there it is again in an omnibus in the uproar of Piccadilly,"[9] she wrote. The world of silence and the world of Piccadilly or, to use terms she employs more frequently, the world of vision and the world of fact—this dualistic yet unified world is for ever reexplored in her writing. Thus to examine the terms and see how the two worlds meet and merge in each of her novels is an illuminating way to penetrate to the core of one of Virginia Woolf's central concerns: the search for pattern in the life of man.

The factual world is, most simply, the world of solid objects. It is also the world of the social actions that get one from breakfast to lunch and from lunch to dinner, the events that make one a social being. Within the world of fact, identity is that which distinguishes one, separates one, from others. In extreme cases, and negative cases in the eyes of Virginia Woolf, identity can be limited to this social self until an individual becomes more mannequin than man.

The factual world is also the world of the intellect that perceives the isolation of men and objects and attempts to find order, using only the tools of objective reason. In Virginia Woolf's novels there are two kinds of individuals who inhabit this intellectual world almost exclusively. The first is the man (or woman) who, seeing the disjointed and isolated state of members of his world, attempts to force an order on the unordered and unconnected beings about him. By devising inflexible laws and enforcing them through possession and conversion, such a man imposes even greater limitations on a world already bounded by the inescapable facts of time, death, and isolation—inescapable at least at the level of fact. The second inhabitant of the objective world is the man who devotes his life to a search for truth without illusion, for an intellectually visible order. Often a scholar, he removes himself as much as possible from the actual world around him in order to avoid the distraction of less rational attributes of people and objects —beauty, for example, or ugliness—and attempts to find some solid law in abstractions or classifications. Honest enough to admit that nearly any system he may devise is imperfect, he continues to search, unfortunately often overlooking actual people and things in his life and thus, of necessity, neglecting many important truths.

In the world of vision, physical objects are not bounded, but instead transcend themselves to take on universal significance. Identity in the world of vision is unity, merging, a combining of all things. Only one kind of person can inhabit the visionary world exclusively while alive, and that is the madman whose sole identity is subsumed in the world around him. The world of vision does, however, exist for others. Most often it is discovered in moments of mystical understanding in which a person or object suddenly discloses the existence of a unity that transcends the bounded life of an individual. This sense of boundlessness pervades the lives of those attuned to the world of vision. It also reveals itself in patterns outside the individual life, in patterns of history, of a certain sort of immortality, and in the pattern of accumulated moments of vision.

Thus, to recapitulate, for Virginia Woolf the world of fact

is the world of physical isolation and limitation; the world of vision is the spiritual world of unity and pattern. But neither world can exist without the other if any order or meaning is to be discovered in life. Fact needs vision to help it transcend the limits of objective, physical truth. Vision needs fact as the solid base from which to leap into unity, or, as Virginia Woolf puts it, "the paraphernalia of reality have at certain moments to become the veil through which we see infinity."[10] Vision, to have any meaning, must be seen to function within the disordered factual world.

Within the lifetime of an individual, as Virginia Woolf sees it, fact and vision create a miniature pattern of their own. The child, being unaware of any distinction between himself and the world around him, is in a state not unlike that of vision; but it is an unseeing state and must experience its own "fortunate fall" (a term Virginia Woolf would never use) in order to understand the greater truth of a greater vision. As he grows, the child is forced to realize his own boundaries as he is exposed to the limits of other people and objects and must define himself in relation to them. Only after he has seen his own separateness can he begin to recreate the world of vision that can transcend that isolation.

If vision is total unity with other people and objects, it can never be achieved perfectly within the physical lifetime of a single man: the fact of the body always interferes. Thus death is, in a sense, the realm in which unity is most possible. Death, however, destroys that carefully nurtured self that experience builds, that self that can grasp with the mind or intuition what the spiritual vision reveals. So, although death does make true unity possible, the man who has reached the point at which he can appreciate the vision can never embrace death without pain.

Thematically, then, Virginia Woolf presents a dual world of fact and vision that can function within the life of the individual or create a larger pattern in the realm of history—the life of mankind as a whole. Stylistically, this same pattern of fact and vision grows within her novels in at least two ways. First of all, the pattern emerges through her use of image. Solid objects in Virginia Woolf's novels demonstrate her notion that fact may become vision either directly, by taking on universal meaning for one of her characters in a moment of vision or, indirectly, by recurring throughout one or more works to give a pattern of order and meaning similar to that created by accumulating, recurrent visions in the lives of her men and women. Second, pattern grows out of the use of repeated character types in her different novels. As we encounter again and again the man who searches for order in fact or the woman who sees unity in vision, this repetition mirrors the pattern of history in which one age seeks truth through the vision of faith or of love, the next in the fact of reason or action, the third again in some form of vision, until the emerging pattern of effort creates a whole. So Mr. Ramsey is cousin to Mr. Ambrose, St. John Hirst, William Rodney, and others, while his wife is sister to any number of visionary women from Mrs. Hilbery to Lucy Swithin. By pairing the conflicting approaches to life in each of her works, Virginia Woolf suggests that to combine these types is to see an ordered world in which the paradoxical states are balanced and united.

The definitions of the factual visionary aspects of life that Virginia Woolf treats in her novels[11] are useful, but it is only by seeing these working terms in action that we can fully understand both the problems she sees in the modern world and the solutions she proposes. For while every novel presents the duality of fact and vision in some form, each one emphasizes a different aspect of this relationship or offers some new insight into the reconciliation of the two. Her early novels tend to stress the isolation, the aimlessness, of modern people while offering the balance of fact and vision as a possible cure for this condition. Those written in the middle of her career put less emphasis on generalized separation of individuals in order to give greater care to refining the vision and better defining the factual world. Her last three novels work toward a final vision that, in the face of facts, can offer solace to a world threatened by chaos and disaster.

1

The Voyage Out

ALTHOUGH many critics of Virginia Woolf's novels give little or no attention to her first major work, *The Voyage Out,* those who do generally agree with Jean Guiguet, who says: "Basically, the essence of this first novel, what it is seeking for, and what it is trying to express, is what Virginia Woolf seeks and tries to express in each of her books."[1] Of course few critics can agree as to what this thematic essence actually is, since, as I have indicated above, few approach her work from the same point of view. Most, however, do recognize "the voyage out" as the symbolic theme of the story, and each tries to explain this symbol from his own position.

To Guiguet himself, the voyage is one that takes Rachel from a world of events and society to a world of essences and inner life.[2] There is, however, an important microsociety in Santa Marina, whose inhabitants, like many Londonites, are represented by people such as Mrs. Hughling Elliot, "who depended so implicitly upon one thing following another that the mere glimpse of a world where dinner could be disregarded, or the table moved one inch from its accustomed place, filled her with fears for her own stability."[3] Seeing the contrast between the hotel society of the Elliots and the isolated world of the villa, James Hafley feels that "it is this dispute between the individual and society with which the novel is primarily concerned."[4] For him, Rachel's personal voyage is one in which love helps her to discover herself but to reject the world outside herself; and her tragedy then lies in her inability to unite her own world with the world around her.[5] Thus from Hafley's viewpoint, the essence of the novel can be summed up in the theme: "to see oneself as reality and the social world as illusion . . . is fatal."[6]

Other critics, too, see the conflict of the individual with various elements in the social world as the stormy waters upon which the voyage takes place. To C. B. Cox, then, Rachel's rejection of conventional middle-class Christianity is essential to the main theme, since it symbolizes her movement "away from a limited Victorian upbringing towards wider horizons."[7] Another social struggle is recognized by Edwin Burgum, who feels that the theme is "clearly the hesitation a girl of spirit and breeding felt at yielding in marriage to one of the traditionally dominant sex."[8]

Such socially oriented approaches, although they illuminate one aspect of Virginia Woolf's theme, often overlook the importance of the spiritual meaning of the voyage. "To feel, to love, to live—what do they mean?"[9] These questions, seen by Guiguet as the spur to the inward voyage, have more weight in Woolf's eyes than questions of male dominance or social reality; and several critics have focused their attention on these questions rather than on those of social import. Floris Delattre, for example, sees the central theme of the novel as "l'éclosion tourmentée d'une âme de jeune fille;"[10] while Melvin Friedman's discussion of the novel as "a renewal of the imaginary voyage of the soul"[11] stresses the spiritual quest and finds the key to Rachel's death in her having grown in sensibility to the point at which her soul literally exceeded the bounds of her own person.[12]

Each of these attempts to explain *The Voyage Out* sheds some light on one or more aspects of the work. But a single beam focused on a single object of necessity distorts the objects that surround it. Nevertheless, each new study of the novel, following the voyage from yet another point of view, helps in the struggle eventually to illuminate the whole.

Certainly no one would disagree that Rachel is at the core of *The Voyage Out,* that her personal growth is central to the theme of the novel as a whole. To see this growth as defined in terms of the relationship of fact to vision is to gain new insight not only into this one work, but also into those that follow it. By working through the novel, noting each new aspect of the relationship as it occurs, one comes as close as is possible in a single study to understanding much of Virginia Woolf's purpose.

The first chapter opens with a very unusual description of Helen and Ridley Ambrose, walking together through the streets of London. What makes this description unusual is that from the moment this couple enters the scene, they take on the proportions of gods rather than of man and woman. The clerks and typists who surround them, says Woolf, seem insignificant, "for in comparison with this couple most people looked small . . ." (1). In fact these two seem to be moving in a world of their own:

> . . . some enchantment had put both man and woman
> beyond the reach of malice and unpopularity. In his case
> one might guess from the moving lips that it was thought;
> and in hers from the eyes fixed stonily straight in front of
> her at a level above the eyes of most that it was sorrow (1–2).

Jean Guiguet, overlooking these clues, finds this opening somewhat misleading in seeming to put emphasis on characters who are not the most important in the novel;[13] but as the story progresses, the role of this unusual couple grows clearer. In fact, the key to their symbolic significance can be found in this opening description, a description that labels them the embryonic representatives of fact and vision, who will grow to adulthood in Virginia Woolf's later novels.

What sets Ridley Ambrose apart from others is his devotion to thought, the ordering principle in the factual world. Once he sets himself up in his private room in Santa Marina, the influence of this approach to life becomes immediately obvious in the life of the villa:

> Every one in the house was vaguely conscious that something
> went on behind that door, and without in the least knowing
> what it was, were influenced in their own thoughts by the
> knowledge that if they passed it the door would be shut,

and if they made a noise Mr. Ambrose inside would be disturbed. Certain acts therefore possessed merit, and others were bad, so that life became more harmonious and less disconnected than it would have been had Mr. Ambrose given up editing *Pindar* . . . (200).

If single-sighted adherence to truth has a harmonizing effect from one point of view, it has equal disadvantages from another. Like the fact-driven characters who will follow him, Ridley Ambrose often inflicts pain in his insistence upon speaking the facts. For example, upon meeting Rachel he remarks audibly on her lack of resemblance to her beautiful, graceful mother. His less godly side comes out again in his fear that his work will be "ignored by the entire civilised world"; (111) a fear shared by Mr. Ramsay, who, like other truth-seekers in fact, sees only the decaying effects of factual time. Like others of his type, too, Mr. Ambrose recognizes the isolation of men, and pictures himself as "a commander surveying a field of battle, or a martyr watching the flames lick his toes . . ." (112). So, if he is a god of order, his powers are limited and his life difficult in its isolation. Thus his wife, who is symbolically his opposite, may say in the light of these painful limitations: "If ever Miss Rachel marries . . . pray that she may marry a man who doesn't know his ABC" (27), in other words, a man who is not devoted entirely to the factual search for truth. It will take the far-sighted Rachel, brought to selfhood under the influence of her aunt and uncle, to unite their opposing views by combining fact with vision in her own life.

Helen Ambrose, whose emotion sets her against the logic of her husband, is, in her symbolic role, the goddess who oversees the action of this novel. As she enters the cabin of the *Euphrosyne*, she is described in terms that set her unmistakably among the more-than-human: "Tall, large-eyed, draped in purple shawls, Mrs. Ambrose was romantic and beautiful; not perhaps sympathetic, for her eyes looked straight and considered what they saw" (7–8). Emphasis on her eyes and her clarity of sight has already been established in her initial appearance as she looked over the heads of the little Londoners and "knew how to read the people who were passing her" (4). That this vision sees the ugliness of life as well as the beauty is also made clear in this passage; for as she looks at the tattered poor about her she realizes that "When one gave up seeing the beauty that clothed things, this was the skeleton beneath" (4).

But if, in her greater moments, Helen is an all-seeing goddess, at others she shares the lack of perception common to all the characters in this novel at one time or another. Virginia Woolf has not yet decided to give one character total visionary weight. As ruling deity, Helen can shape Rachel's world to allow the girl to grow, but she has no control over her creation once she sets it going, nor does her vision extend beyond the life of this creation. The extent and the limitations of Helen's sight are best represented by the fact that, after a few days of the voyage have passed, she correctly judges Mr. Pepper as a bore, who is only half alive, while at the same time failing to grasp the depth of Rachel's potential and seeing her as an ordinary, sentimental, "unlicked girl" (18) instead of an incipient visionary. Like that of ordinary mortals, Helen's insight extends only as far as her own vision.

Her total rejection of any sort of ideal or religion marks this visionary limitation, a limitation that will not be common to the rest of Virginia Woolf's visionaries. Even when Rachel turns against the Christianity of Reverend Bax, she recognizes the existence of an ideal that this religion aimed for and missed, while Helen answers Ridley's "Oh, surely, Helen, a little religion hurts nobody," with "I would rather my children told lies" (23). Thus although Helen resembles Mrs. Hilbery, Mrs. Ramsay, and Lucy Swithin in her ability to guide others toward an apprehension of visionary unity, she falls far short of these in her own personal insight. The actual moments of transcendent vision are reserved for Rachel.

If Helen, then, is not goddess of vision, she is creator of the path to vision; and her extraordinary foresight, necessary to one who molds the fortunes of others, extends far enough into the future for her to foresee a tragic ending to the voyage out. She and her husband approach the *Euphrosyne* by rowboat, and as they draw close enough to see the ensign flying, "the blue flag appeared a sinister token, and this the moment for presentiments . . ." (7). Then, as they descend into the cabin of the ship, the first words the other passengers hear from them are " 'On a dark night one would fall down these stairs head foremost,' to which a woman's voice added, 'And be killed' " (7).

It soon becomes evident that this threat of death is associated with Rachel, and as we watch her grow, we are constantly made aware of the fact that her personal spiritual voyage must end in tragedy. David Daiches, in his book *Virginia Woolf,* makes an illuminating comment that may be applied to this nearness of Rachel to death: "Death for this writer was always the illuminator of and commentator on life, so that an adequate insight into any character is only given if he is shown not only living but also in some connection with death."[14] Once the visionary aspect of death is revealed with Rachel's actual dying, all earlier hints of tragedy take on a deeper significance, but they remain tragic in their suggestion that the true voyage to vision cannot end in any other way.

This paradoxically tragic/visionary destination toward which the *Euphrosyne* sails is foreshadowed by an equal number of threatening and favorable presentiments felt by the passengers on board. If at times disaster seems to loom over the horizon, at others exultation is the ruling sensation: "They were free of roads, free of mankind, and the same exhilaration at their freedom ran through them all" (23). So death, too, is both destructive and liberating, and the *Euphrosyne* becomes "a ship passing in the night—an emblem of the loneliness of human life . . ." (99), a symbol of the human voyage toward death and freedom.

Once the ruling deities have been introduced and the vessel boarded for the momentous journey, the voyager can be brought on stage. Our immediate impression of Rachel Vinrace is one of formlessness: "Her face was weak rather than decided, saved from insipidity by the large enquiring eyes; denied beauty, now that she was sheltered indoors, by the lack of colour and definite outline" (14). As she moves away from the strictly bounded world of her Victorian aunts, she, like the ship, is "a bride going forth to her husband, a virgin unknown of men . . ." (29), but she needs to find an identity distinct from the rest of the world before she will be ready to unite herself with another. Although she is technically an adult, Rachel, like most of Virginia Woolf's children, is suspended in that unconscious world of vision in which one is merged with others simply through lack of awareness of any limitations to be transcended. There are signs, however, that she is ready to find an identity in the factual world, and even more important signs that she has the potential to move from that identity into the world of conscious visionary unity.

As Rachel faces the world around her and the people who inhabit that world, she is alive with questions: "Why did they do the things they did, and what did they feel, and what was it all about?" (34). These questions show an awakening to the existence of others if not yet to self, and the mere asking is a beginning of her voyage into reality. As this voyage begins, Rachel has only the puzzle, no solution; yet she does sense an answer that demonstrates her closeness to the greater world of vision: "It appeared that nobody ever said a thing they meant, or ever talked of a feeling they felt, but that was what music was for" (35). Music, the most visionary of all the arts, the most capable of capturing for a moment the unity that underlies human diversity; music is Rachel's tool for building truth. Images that Virginia Woolf uses to describe her music indicate its creative importance: ". . . an invisible line seemed to string the notes together, from which rose a shape, a building" (61); and in fact the visionary powers of this art affect Rachel even before she is aware of the significance of the experience. "Inextricably mixed in dreamy confusion, her mind seemed to enter into communion, to be delightfully expanded and combined with the spirit of the whitish boards on deck, with the spirit of the sea, with the spirit of Beethoven Op. 112, even with the spirit of poor William Cowper there at Olney" (35). As yet, however, this visionary experience of unity is mere dreamy confusion. Rachel needs the sharpness of fact to carve a definite self from her yet unformed being before she can experience the vision in its full intensity. Her face, which reflects her identity, is still only a "smooth unmarked outline" (20).

Rachel's first encounter with this incisive world of fact occurs with the appearance of Mr. and Mrs. Richard Dalloway, and she feels their impact immediately: ". . . she had come to the depressing conclusion, since the arrival of the Dalloways, that her face was not the face she wanted, and in all probability never would be" (41). This sudden, unusual self-awareness is sparked by both Clarissa and Richard, each of whom represents one aspect of the world of society.

Clarissa, like her deeper, older, more visionary self in *Mrs. Dalloway,* possesses that illuminated selfhood that implies her control over her destiny: ". . . she seemed to be dealing with the world as she chose; the enormous solid globe spun round this way and that beneath her fingers" (47); and her entrance into a room always sends "a little flutter like a breath of air" (58) through those who are already there. Such overwhelming presence cannot fail to have some effect on Rachel, whose own selfhood is so unformed. Yet unlike the older Mrs. Dalloway in the later novel, this woman's message is not vision but action, and she serves primarily as a bridge between her husband and Rachel. One of the first facts told us about this Clarissa is that "she photographed Fielding's grave, and let loose a small bird which some ruffian had trapped, 'because one hates to think of anything in a cage where English people lie buried' " (39). No one who remembers the odious Blifil in *Tom Jones* with his hypocritically pious freeing of Sophia's bird can fail to catch the negative note in this element of Clarissa's character. Her excessive reaction to the little poor child, too, suggests a touch of hypocrisy that confirms our suspicions that in this novel her answer is not the ultimate solution: "I should like to stop all the painting and writing and music until this kind of thing exists no longer" (45), she says, a thought directly opposed to Rachel's inchoate beliefs. Here Clarissa's ability to create unity in others is unstressed because her function is to introduce Rachel to the inflexible fact of Richard, a man who stands solidly for fact and action as against vision and intuition. Only by seeing what vision is not can one recognize consciously what it is; only by recognizing what one's self is not, can one form a complete identity and choose one's path toward reality. And if one is defined by one's opposite, the potentially visionary Rachel, feminine and intuitive, will best be defined against a man, a masculine, factual man.

Rachel's first impression of Richard Dalloway, unlike her awareness of the exciting essence of his wife, is of the solidity of his physical being. "She was curiously conscious of his presence and appearance—his well-cut clothes, his crackling shirt-front, his cuffs with blue rings round them, and the square-tipped, very clean fingers, with red stone on the little finger of the left hand" (58). And if the precision of his appearance indicates his allegiance to the objective world, his association with the tools of fact makes this all the clearer: "He seemed to come from the humming oily centre of the machine where the polished rods are sliding, and the pistons thumping . . ." (48). So Rachel, sensing the solid reality of his personality, turns to him for aid in finding out the truth about life. " 'Please tell me—everything.' That was what she wanted to say" (60). So Richard Dalloway proceeds to tell her "everything" in his own terms, terms that begin to make her profoundly aware of their differences. He has cut the working hours of some thousands of Lancashire working girls and is prouder of that fact than he would be of having written Keats and Shelley both. Rachel senses painfully that she is "one of those who write Keats and Shelley" (70). So she attempts to bring her emerging view of life closer to his, and hypothesizes a lonely widow whose mind and affections are untouched by his activities. His answer, ". . . conceive the state as a complicated machine; we citizens are parts of that machine" (72), is irreconcilable with Rachel's image of a lean, black-clothed widow, "gazing out of her window. . . The attempt at communication had been a failure" (72).

The voyage, however, has begun. "The ship was making her way steadily through small waves which slapped her and then fizzled like effervescing water, leaving a little border of bubbles and foam on either side" (23). So, Rachel too is beginning to be marked by her contact with the human waves around her. Then comes the storm, and human contact ceases, leaving people to fall back on their own identities. But Rachel is not yet ready for this. She "had just enough consciousness to suppose herself a donkey on the summit of a moor in a hail-storm, with its coat blown into furrows; then she became a wizened tree, perpetually driven back by the salt Atlantic gale" (78). She is not yet a fully formed human being. Her next direct contact with fact will begin to make her one.

This contact is Richard's kiss, a kiss that makes her suddenly very aware not only of his body, but of her own. The door to selfhood has been opened and "Life seemed to hold infinite possibilities she had never guessed at" (85). Although the Dalloways leave just after this crisis in her life, Rachel has had the experience, and its impact has been terrific: "By this new light she saw her life for the first time a creeping hedged-in thing, driven cautiously between high walls . . ." (91–92). This introduction to sex has its frightening as well as its exciting aspects, and Rachel's initial reaction to her encounter is a horrible nightmare, full of damp tunnels, "with a little deformed man who squatted on the floor gibbering . . ." (86); but fear as well as joy makes the realities of life more clear. Thus her identity has begun to take on form, and she is ready for the tutelage of her aunt.

Helen, extremely interested in her niece's awakening, understands the importance of the encounter with Richard Dalloway. "Her conclusion was that she would very much like to show her niece, if it were possible, how to live, or as she put it, how to be a reasonable person" (94). She begins by saying, " 'So now you can go ahead and be a person on your own account . . .' " (94), and the words work wonders in Rachel's mind. "The vision of her own personality, of herself as a real everlasting thing, different from anything else, unmergeable, like the sea or the wind, flashed into Rachel's mind, and she became profoundly excited at the thought of living" (94–95). By colliding sharply with fact, then having the experience explained to her by her guardian deity, Rachel is ready to begin the second stage of her voyage.

When she first set out on the Atlantic cruise with her father, Rachel began a trip that could have ended back in London where she would have continued as a social being with no life of her own. Only after she had broken through the shell of her chrysalis with the assistance of Richard Dalloway was she ready to complete her voyage of awareness. Helen, seeing that Rachel is ripe for further self-education, makes preparations, both symbolically and practically, for this second phase of the girl's journey; for she is determined that her niece must have all the free rein she needs, away from unyielding social demands, in order that she may define herself and approach life with an awakened consciousness. This symbolic preparation begins when Helen first sits down to her embroidery:

> She chose a thread from the vari-coloured tangle that lay
> in her lap, and sewed red into the bark of a tree, or yellow
> into the river torrent. She was working at a great design
> of a tropical river running through a tropical forest, where
> spotted deer would eventually browse upon masses of fruit,
> bananas, oranges, and giant pomegranates, while a troop
> of naked natives whirled darts into the air. Between the
> stitches she looked to one side and read a sentence about
> the Reality of Matter, or the Nature of Good (30).

It will take many months before the design that was begun at the outset of the voyage is complete, many months before Rachel is ready for the final stage of her journey; but from the moment Helen picks up her needle and assumes the character of goddess, the future seems to unroll in a steady and inevitable flow: "With one foot raised on the rung of a chair, and her elbow out in the attitude for sewing, her own figure possessed the sublimity of a woman's of the early world, spinning the thread of fate . . ." (245–46). Creating pattern out of tangle and weaving the essences of life into the whole, Helen guides Rachel toward the physical jungle where the girl will experience the most crucial event of her life.

When Rachel stands at the threshold of the Santa Marina world that Helen offers her as the next step in her education, images of this river loom large in the girl's mind, and Helen,

by promising that the dream will become fact, persuades
Rachel to leave the ship and continue her voyage out:

> Visions of a great river, now blue, now yellow in the tropical
> sun and crossed by bright birds, now white in the moon,
> now deep in shade with moving trees and canoes sliding out
> from the tangled banks, beset her. Helen promised a river.
> Then she did not want to leave her father. That feeling
> seemed genuine too, but in the end Helen prevailed,
> although when she had won her case she was beset by doubts,
> and more than once regretted the impulse which had
> entangled her with the fortunes of another human
> being (98).

Thus at the outset of the second stage of the voyage, premoni-
tions of disaster again hover below the surface of Helen's mind.
Once the family is settled in the villa, too, another menacing
note is sounded as Mr. Pepper, who more than once has assumed the character of a "malicious old ape" (11), abandons
the private house over a matter of unwashed vegetables and
leaves for the hotel, saying, " 'If you all die of typhoid I won't
be responsible!' " (107).

But this small cloud soon disperses; and Rachel is free to
pursue her own thoughts and wishes as Helen sweeps clear the
path before her. "Among the promises which Mrs. Ambrose
had made her niece should she stay was a room cut off from
the rest of the house, large, private—a room in which she could
play, read, think, defy the world, a fortress as well as a sanc-
tuary" (142). Having spent her entire youth in the strictly
regimented home of her aunts, Rachel needs room to expand
and the option to go out and see life or retreat into herself
instead if she chooses. In the Villa San Gervasio in Santa Marina, Rachel first experiences the luxury of privacy and begins,
as a result, to discover her own identity.

Since personal growth in such an atmosphere is steady but
slow, Virginia Woolf skips quickly over the first few months
of Rachel's adventure and reintroduces the reader to the family some time later. "Three months had made but little difference in the appearance either of Ridley or Rachel; yet a keen

observer might have thought that the girl was more definite and self-confident in her manner than before. Her skin was brown, her eyes certainly brighter, and she attended to what was said as though she might be going to contradict it" (111). When the novel began, Rachel was swayed by the tide of any person she was with because she had no self with which to oppose distasteful ideas or opinions. Her encounter with Richard Dalloway began the shaping process that would slowly create for her a definable selfhood. Now in her private room she collides with fact after fact as she makes her way through any number of books, tempering her reading with forays out into the town of Santa Marina.

> Rachel read what she chose, reading with the curious
> literalness of one to whom written sentences are unfamiliar,
> and handling words as though they were made of wood,
> separately of great importance, and possessed of shapes like
> tables or chairs. In this way she came to conclusions, which
> had to be remodelled according to the adventures of the
> day, and were indeed recast as liberally as any one could
> desire, leaving always a small grain of belief behind
> them (144).

Virginia Woolf could not put more clearly her theory that the individual grows through encounter with the world of fact. Each new object, be it sentence or adventure, must evoke a reaction and that reaction serve to define more clearly the growing outline of the self.

At last Rachel emerges one day into an overwhelming self-awareness that can then proceed into the greater vision in which the definite self becomes one with the world around it, an illuminating experience quite unlike the unconscious unity felt by the undefined child. The experience begins as she sets aside a book she has been reading:

> The landscape outside, because she had seen nothing but
> print for the space of two hours, now appeared amazingly
> solid and clear, but although there were men on the hill
> washing the trunks of olive trees with a white liquid, for the

moment she herself was the most vivid thing in it—an heroic statue in the middle of the foreground, dominating the view (143).

After the sudden reality of her own existence engulfs her, she begins to sense the even greater reality of a life which is larger than space or time:

> She was next overcome by the unspeakable queerness of the fact that she should be sitting in an arm-chair, in the morning, in the middle of the world. Who were the people moving in the house—moving things from one place to another? And life, what was that? It was only a light passing over the surface and vanishing, as in time she would vanish, though the furniture in the room would remain. Her dissolution became so complete that she could not raise her finger any more, and sat perfectly still, listening and looking always at the same spot. It became stranger and stranger. She was overcome with awe that things should exist at all. . . . She forgot that she had any fingers to raise. . . . The things that existed were so immense and so desolate (145).*

Here Rachel has reached an important plateau in her climb toward full vision, but she has achieved this level within herself alone and only as a kind of abstraction. It still remains for her to define herself by, then unite herself to, actual people in the social world before she will have come to her final destination.

Because Santa Marina is only a microcosm, most of the people there must act as representatives of a larger class. The man who will serve as the sharp-cutting edge of intellectual fact against whom Rachel must measure herself is St. John Hirst, who, according to Terence Hewet, has "a mind like a torpedo . . . aimed at falsehood" (361). When the reader first makes Mr. Hirst's acquaintance, St. John is reading, but not with Rachel's exploratory instinct. "As he read he knocked the ash automatically, now and again, from his cigarette and

* The suspension points here are Virginia Woolf's, to indicate a break in thought, not ellipses indicating an omitted word or phrase.

turned the page, while a whole procession of splendid sentences entered his capacious brow and went marching through his brain in order" (121). Helen, upon meeting and talking to him, recognizes immediately that his is the orderly mind to which Rachel must be exposed in order for her to continue to grow; and she asks that he assist Rachel in her self-education. Helen appreciates the fact that "He took her outside this little world of love and emotion. He had a grasp of facts" (373). Yet if she sees St. John's merits, she also recognizes his limitations and regrets them:

> . . . she was thinking of the clever, honest, interesting young men she knew, of whom Hirst was a good example, and wondering whether it was necessary that thought and scholarship should thus maltreat their bodies, and should thus elevate their minds to a very high tower from which the human race appeared to them like rats and mice squirming on the flat (242).

Thus, although St. John may test Rachel successfully in the realm of fact, he is too detached physically and mentally to accompany her in any way into the world of vision. As his closest friend laughingly puts it: " 'Nothing moves Hirst . . . unless it were a transfinite number falling in love with a finite one . . .' " (166).

And so at the mountain picnic St. John Hirst, with the tools of fact, begins to force Rachel into articulating and defining her beliefs about herself and the world around her. " 'You believe in a personal God?' Hirst demanded, turning round and fixing her with his eyeglasses. 'I believe—I believe,' Rachel stammered, 'I believe there are things we don't know about, and the world might change in a minute and anything appear' " (168). Each time she slips into some vagueness of thought or speech, Hirst turns on her with " 'What d'you mean?' " (237). At first her reaction to this treatment is awe, then, as she gains more self-confidence under his strict tutelage, she becomes angry. The peak of this stage comes at the hotel dance as Hirst considers whether or not to lend Rachel his Gibbon: " 'It's awfully difficult to tell about women,' " he says to her, " 'how much, I mean, is due to lack of training, and how much is native incapacity. I don't see myself why you shouldn't understand—only I suppose you've led an absurd life until now—you've just walked in a crocodile, I suppose, with your hair down your back' " (180–81). To see the bare, cold facts of her previous life set before her with no compromise makes her furious, and her immediate reaction is to reach out for something to confirm her belief that there is more to life than bald fact. " 'There are trees,' she said aloud. Would the trees make up for St. John Hirst? She would be a Persian princess far from civilisation, riding her horse upon the mountains alone, and making her women sing to her in the evening, far from all this, from the strife and men and women . . ." (181). But as she becomes accustomed to St. John's method she no longer flees into dreams away from men but instead appreciates him for his courage and uncompromising devotion to truth while pitying him "as one pities those unfortunate people who are outside the warm mysterious globe full of changes and miracles . . ." (361).

If Hirst misses the spiritual truths that pervade life, he is keenly perceptive about factual affairs. His early conversation with Terence Hewet in their hotel room sets these two kinds of truth against each other: " '. . . that's where we differ,' said Hewet. 'I say everything's different. No two people are in the least the same. Take you and me now.' 'So I used to think once,' said Hirst. 'But now they're all types. Don't take us,— take this hotel. You could draw circles round the whole lot of them, and they'd never stray outside' " (123). The truth in Hirst's point of view is substantiated by an authorial comment some pages later: ". . .by this time the society at the hotel was divided so as to point to invisible chalk-marks such as Mr. Hirst had described . . ." (175). And if he is not able to participate in the more visionary view of life, he can appreciate its significance objectively. Not long before Rachel dies, after she and Terence have become engaged, St. John admits his understanding of a vision that his insistence on pure fact will not let him share:

"It was here we sat, and you talked nonsense, and Rachel made little heaps of stones. I, on the other hand, had the whole meaning of life revealed to me in a flash." He paused for a second, and drew his lips together in a tight little purse. "Love," he said. "It seems to me to explain everything. So, on the whole, I'm very glad that you two are going to be married" (382).

This rare instance in Woolf's novels of fact fully recognizing the value of vision, indicates the importance of Hirst's role as both goad to Rachel's growth and perceptive spectator of the outcome. It also enables him to understand the visionary implications of the pattern with which the book ends.

Terence Hewet, the man who can bring Rachel's personal growth to fruition through the visionary power of love, is linked symbolically to her at his first appearance.

"The truth of it is that one is never alone, and one never is in company," he concluded.

"Meaning?" said Hirst.

"Meaning? Oh, something about bubbles—auras— what d'you call 'em? You can't see my bubble; I can't see yours; all we see of each other is a speck, like the wick in the middle of that flame. The flame goes about with us everywhere; it's not ourselves exactly, but what we feel; the world is short [*sic*], or people mainly; all kinds of people. . . . And supposing my bubble could run into some one else's bubble——"

"And they both burst?" put in Hirst.

"Then—then—then—" pondered Hewet, as if to himself, "it would be an e—nor—mous world . . ." (125).

Rachel, too, looks for the spiritual uniting of two people and sees the event in terms of bubbles. During her abortive union with Richard Dalloway, she sits stirring her tea round and round; "the bubbles which swam and clustered in the cup seemed to her like the union of their minds" (60). And Terence's picture of the world as a great teetotum that collects everything into itself (124) is not unlike Rachel's semiarticulated idea that "if one went back far enough, everything perhaps was intelligible; everything was in common; for the mammoths who pastured in the fields of Richmond High Street had turned into paving stones and boxes full of ribbon, and her aunts" (73). Both Rachel and Terence tend toward the ill-defined boundaries that characterize vision; both grow under the unwinking eye of the truth-seeker Hirst; and together, with his help and that of Helen (whom Terence sees as standing out from others like a great stone woman [157]) they can find in unity an answer to their mutual awareness of the uncertainty of the world.

The fact that their unity will end in death is revealed as the incipient tragedy of the novel almost as soon as it is hinted that they will fall in love. Just before leaving Hirst for the night after their theoretical discussion about life, Terence reads aloud the following poem:

> I speak as one who plumbs
>   Life's dim profound,
> One who at length can sound
>   Clear views and certain.
> But—after love what comes?
>   A scene that lours,
> A few sad vacant hours,
>   And then, the Curtain (127).

Seen in the context of what is to come, these lines sum up Rachel's voyage from quest to definition to love and finally to death.

But love is still far from the minds of both the persons concerned. There must be further preparation, false starts, and retreats before the delicate bridge can be forged between them. Two other characters, peripheral to the central action, take the first step by falling in love themselves and thus setting the thoughts of all who are acquainted with them on the power of love. Susan Warrington and Arthur Venning, although their love for each other soon grows a hard shell of limited domesticity, experience for a moment the visionary possibilities inherent in their intimacy. At the instant of their engagement, Susan becomes conscious of an "excitement . . . which seemed not only to lay bare something in her, but in the trees and the sky . . ." (161); while Arthur "looked as if he were trying to put things seen in a dream beside real things" (161). Unfortunately, neither has the insight to keep the vision alive, so that before long the exhilaration dies and their intimacy dwindles to the breakfast-table variety, manifested in Susan's trotting after Arthur, urging him to put on a sweater.

Nevertheless, love has been introduced; and before long Rachel and Terence begin the subtle, formal dance steps of courtship. Because they share a general uncertainty about the less tangible aspects of life, they both attempt to use solid facts as an entrance to intimacy. Terence begins by describing his family, Rachel by presenting a sketch of her aunts: "They are small, rather pale women . . . very clean . . . They are always going to church. They tidy their drawers a good deal" (165). But no matter how much the family circle may influence one's life, no one can be defined by his aunts. Communication, as Woolf sees it, is always exceptionally difficult, especially the communicating of the self:

> We all indulge in the strange, pleasant process called thinking, but when it comes to saying, even to some one opposite, what we think, then how little we are able to convey! The phantom is through the mind and out of the window before we can lay salt on its tail, or slowly sinking and returning to the profound darkness which it has lit up momentarily with a wandering light.[15]

So it will take many unsatisfactory efforts before Rachel and Terence can begin to talk to each other in earnest.

At the hotel dance in honor of Susan and Arthur's engagement, the perils and pleasure of sharing oneself with another lead Terence and Rachel to their first important encounter. It is here that Hirst confronts Rachel with his unflattering picture of her life, and she, still vibrating with anger, bursts out with her momentary view of the relationships between men and women: " 'It's no good; we should live separate; we cannot understand each other; we only bring out what's worst' " (182). In spite of the tone of this statement, the fact that she has shared her emotion with Terence seems to unite them far better than any number of careful and objective self-portraits. And if emotion begins to build the bridge, music, already established as a visionary force, continues the process. After the musicians have left and Rachel has stopped improvising dance tunes for the couples who remain, she sits at the piano playing Bach to herself and a small audience of her friends. "They sat very still as if they saw a building with spaces and columns succeeding each other rising in the empty space. Then they began to see themselves and their lives, and the whole human life advancing very nobly under the direction of the music" (196). At the dance, then, emotion and music " 'say all the things one can't say oneself' " (197) and unite those who are factually separate from one another.

Although the events at the dance have done no more than allow the seed of love to be planted, Rachel's new closeness to Terence and others leads her nearer to vision and enables her to experience one of those visionary moments common to Woolf's enlightened characters. On the morning after the dance, Rachel wanders aimlessly and dreamily with no goal in mind.

So she might have walked until she had lost all knowledge of her way, had it not been for the interruption of a tree, which, although it did not grow across her path, stopped her as effectively as if the branches had struck her in the face. It was an ordinary tree, but to her it appeared so strange that it might have been the only tree in the world. Dark was the trunk in the middle, and the branches sprang here and there, leaving jagged intervals of light between them as distinctly as if it had but that second risen from the ground. Having seen a sight that would last her for a lifetime, and for a lifetime would preserve that second, the tree once more sank into the ordinary ranks of trees, and she was able to seat herself in its shade and to pick the red

flowers with the thin green leaves which were growing
beneath it (204–5).

Here a factual object has suddenly transcended its physical
boundaries to take on gigantic and symbolic importance; it
has stopped the flow of time, frozen into eternity the tumultuous life represented by the dance, and has given Rachel another
glimpse of the timeless, universal world of vision. Bernard
Blackstone finds no illuminating "spots of time" in *The Voyage Out*,[16] but surely this moment has all the true visionary
import of the miniature revelations in Woolf's later novels.
Nor is it unique in this work, as later instances of revelation
will show. The significance of this particular tree-vision is
emphasized by the fact that Helen, in her capacity as seer, has
foretold the importance of the trees. Before setting out on her
walk, Rachel surveys the landscape around her and takes special note of "those trees which Helen had said it was worth the
voyage out merely to see" (204). Then, while sitting under
the wonderful tree, she reads a few random sentences in Gibbon that reveal a further meaning to her vision. The words
seem "to drive roads back to the very begining of the world, on
either side of which the populations of all times and countries
stood in avenues, and by passing down them all knowledge
would be hers, and the book of the world turned back to the
very first page" (206). The vision extends from the beginning
of time to eternity.

The fact that these visions of unity are no longer merely
abstractions is quickly revealed by the turn Rachel's thoughts
next take.

"What is it to be in love?" she demanded, after a long
silence; each word as it came into being seemed to shove
itself out into an unknown sea. Hypnotised by the wings of
the butterfly, and awed by the discovery of a terrible
possibility in life, she sat for some time longer. When the
butterfly flew away, she rose, and with her two books beneath
her arm returned home again, much as a soldier prepared
for battle (207).

Thus her closeness to others at the dance has opened the way to vision; and the vision has pointed to love as the possibility of achieving vision in life. And because the butterfly was present at Rachel's realization of love, it seems to share in her awakening until moths and butterflies come to symbolize her enlightened spirit throughout the rest of the novel.

If the dance has planted the vision of love in Rachel's mind, it has done the same for Terence who wanders up to the villa the next evening, overhears Rachel and Helen speaking, and then returns to the hotel repeating half-consciously as he walks, " 'Dreams and realities, dreams and realities, dreams and realities . . .' " (222); and, like Rachel, recognizing that there is danger in bringing the dream world of love into the factual world of life. This dangerous aspect of love appeared symbolically just before he set out for the villa, for in the main sitting room of the hotel, the flight of a large moth about the lights provoked cries of " 'Some one ought to kill it!' " (216) from several young women. This symbol of the moth as the struggling spirit of the visionary is not uncommon in Woolf and reappears in *Jacob's Room* and "The Death of the Moth."

Once Rachel and Terence resolve to brave the dangers and learn to know each other, they begin to talk about things that matter very much not only to them but also to Virginia Woolf. Terence, for example, reveals to Rachel his dream of becoming a novelist and shows her that he (like his creator) is concerned with capturing the vision in his art. " 'I want to write a novel about Silence,' " he says, " 'the things people don't say' " (262). He perceives that Rachel, with her music, is attempting much the same thing and says

> "What I want to do in writing novels is very much
> what you want to do when you play the piano, I expect. . . .
> We want to find out what's behind things, don't we?—
> Look at the lights down there . . . scattered about anyhow.
> Things I feel come to me like lights. . . . I want to combine
> them. . . . Have you ever seen fireworks that make figures?
> . . . I want to make figures" (266).

But for all the importance of sharing ideas about vision, the vision itself is not complete until love has been established, and each meeting that ends before this can take place seems to end in interruption. Love, however, does not come easily, and Rachel in particular has several hurdles to overcome before she can achieve it. First of all she needs to understand more clearly the proper way to approach the vision. This understanding comes one Sunday morning at church, when, by seeing how far short the limited Christianity of her fellow-worshipers falls in trying to achieve true adoration and true vision, she realizes that "All round her were people pretending to feel what they did not feel, while somewhere above her floated the idea which they could none of them grasp, which they pretended to grasp, always escaping out of reach, a beautiful idea, an idea like a butterfly" (278). By learning from the bad example of others, Rachel sees that the vision in any form cannot be possessed, clung to, limited. Having abandoned religion as a means of reaching the truth, she is lost for a moment and must find some new method to employ. That afternoon in the hotel, hoping that "each new person might remove the mystery which burdened her" (308), she examines the answers provided by the other women there, but finds none of them satisfactory. Evelyn's desire for activity on the social level she has already experienced and rejected in Richard Dalloway. Miss Allan's kindly offer of ginger, books, and conversation is no help; for in her well-meaning way she only points out diversity when Rachel desires unity. "As they walked down the passage they passed many pairs of boots and shoes, some black and some brown, all side by side, and all different, even to the way in which they lay together. 'I always think that people are so like their boots," said Miss Allan" (314). Only the exuberant Alice Flushing with her plan of a river expedition that would include Terence brings any light into the darkness, but the momentous nature of the trip is as yet invisible to Rachel. As the afternoon draws to a close and she has not yet recognized love as the path to her vision, Rachel releases her frustration in an attack upon Helen, which Helen rather enjoys since it indicates the activity going on in her niece's mind.

Terence, meanwhile, is fighting his own battles, trying to see whether love can avoid solidifying into the fossilized affection of Susan and Arthur. At first all his mental images show married people "walled up in a warm firelit room" and single people as "active in an unlimited world" (295). This leads him to consider love without marriage; but this separation of vision from fact, of love from the real world, is unsatisfactory. At last in a moment of exultation he recognizes that he and Rachel could both love each other and maintain their individual freedom as well. He is now ready for the jungle expedition in which their love will flower.

As Helen watches love begin to bud between Rachel and Terence, she sees that her days as tutor and guide are drawing to a close; and as Rachel slips out of her protective care, visions of disaster begin to spring up thick and fast. "Her sense of safety was shaken, as if beneath twigs and dead leaves she had seen the movement of a snake. It seemed to her that a moment's respite was allowed, a moment's make-believe, and then again the profound and reasonless law asserted itself, moulding them all to its liking, making and destroying" (322). In spite of her fears of the outcome of the river voyage, Helen agrees to go, and she, with Rachel and Terence, St. John and the Flushings, enters a world in which the vision is all reality. This visionary quality of the jungle river is evident from the uniting of all time in its landscape.

> Since the time of Elizabeth very few people had seen the river, and nothing had been done to change its appearance from what it was to the eyes of the Elizabethan voyagers. The time of Elizabeth was only distant from the present time by a moment of space compared with the ages which had passed since the water had run between those banks, and the green thickets swarmed there, and the small trees had grown to huge wrinkled trees in solitude (323).

Here in her embroidery world where the winding river leads the boat into the "heart of the night" (325) of vision, Helen watches Rachel and Terence accept love as the only realistic way to unity in the objective world and feels the presentiments of disaster grow stronger. "A falling branch, a foot that slips, and the earth has crushed them or the water drowned them. Thus thinking, she kept her eyes anxiously fixed upon the lovers, as if by doing so she could protect them from their fate" (350). But once the two have declared their love, Rachel has passed beyond Helen's guardianship.

After their return to the life of hotel and villa, Rachel and Terence continue to fulfill each other in the free exchange of intimacy. "In return for what he could tell her she brought him . . . curiosity and sensitiveness of perception" (367) in a miniature union of fact and vision that Virginia Woolf will expand in her later novels. But this union is never uninterrupted—only for brief moments does the vision become reality. These moments, however, are far reaching in their significance. As Rachel contemplates her new sense of direction, she begins to see a pattern that underlies everything. "When she looked back she could see that a meaning of some kind was apparent in the lives of her aunts, and in the brief visit of the Dalloways whom she would never see again, and in the life of her father" (385). Love gives her a sense of independence, of calm, of certainty, until for a moment she feels as though she has reached the ultimate point of vision: "For the moment she was as detached and disinterested as if she had no longer any lot in life, and she thought that she could now accept anything that came to her without being perplexed by the form in which it appeared" (385). Terence, too, finds a new order in life through love; but invariably, just as the two discover an all-pervading pattern, something shatters the vision: they move to the mirror to see reflected the immensity of their unity, but "instead of being vast and indivisible they were really very small and separate, the size of the glass leaving a large space for the reflection of other things" (371). Each time that this happens they feel that "they could never love each other sufficiently to overcome all these barriers, and they could never be satisfied with less" (371).

There is only one way for them to stop the repeated destruction of their vision, and that is for one or both of them to escape the factual world in which the vision can exist only sporadically. Because it is Rachel whose voyage to vision is at the heart of this novel, it is she who must escape; and she can do so only by dying. Her river journey has led her to the point at which she sees the full power of love and vision, and her refusal to accept anything less can lead only to death. But having developed in the course of her voyage out a definite self that enabled her to love, she cannot experience the dissolution of that self without some fear. Just as her first step toward self-hood evoked a nightmare of restriction and deformity, so her final step toward unity calls forth an almost identical dream: she "found herself walking through a tunnel under the Thames, where there were little deformed women sitting in archways playing cards, while the bricks of which the wall was made oozed with damp . . ." (404). Just before she dies, how-ever, her fear leaves her, and her actual dying creates for both her and Terence the moment of perfect vision:

> . . . they seemed to be thinking together; he seemed to
> be Rachel as well as himself; and then he listened again;
> no, she had ceased to breathe. So much the better—this
> was death. It was nothing; it was to cease breathe. It was
> happiness; it was perfect happiness. They had now what they
> had always wanted to have, the union which had been
> impossible while they lived. . . . It seemed to him that their
> complete union and happiness filled the room with rings
> eddying more and more widely (431).

Rachel has completed her voyage out and has become one with her vision. But life does not stop when one life ends or the pattern would be broken, the vision denied. So Terence must face the world alone as a new day dawns with Rachel dead. Ridley will continue his struggle with facts, including the fact of death, as he marches up and down reciting signifi-cantly,

> They wrestled up, they wrestled down,
> They wrestled sore and still:
> The fiend who blinds the eyes of men,
>   That night he had his will (427).

Mrs. Flushing will refuse to submit to dark and nothingness; and life at the hotel and villa will go on without Rachel. Yet, true to the unity of the vision, she is gone only in fact. The moth still flutters about the lamps in the lounge, and Evelyn Murgatroyd, in her own moment of vision, feels Rachel's presence in the room with her and senses the unity of the factual world with the unseen world beyond. As the novel ends, St. John Hirst, whose objective mind can see the vision even though he cannot experience it, sits watching the pattern reform: "The movements and the voices seemed to draw together from different parts of the room, and to combine themselves into a pattern before his eyes; he was content to sit silently watching the pattern build itself up, looking at what he hardly saw" (456).

So *The Voyage Out* portrays the individual struggle of one girl to work her way through the seemingly conflicting worlds of fact and vision, while presenting that single struggle as part of a pattern in which every person living must make his own voyage out, some finding the vision before they die as did Rachel, some content to do battle with the puzzle of fact. As Virginia Woolf described this novel when writing to Lytton Strachey, "I wanted to give the feeling of a vast tumult of life, as various and disorderly as possible, which should be cut short a moment by the death, and go on again—and the whole was to leave a sort of pattern, and be somehow controlled."[17]

2

Night and Day

In *The Voyage Out* Virginia Woolf moved a young girl out
of the tumultuous London world and into a more peaceful
symbolic society, then traced her spiritual growth from unconscious unity with others to conscious vision, a development
made possible by participation in the factual world and the
formation of a defined self. In *Night and Day* she again tackles
the problem of joining fact and vision, but this time she
determines to achieve her aim in London where a sense of infinite unity is continually threatened by social restriction. By
placing her characters in this world of tea parties, offices, and
daily regimentation, she makes it more difficult for them to
apprehend the vision, and some critics feel that her mystical
message is obscured by its worldly setting. David Daiches, for
example, seeing the contradiction between the vision Woolf
attempted to present and the factual world in which she
wrapped it, finds *Night and Day* "a heavy, protracted piece of
work with a quite glaring disparity between form and content."[1] Yet even in her most visionary novels Virginia Woolf
insisted upon the need for fact to give direction to vision.
Because she felt that she was dealing with a real problem, not
merely a literary toy, she tried to present it as it actually
existed in the world around her.

Because *Night and Day* is concerned with the fact/vision
duality as it exists in a social setting, it is not surprising that
many critics approach the work either as a novel of social
comment or as one in which the central struggle is not between
vision and fact but between the private individual and the

public world. Irma Rantavaara, for example, says: "I find the real interest to lie in the fact that it conveys the atmosphere of security and culture in the respectable middle-class intellectual family of pre-war London and describes the gradual change into a disintegrating society where the younger generation begins to make their own way."[2] Admittedly, this social change exists on the surface of the novel, but such a view ignores the fact that as the story draws to a close, one of the oldest characters, Mrs. Hilbery, is the person who untangles the problems of the young, showing as "progressive" an attitude as anyone in the book. Dorothy Brewster, recognizing a deeper level to the social theme, feels that "the *night* is the inner, the *day* the outer, in the perpetual interplay between the self and its environment"[3]; and C. B. Cox, working along the same lines, sees this central question haunting Katharine and Ralph, the two lovers: "How can they connect the inner world of the imagination with the outer world of society?"[4] This relationship of the outer world to the inner is at the core of James Hafley's approach to the novel as well. He sees *Night and Day* as being "concerned for the most part with the 'organized society' of London, whose codes and conventions no longer spring from the individuals who compose it, but rather are superimposed upon them. Here the individual must deny himself if he is to make peace with the dead organism of his society."[5] It is true, as all these views indicate, that society, the need to earn a living or keep a house, does hamper the progress of the inner man; but there is more to *Night and Day* than a struggle between social obligations or limitations and personal fulfillment. There is the vision, as no one who watches the progress of Mrs. Hilbery can deny. And vision, as we have seen before, goes beyond the personality into a greater world.

Jean Guiguet, whose treatment of Virginia Woolf's novels shows a great deal of perception, sweeps aside "the social setting, the teas and dinners in Cheyne Walk or at Stogdon House, at the Denhams', the meetings in the suffragette's office or at Mary's" as merely "a background of illusory realism, against which, in the foreground, the human drama is played out."[6] Whether or not this realism is "illusory," it is certainly not Virginia Woolf's central concern. It is there to provide the challenging circumstances in which the problem of reconciling fact to vision must be worked out. Those critics who, like Guiguet, set aside the social element to puzzle over the deeper questions that this novel raises, see more intangible themes at its base. Bernard Blackstone emphasizes "the nature of freedom and the nature of love"[7] at the heart of *Night and Day,* and recognizes the power of love to enable two minds to "share the vision of reality which hitherto had seemed open only to the solitary mind."[8] J. K. Johnstone, attacking another angle of this same approach, sees "the difficulty of communicating, the difficulty of knowing even those closest to us"[9] as the major theme of the novel. These two critics see either the fact of separateness or the power of love to unite the divided, but neither goes that next step to recognize love as only a symbolic example of the unity that vision shows to be infinite.

In *Night and Day* Virginia Woolf goes further than she did in her earlier work to make each of her characters representative of some aspect of fact or vision. Several critics, although not seeing the factual/visionary element in this technique, have recognized the divisions and have presented their own interpretations of the characters. Harvena Richter, for example, looks at the five young people in the novel as constituting "differing aspects of the masculine and feminine worlds."[10] James Hafley, who includes Mrs. Hilbery among the symbolic five, assigns each one a specific role: Katharine is creative and purposeful reason, Ralph creative emotion; Mrs. Hilbery is uncreative emotion, William uncreative reason; and Mary, the last of the five, is reason denying emotion.[11] To categorize the characters according to Hafley's scheme forces one to overlook the fact that Mrs. Hilbery's ruling vision is far greater than mere emotion and that Ralph and Katharine are both noteworthy for embracing conflicting views of life. When one remembers that "Dreams and Realities" was the original title for this novel,[12] to approach the work as a study of vision and fact becomes both justifiable and potentially enlightening.

If there is a goddess of vision in this novel—for gods and

goddesses are rare in the factual world—she is Mrs. Hilbery, a woman with a never-failing sense of unity that defies time, space, and the barriers between individuals or generations. Herbert Marder senses her talent, but sees it only as "the fine discrimination of feelings and the ability to bring about adjustments in personal relations."[13] These she has, of course; but the sum of her being is far greater than a composite of "the domestic arts."[14] Mrs. Hilbery is a visionary, first and last. That she is not mad or suicidal like the rest of Woolf's pure visionaries is partly because her creator has not yet begun to feel that total vision is impossible in the factual world; it is also because Mrs. Hilbery has a grasp of fact, although that grasp is of the visionary kind that does not see objects or actions as self-contained but as extending beyond external limits to weave themselves into a whole. As a woman who lives completely in the world of vision, then, she is not mad; but she plays, in part, the fool—the wise fool who sees the world clearly but with an extraworldly eye:

> She was beautifully adapted for life in another planet. But the natural genius she had for conducting affairs there was of no real use to her here. Her watch, for example, was a constant source of surprise to her, and at the age of sixty-five she was still amazed at the ascendancy which rules and reasons exerted over the lives of other people. She had never learnt her lesson, and had constantly to be punished for her ignorance. But as that ignorance was combined with a fine natural insight which saw deep whenever it saw at all, it was not possible to write Mrs. Hilbery off among the dunces; on the contrary, she had a way of seeming the wisest person in the room.[15]

As a visionary, then, she is infinitely wise. She recognizes the false limitation of clock time, saying, " 'After all, what *is* the present? Half of it's the past, and the better half, too, I should say . . .' " (7). She sees that objects are not mere inanimate shapes: " 'Dear things!' she exclaimed. 'Dear chairs and tables! How like old friends they are—faithful, silent friends' " (15).

In her pure vision, essence is better than action: " 'They *were*,' " she says of the sensitive Victorian wives and mothers, " 'and that's better than doing' " (117).

Yet in the real world, this insight into the truth of things has its own limitations, as the reader can quickly see. "A single glance was enough to show that Mrs. Hilbery was so rich in the gifts which make tea-parties of elderly distinguished people successful, that she scarcely needed any help from her daughter, provided that the tiresome business of teacups and bread and butter was discharged for her" (1). A master of the delicate art of uniting the separated, she is hopeless when it comes to fulfilling the more practical duties of life. As the only daughter of a great Victorian lyric poet, she is the one person who could write an authoritative biography of the man—could, that is, if she did not share his vision. Each day when she sets about giving the public a flawless picture of her father, she is at first caught up in a torrent of inspiration. "These spells of inspiration never burnt steadily, but flickered over the gigantic mass of the subject as capriciously as a will-o'-the-wisp, lighting now on this point, now on that" (35). Since the visionary sees a world without boundaries, it is impossible for such a person to draw circles around anyone to define him, or even to present one definitive side of that person's character. So if anyone could march directly through the life of the poet Richard Alardyce from birth to death, Mrs. Hilbery is not the one.

Another disadvantage to being a woman of vision in a world of fact is that facts continually contradict any sense of unity, so that Mrs. Hilbery is often forced into a seemingly false position by her own vision. She "seemed to regard the world with an enormous desire that it should behave itself nobly, and an entire confidence that it could do so, if it would only take the pains" (14). Then, too, though she welcomes the younger generation, she "weaved round them romances which had generally no likeness to the truth" (32). Nevertheless, though her individual romances may be objectively false, they are essentially true and show a keen insight into the greater meaning behind the disparate factual world.

Because Virginia Woolf's visionaries see beyond the boundaries of the objective world, they almost invariably have some sort of religion that directs their lives. Not until Lucy Swithin appears in *Between the Acts* does this religion correspond to anything even vaguely orthodox, but the force is there behind each of them nevertheless. Herbert Marder has pointed out that Woolf often presents Shakespeare, "the man of luminous mind," as her "symbol of reconciliation, combining the opposites";[16] and it is Shakespeare who is Mrs. Hilbery's god. When she returns from her visit to his tomb, Mrs. Hilbery brings with her the spiritual strength needed to unravel all the problems that have knotted themselves together during her absence.

> "So much earth and so much water and that sublime spirit brooding over it all," she mused, and went on to sing her strange, half-earthly song of dawns and sunsets, of great poets, and the unchanged spirit of noble loving which they had taught, so that nothing changes, and one age is linked with another, and no one dies, and we all meet in spirit, until she appeared oblivious of any one in the room. But suddenly her remarks seemed to contract the enormously wide circle in which they were soaring and to alight, airily and temporarily, upon matters of more immediate moment (526).

If Shakespeare is the godly spirit brooding upon the waters, Mrs. Hilbery, as she says of herself, is "quite a large bit of the fool, but the fools in Shakespeare say all the clever things" (324); and in this unique religion of hers, "fool" may well be read as "angel"; for it is she who brings Shakespeare's message of unity down into the factual world about her. That this message is one of vision, and vision that must battle constantly or be swallowed up in fact, is made clear directly when Mrs. Hilbery says to Katharine: " 'We have to have faith in our vision,' . . . glancing at the figures, which distressed her vaguely, and had some connexion in her mind with the household accounts, 'otherwise, as you say——' She cast a lightning glance into the depths of disillusionment which were, perhaps, not altogether unknown to her" (513).

Like Helen Ambrose, Mrs. Hilbery is married to a man who

is her opposite, who rules his life by the laws of mental accuracy in an abstract, factual realm, detached from the contradictions of the outside world. As he is first described to us by Virginia Woolf, this detachment is Mr. Hilbery's most outstanding feature.

> He played constantly with a little green stone attached to his watch-chain, thus displaying long and very sensitive fingers, and had a habit of moving his head hither and thither very quickly without altering the position of his large and rather corpulent body, so that he seemed to be providing himself incessantly with food for amusement and reflection with the least possible expenditure of energy (4–5).

He, like Mr. Ambrose or St. John Hirst, is not a participant in life but an observer. As a scholar, his specialty is the Romantic poets; but, as we can see from Virginia Woolf's summary of his work, his concern is not with lyricism but with fact and again fact. Presenting the reader with his study—for rooms in Mrs. Woolf's novels often reflect the soul of a man—she writes:

> Here Mr. Hilbery sat editing his review, or placing together documents by means of which it could be proved that Shelley had written "of" instead of "and," or that the inn in which Byron had slept was called the "Nag's Head" and not the "Turkish Knight," or that the Christian name of Keats's uncle had been John rather than Richard, for he knew more minute details about these poets than any man in England, probably, and was preparing an edition of Shelley which scrupulously observed the poet's system of punctuation. He saw the humour of these researches, but that did not prevent him from carrying them out with the utmost scrupulosity (108–9).

As for his observations about the world around him, they evince an awareness of objective fact, and even of the existence of the soul, in a figurative sense (" 'Yes, the office atmosphere is very bad for the soul,' said Mr. Hilbery" [99]); but when he is called upon to become personally involved in situations that directly concern him, that he cannot do. For example, when Katharine confronts him with the fact that her cousin Cyril has had several children by a woman who is not his wife, Mr. Hilbery avoids the individuality of the case by immediately setting it into a ready-made factual category:

> What a distance he was from it all! How superficially he smoothed these events into a semblance of decency which harmonized with his own view of life! He never wondered what Cyril had felt, nor did the hidden aspects of the case tempt him to examine into them. He merely seemed to realize, rather languidly, that Cyril had behaved in a way which was foolish, because other people did not behave in that way. He seemed to be looking through a telescope at little figures hundreds of miles in the distance (111).

So, too, when Katharine breaks her first engagement in an unorthodox way, her father can only approach the problem by the social rulebook, creating extra confusion for his vision- ary wife to rectify.

The visionary Mrs. Hilbery and her fact-loving husband are the perfect parents for Katharine, the central female figure in this novel; for as their daughter, she has the potential to com- bine both world views in herself and so to effect the reconcilia- tion of fact and vision. Ralph Denham, seeing her for the first time at her mother's tea-party, has the perspicacity to recognize that

> Katharine . . . had a likeness to each of her parents, and these elements were rather oddly blended. She had the quick, impulsive movements of her mother, the lips parting often to speak, and closing again; and the dark oval eyes of her father brimming with light upon a basis of sadness, or, since she was too young to have acquired a sorrowful point of view, one might say that the basis was not sadness so much as a spirit given to contemplation and self-control (5).

That her inward being is reflected in these outward manner- isms is made clear as the novel progresses, but that Katharine herself is unaware of her inheritance is demonstrated soon after the story opens. As her perceptive cousin says of her, " 'Katharine hasn't found herself yet' " (215).

The main reason for Katharine's failing to recognize the traits of both her parents in herself is the fact that she is too much involved in her mother's world to be able to achieve any sense of perspective.

> Circumstances had long forced her . . . to consider, painfully and minutely, all that part of life which is conspicuously without order; she had had to consider moods and wishes, degrees of liking or disliking, and their effect upon the destiny of people dear to her; she had been forced to deny herself any contemplation of that other part of life where thought constructs a destiny which is independent of human beings (350).

Caught in the backwash of vision, feeling the emotion but missing the perception of unity that evokes it, Katharine's initial desire is not, as Herbert Marder puts it, "to find a place in her life for the life of the mind, to combine her mother's kind of wisdom with more impersonal knowledge";[17] instead, she wishes to escape completely from her mother's approach to life.

Thus although the reconciling of fact and vision may be Katharine's destination, her original impetus is toward fact alone; and many of her likes and dislikes, actions and dreams, are results of this urge to be free of Mrs. Hilbery's all-embracing influence. For example, "She did not like phrases. She had even some natural antipathy to that process of self-examination, that perpetual effort to understand one's own feeling, and express it beautifully, fitly, or energetically in language; which constituted so great a part of her mother's existence. She was, on the contrary, inclined to be silent; she shrank from expressing herself even in talk, let alone in writing" (38). This fear and dislike of the very communication that makes vision possible is compounded by a love of precise, impersonal fact: "She would not have cared to confess how infinitely she preferred the exactitude, the star-like impersonality, of figures to the confusion, agitation, and vagueness of the finest prose" (40). What is ironic about Katharine's fleeing to this mathematical dream world of fact to escape from her mother's world, what Katharine herself senses but does not fully recognize, is that she approaches algebra or astronomy not as pure, self-contained fact, but as fact that sends out limitless waves of implication. In other words, mathematical problems to Katharine, like the wonderful tree to Rachel, serve as a path not to objective, bounded truth, but to infinite vision. Thus when Mrs. Hilbery and her daughter sit down to attack the daily problem of the Alardyce biography, Katharine often finds herself floating unconsciously into her mother's unearthly atmosphere.

> Again and again she was thinking of some problem when she should have been thinking of her grandfather. Waking from these trances, she would see that her mother, too, had lapsed into some dream almost as visionary as her own. . . . But, seeing her own state mirrored in her mother's face, Katharine would shake herself awake with a sense of irritation. Her mother was the last person she wished to resemble, much though she admired her (41).

Katharine is caught in a most uncomfortable position as the novel opens. Because Mrs. Hilbery is totally impractical, her daughter is forced to take on all the duties of a large household and so cannot enjoy the unalloyed vision her mother achieves. At the same time she is too close to her mother, too much like her, actually, to be able to become totally immersed in the factual world either in action or in abstraction. Thus, in order to attain to any identity that can include the visionary, Katharine feels she must deny the impractical vision upon which her mother thrives and under which she herself becomes the sensible daughter. "She reviewed her daily task, the perpetual demands upon her for good sense, self-control, and accuracy in a house containing a romantic mother. Ah, but her romance wasn't *that* romance. It was a desire, an echo, a sound; she could drape it in colour, see it in form, hear it in music, but not in words; no, never in words" (303). Seeing the cloudy nature of Mrs. Hilbery's approach to life, Katharine attempts to discover her own fulfillment in precision, and self-assertion. When confronted with a room full of people all emotionally involved in some argument, she cries out, " 'Don't you see how many different things these people care about? And I want to beat them down—I only mean . . . that I want to assert myself . . ." (54). Emotion, involvement, and caring, because they are all so deeply set into her mother's life and thus have been such a burden to Katharine, become a threat to her selfhood and to her personal vision. So, until she can step back from her mother and see the truth in a vision that is based upon human unity, Katharine weaves a dream by casting "her mind out to imagine an empty land where all this petty intercourse of men and women, this life made up of the dense crossings and entanglements of men and women, had no existence whatever" (106). At the height of this unspoken struggle with her mother, Katharine confides in her cousin Henry Otway: " 'I don't care much whether I ever get to know anything—but I want to work out something in figures —something that hasn't got to do with human beings' " (203).

Because Katharine's dreams, at the outset of her struggle, all run to barren wastes and equally barren numbers, she rejects love as being too close to her mother's vision, and chooses to marry a man for whom she has little affection but who will allow her the independence she craves. When William Rodney first enters the scene, he, like St. John Hirst, is immediately recognizable as one of those mentally alert, physically twisted men who inhabit the scholarly world of precise fact, a man perfectly suited to Katharine's mathematical self, but totally unfit to be husband to the whole woman.

> He was scrupulously well dressed, and a pearl in the centre of his tie seemed to give him a touch of aristocratic opulence. But the rather prominent eyes and the impulsive stammering manner, which seemed to indicate a torrent of ideas intermittently pressing for utterance and always checked in their course by a clutch of nervousness, drew no pity, as in the case of a more imposing personage, but a desire to

laugh, which was, however, entirely lacking in
malice (47–48).

Like Katharine's father, William, who aspires to be a poet,
approaches poetry through fact rather than through lyrical
vision, and even emotion conforms to clear-cut rules in his
verse.

> His theory was that every mood has its metre. His mastery
> of metres was very great; and, if the beauty of a drama
> depended upon the variety of measures in which the per-
> sonages speak, Rodney's plays must have challenged the
> works of Shakespeare. Katharine's ignorance of Shakespeare
> did not prevent her from feeling fairly certain that plays
> should not produce a sense of chill stupor in the audience,
> such as overcame her as the lines flowed on, sometimes
> long and sometimes short, but always delivered with the
> same lilt of voice, which seemed to nail each line firmly
> on to the same spot in the hearer's brain (143).

If Katharine were really as fond of precision as she imagines
herself to be, William's poetry should satisfy her; yet, although
she avoids her mother's immersion in Shakespeare, she cannot
avoid looking for the soul in verse.

But Katharine does not agree to marry William because he
fulfills her ideal vision of a husband. She is not looking for
someone to love, but for someone who will let her live her own
life, who will not demand that she share her inward self with
him. Although William insists that he loves her, his method of
proposal indicates that he does not look upon marriage as a
visionary, poetic life of spiritual union but as a practical compromise for those to whom that life is inaccessible. "Perhaps
if you married me—I'm half a a poet, you see, and I can't pretend not to feel what I do feel. If I could write—ah, that would
be another matter. I shouldn't bother you to marry me then,
Katharine,' " he says. " 'But for me I suppose you would rec-
ommend marriage?' " she answers. " 'Certainly I should. Not
for you only, but for all women. Why, you're nothing at all

without it; you're only half alive; using only half your faculties . . .' " (62–63). Marriage, then, as he presents it, is not a union of souls as it might appear to Mrs. Hilbery, but a recommended state for all young ladies, a life that employs unused talents and gives an arbitrary identity to those who cannot create their own. Katharine sees, both from this unusual proposal and from William's excessive concern with the social proprieties, that Mr. Rodney's world is limited by social and intellectual fact. If he is half poet, he is also half prig; and this combination makes a man who would be satisfied with a wife who would go through the motions of marriage. She sees that "She would come to feel a humorous sort of tenderness for him, a zealous care for his susceptibilities . . ." (107), and so, finally, accepts his offer, thinking that in a life with him she can extricate herself completely from her mother's vision.

If Katharine's approach to marriage with William is not strictly candid, either to herself or to him, his own attitude toward her shows an equal lack of honesty. " 'I should never think of telling Katharine the truth about herself,' " he says. " 'That wouldn't do at all. One has to be in an attitude of adoration in order to get on with Katharine' " (68). That their resulting relationship is built on distance rather than intimacy is reflected symbolically in the lines from Sidney's *Astrophel and Stella* that leap to William's mind as he walks by the river with Katharine, looking at the moon: "With how sad steps she climbs the sky,/How silently and with how wan a face" (63). The sonnet from which these lines, slightly misquoted, are taken bemoans the fact that on earth constancy in love is despised and proud Beauties "love to be lov'd, and yet/Those Loves scorne whom that Love doth possesse." William's love for Katharine, though superficial, deserves a greater return than it is granted; for in spite of his prudishness and fastidious concern with society's dictates, the man has his good points. He is generous, in spite of having little money of his own. He has the capacity to love another less visionary than Katharine. And Katharine, too, deserves and needs a far greater man than William will ever be.

Mrs. Hilbery, as might be expected, senses that all is not well between her daughter and William. But she knows that no one can be converted by force to any view of life; and so she waits patiently, saying, "One doesn't know any more, does one? One hasn't any advice to give one's children. One can only hope that they will have the same vision and the same power to believe, without which life would be so meaningless. That is what I ask for Katharine and her husband" (148). Katharine, as Virginia Woolf has already indicated, has inherited this vision, although she is not yet ready to recognize its strength. Nevertheless, soon after she has committed herself to a loveless marriage, she recognizes her mistake; and "when her mother said that marriage was the most interesting life, Katharine felt, as she was apt to do suddenly, for no definite reason, that they understood each other, in spite of differing in every possible way" (224).

In her desire to shake off the imprecision of her mother's views, Katharine may feel that she has little in common with Mrs. Hilbery, but in fact her mathematical approach to reality is only a different form of the same vision. When she visits the thoroughly practical world of Mary Datchet's suffragette office, Katharine's own aura of romance grows up in sharp contrast to the factual atmosphere. "Her figure in the long cloak, which took deep folds, and her face, which was composed into a mask of sensitive apprehension, disturbed Mary for a moment with a sense of the presence of some one who was of another world, and, therefore, subversive of her world" (83). That her fact is not that of social action but rather the fact that blossoms into vision is made finally clear to the reader in the Christmas scene describing Katharine's star-gazing. Although she turns to the stars to escape from the world around her, she soon senses a sympathetic unity between herself and the heavens, suitable to the Christmas season. Then,

⌣ . . . after gazing for another second, the stars did their usual work upon the mind, froze to cinders the whole of our short human history, and reduced the human body to an ape-like, furry form, crouching amid the brushwood of a barbarous clod of mud. This stage was soon succeeded by

another, in which there was nothing in the universe save
stars and the light of stars; as she looked up the pupils of her
eyes so dilated with starlight that the whole of her seemed
dissolved in silver and spilt over the ledges of the stars for
ever and ever indefinitely through space. Somehow simultaneously, though incongruously, she was riding with the
magnanimous hero upon the shore or under forest
trees . . . (205).

"Astronomy," then, has led her to vision—vision that defies the
laws of historical time and absorbs the individual into a
universal, spiritual whole. The magnanimous hero, riding
through this moment of revelation, indicates that love, as in
The Voyage Out, is the smaller unity that reenacts the greater
in the factual world.

Throughout the novel, even during her arid relationship
with William Rodney, Katharine dreams of the bold rider
and connects him with an overwhelming love extending beyond the limits of factual truth.

Spendid as the waters that drop with resounding thunder
from high ledges of rock, and plunge downwards into the
blue depths of night, was the presence of love she dreamt,
drawing into it every drop of the force of life, and dashing
them all asunder in the superb catastrophe in which
everything was surrendered, and nothing might be re-
claimed. The man, too, was some magnanimous hero, riding
a great horse by the shore of the sea. They rode through
forests together, they galloped by the rim of the sea (107–8).

Because she is too close to her mother, Katharine does not see
that her vision of love is very much like Mrs. Hilbery's idea of
total unity. But when she looks at the portait of her grand-
father, Katharine can imagine "what he was looking for; were
there waves beating upon a shore for him, too, she wondered,
and heroes riding through the leaf-hung forests?" (337–38).
Little by little as her self-awareness grows, Katharine begins
to "cast her mind alternately towards forest paths and starry
blossoms, and towards pages of neatly written mathematical

signs" (226) and to realize that perhaps fact and vision are not irreconcilable. Until she falls in love herself, however, she cannot make the leap from the thought of theoretical unity to the possibility of its enactment in the outside world.

> Why, she reflected, should there be this perpetual disparity between the thought and the action, between the life of solitude and the life of society, this astonishing precipice on one side of which the soul was active and in broad daylight, on the other side of which it was contemplative and dark as night? Was it not possible to step from one to the other, erect, and without essential change? (358–59).

It is this night and day that Katharine's eventual love and engagement move to reconcile.

But Katharine, like Rachel Vinrace, grows slowly into love. Being so firmly set against her mother's ways at first, she will come to recognize her spiritual inheritance only by gradual stages. As a first step away from devotion to the factual dream and toward an acceptance of the equal power of vision, Katharine makes it possible for William to find a wife who will share his love and his interests, thus giving up a life of detachment that formerly seemed ideal. The woman whom William chooses is Cassandra Otway, a girl who shares Mrs. Hilbery's social talent without her vision and who is as unlike Katharine as possible. "Where Katharine was simple, Cassandra was complex; where Katharine was solid and direct, Cassandra was vague and evasive. In short, they represented very well the manly and the womanly sides of the feminine nature . . ." (362). Possessing devotion to truth combined with her mother's sense of vision, Katharine will be able, as much as is possible, to combine that vision with life in the practical world. Cassandra, living in a world of smaller scope, can create her own social unity in the world of protocol. Thus the more limited girl will be able to soothe William's fears about propriety and think his poetry second only to that of Shakespeare without seeing his shortcomings or longing for a more fulfilling existence.

Once William is prepared to be happily settled with Cassandra, Katharine is free to discover a man who, like herself, is capable of reconciling fact and vision in his own life. And, because Katharine approaches vision through fact, her choice should be someone who approaches fact through vision in order that the balance between the two world-views may be precise. This man, as complex in his own way as Katharine is in hers, is Ralph Denham.

Like Katharine, Ralph is originally introduced by a description that shows his potential ability to see the world from two distinct points of view. "His eyes, expressive now of the usual masculine impersonality and authority, might reveal more subtle emotions under favorable circumstances, for they were large, and of a clear, brown colour—they seemed unexpectedly to hesitate and speculate . . ." (9). As the novel progresses the reader learns that the factual side of his life includes an extensive amateur knowledge of botany, heraldry, and the breeding of bulldogs. But for Ralph fact is not primarily a hobby as it is for Katharine; instead it is a way of life imposed upon him from outside. If Katharine, living daily in her mother's shadow, is hemmed in by the emotion that surrounds the vision and so is unable to see the true value of this vision from over-exposure to its drawbacks, Ralph is equally restricted from seeing the merits of fact because he is continually subjected to the demands of a regimented, factual life. "He had always made plans since he was a small boy; for poverty, and the fact that he was the eldest son of a large family, had given him the habit of thinking of spring and summer, autumn and winter, as so many stages in a prolonged campaign" (20). Forced into his position by circumstances, he has fulfilled his obligations to the letter, but, like Katharine, he has built his own method of escape. By continual struggle he has salvaged a small spot of privacy—a room of his own to dream in; and the tattered vision he manages to extract from life is symbolized by the room's sole ornament, a tame rook whose lack of feathers and inability to fly represent the sorry state of Ralph's dream world at the outset of the novel.

Ralph's sister, in spite of her brother's devotion to duty, ". . . could fancy Ralph suddenly sacrificing his entire career for some fantastic imagination; some cause or idea or even (so her fancy ran) for some woman seen from a railway train hanging up clothes in a back yard" (127). And her perception is acute.

> . . . it needed all Ralph's strength of will, together with the pressure of circumstances, to keep his feet moving in the path. . . . It needed, in particular, a constant repetition of a phrase to the effect that he shared the common fate, found it best of all, and wished for no other; and by repeating such phrases he acquired punctuality and habits of work, and could very plausibly demonstrate that to be a clerk in a solicitor's office was the best of all possible lives, and that other ambitions were vain (129).

In his private room he can conjure up dreams of heroic deeds, magnanimous gestures, creations of beauty. The rest of his life is fact. The division between the two realms seems firmly fixed: "he thought he could pride himself upon a life rigidly divided into the hours of work and those of dreams; the two lived side by side without harming each other" (130). Thus he and Katharine both begin by attempting to live segmented lives and must learn to unite the isolated halves before their educations are complete.

Ralph's education starts the moment he enters the Hilbery's drawing-room that, compared to the active streets outside, "seemed very remote and still" (2). The influence of this vision-filled house does not end when he shuts its front door behind him, but follows him home and haunts him until "in the miniature battle which so often rages between two quickly following impressions of life, the life of the Hilberys was getting the better of the life of the Denhams in his mind . . ." (26). Because of his existence as breadwinner and head of a household, Ralph cannot afford to be assailed by vision in his daily life. So he fights the dream of Katharine that fills his thoughts until suddenly, running into her in the street after a few casual meetings, ". . . immediately the whole scene in the Strand wore that curious look of order and purpose which is imparted to the most heterogenous things when music sounds . . ." (133). Katharine, unknowingly, has given Ralph his first real glimpse of vision, and from then on he is tossed about by the formerly neatly categorized modes of life that had seemed so sharply and painlessly divided before. This duality existing in himself brings to Ralph's mind an image of "a lighthouse besieged by the flying bodies of lost birds, who were dashed senseless, by the gale, against the glass. He had a strange sensation that he was both lighthouse and bird; he was steadfast and brilliant; and at the same time he was whirled, with all other things, senseless against the glass" (417–18). After a hard struggle, Ralph will finally accept Katharine as the lighthouse to which he must invariably fly; but this acceptance of the vision as part of his factual existence is long in coming.

As Katharine turns to William Rodney for an escape from the visionary world, so Ralph turns to Mary Datchet for protection from the overpowering vision that assails him. With her, he finds respite from the monotonous factual atmosphere of home and office as well as a shield from the too influential dream of Katharine. "Certainly it was very pleasant to be with Mary Datchet and to become, directly the door was shut, quite a different sort of person, eccentric and lovable, with scarcely any likeness to the self most people knew" (131). But because, unknowingly, he is using Mary for his own ends, he is able to see only one side of her, just as Katharine sees only one side of William. The Mary Ralph finds when he visits is the practical woman of committee meetings. "A pleasanter and saner woman than Mary Datchet was never seen within a committee-room. She seemed a compound of the autumn leaves and the winter sunshine; less poetically speaking, she showed both gentleness and strength, an indefinable promise of soft maternity blending with her evident fitness for honest labour" (172). In this capacity Mary, like Katharine in her more factual moods, wants to assert herself over others. This urge to conversion, however, is not at the core of Mary's character. On the contrary, away from the excitement of the meetings, she realizes that "She could not see the world divided into separate compartments of good people and bad people, any more than she could believe so implicitly in the rightness of her own thought as to wish to bring the population of the British Isles into agreement with it" (271). In her own way, Mary reconciles fact and vision better than any of the other characters in the novel, although she never completely experiences the vision herself. Because she, of all the young people in the story, is the only one who finds no fulfillment in love, though having a large capacity for loving, Mary must be able to maintain a balance in herself between the two worlds in order to exist. She may not live in either, but she must recognize both.

The man she loves and cannot have is Ralph; and he, seeing only her practical side, has no idea that his continued visits could spark any romantic thoughts in her. During one quiet evening with her he thinks: " 'How absurd Mary would think me if she knew that I almost made up my mind to walk all the way to Chelsea in order to look at Katharine's windows. She wouldn't understand it, but I like her very much as she is' " (133–34). The truth of the matter is, however, that Mary could sympathize very deeply with the romantic impulse, having a good portion of it herself. For example, in visiting the Elgin marbles that she somehow connects with Ralph, "She looked at them, and seemed, as usual, borne up on some wave of exaltation and emotion, by which her life at once became solemn and beautiful . . ." (80). As the months go by and Ralph turns more and more to Mary in trying to free himself from Katharine, the exaltation focuses and defines itself as love. When she and Ralph walk together down a country road at Christmas time, "It seemed a mere toss-up whether she said, 'I love you,' or whether she said, 'I love the beech-trees,' or only 'I love—I love' " (230). This awareness that love unites more than just the lover and beloved, that it includes everything in its vast scope, this perceptive insight is, in reality, vision. And if Mary is sensitive enough to understand the full implication of love, she is also conscious that she will never achieve this vision with Ralph. In an earlier scene as they sit together, silently working out their own feelings, "She felt that the two lines of thought bored their way in long, parallel tunnels which came very close indeed, but never ran into each other" (136). Sensitized both by her love for Ralph and her love for truth, it is Mary, too, who sees the natural kinship between Ralph and Katharine. As the latter comes to her apartment in a state of confusion as deep as any Ralph may feel, Mary recognizes, looking at Katharine, that there was "something that reminded Mary of Ralph. Oddly enough, he gave her the same feeling, too, and with him, too, she felt baffled" (184). Both Ralph and Katharine share an ability to step completely out of the factual world into pure vision, an ability Mary is denied partly because of her natural practicality, partly because she is forced to let love wither away unfulfilled within her. But though she may not be able to pinpoint rationally what sets Ralph and Katharine together and apart from others, Mary unconsciously answers her own question in associating Ralph with "a young Greek horseman, who reins his horse back so sharply that it half falls on its haunches. He always seemed to her like a rider on a spirited horse" (238). In her imaginings, Mary has, without knowing it, discovered Katharine's magnanimous hero and the man Ralph daydreams of being. But her casual mental images are never allowed to become full-blown dreams as they are for Ralph and Katharine. This transforming of the actual, Mary, in her devotion to unvarnished truth, cannot accept as valid.

The time will come when this one limitation of vision will save Mary from disaster. Ralph, at his blindest moment, proposes to her, admitting, as did William, the compromise inherent in his offer, saying "of course, in an ideal state of things, in a decent community even, there's no doubt you shouldn't have anything to do with me—seriously, that is" (240–41). If Mary were not unyieldingly honest, she might accept this compromise. Earlier she nearly gave in to her love for him, almost confessed her feelings in spite of knowing that his affection for her was only half-hearted.

> She was preserved from doing so only by a stubborn kind of respect for herself which lay at the root of her nature and forbade surrender, even in moments of almost overwhelming passion. Now, when all was tempest and high-running waves, she knew of a land where the sun shone clear upon Italian grammars and files of docketed papers.

Nevertheless, from the skeleton pallor of that land and the rocks that broke its surface, she knew that her life there would be harsh and lonely almost beyond endurance (234).

She will not accept what rightfully belongs to Katharine, and when renouncing her nascent vision after recognizing that it is Katharine whom Ralph loves, she takes refuge in the dry world of fact, recognizing that this narrower life is all that is left to her. By heaping the facts of Ralph's love for another upon herself, insisting on truth at all costs, she achieves a smaller vision with a dimmer glow than that of love, but shining all the same. "The truth seemed to support her; it struck her, even as she looked at his face, that the light of truth was shining far away beyond him; the light of truth, she seemed to frame the words as she rose to go, shines on a world not [to] be shaken by our personal calamities" (243).

Borne up by a new strength found in truth, Mary makes the final sacrifice and lays her love for Ralph bare before Katharine, while admitting that it is Katharine whom Ralph loves. This admission awakens Katharine to the fact that her own conception of love, that her relationship with Rodney, has been totally false: ". . . Katharine perceived far too vividly for her comfort the mediocrity, indeed the entirely fictitious character of her own feelings so far as they pretended to correspond with Mary's feelings" (294). If Mary's personal sacrifice has opened the way to Katharine's fulfillment, it has also given Mary the firm if hollow triumph of discovering that ". . . having renounced everything that made life happy, easy, splendid, individual, there remained a hard reality, unimpaired by one's personal adventures, remote as the stars, unquenchable as they are" (275). So she determines to remain true to this way of life, thinking, "having lost what is best, I do not mean to pretend that any other view does instead. Whatever happens, I mean to have no pretences in my life" (279). Thus Mary's factual world, tempered by the fire of the vision renounced, becomes a viable truth that will serve as a foundation for Ralph's and Katharine's final union and vision.

William now has Cassandra and Mary her work, leaving

Katharine and Ralph free to work out their natural destinies through a gradual process of harmonizing fact and vision within themselves and between each other. In order to achieve this harmony, Katharine, as we have already noted, must learn to see her mathematical abstractions in the context of vision. Ralph, on the other hand, must be able to reconcile his visions with the factual world. Because Ralph's visions, created by love, are concerned almost entirely with Katharine, his education will be complete only after he can understand that she contains as much practical love of fact as she does romantic potential for vision: ". . . how terrible sometimes the pause between the voice of one's dreams and the voice that comes from the object of one's dreams!" (319) he suddenly realizes, and it is this pause that Ralph must bridge by uniting the conflicting sides of his own nature and seeing Katharine in this dual light.

Part of Ralph's inability to see Katharine as she really is stems from the fact that she is engaged to someone else and thus seems totally inaccessible on a realistic plane. "Since the day when he had heard from Katharine's lips of her engagement, he had refrained from investing his dream of her with the details of real life. But the light of the late afternoon glowed green behind the straight trees, and became a symbol of her. The light seemed to expand his heart" (192). Detached from the actual physical and mental world, Ralph's dream of Katharine has the visionary power to intensify and enlarge experience, but until the dream is reconciled with fact, reality always comes as a shock. The image of Katharine that Ralph imagines during her absence grows less and less like her actual self, so that each new encounter with her in the flesh comes as a blow to his dream. "He was struck dumb by finding that Katharine was quite different, in some strange way, from his memory, so that he had to dismiss his old view in order to accept the new one" (246). All this vacillation between dream and reality takes place in the context of Ralph's further division between the world of his office and the world of his private room. At last after attempting at first to deny the vision, then to dispel it by turning it into a conscious daydream, Ralph

decides that he must confront it and work it into his real life.
So he approaches Katharine in person and presents his vision
to her, saying, "I've made you my standard ever since I saw
you. I've dreamt about you; I've thought of nothing but you;
you represent to me the only reality in the world. . . . I see you
everywhere, in the stars, in the river, to me you're everything
that exists; the reality of everything" (313). In telling her of
this all-inclusive ideal, Ralph admits its limitations while
showing that he understands the truth upon which it is based:
" 'Without knowing you, except that you're beautiful, and all
that, I've come to believe that we're in some sort of agreement;
that we're after something together; that we see something"
(315). Ralph sees that his own weakness lies in his ignorance
of Katharine's factual self; but at the same time he recognizes
in her the vision of which she is as yet barely aware.

When Ralph begins this final progress toward uniting fact
and vision in his relationship with Katharine, he starts a similar
process working in her. As she listens to him presenting his case

> . . . all the time she was in fancy looking up through a
> telescope at white shadow-cleft disks which were other
> worlds, until she felt herself possessed of two bodies, one
> walking by the river with Denham, the other concentrated
> to a silver globe aloft in the fine blue space above the scum
> of vapours that was covering the visible world. . . . There
> was no reason, she assured herself, for this feeling of
> happiness; she was not free; she was not alone; she was still
> bound to earth by a million fibres; every step took her
> nearer home. Nevertheless, she exulted as she had never
> exulted before (317).

Here Katharine begins to accept the duality of her nature, to
see that exultation is found not in detachment but in attachment, and to reconcile herself with Denham's help to the visionary world of a home dominated by Mrs. Hilbery. As yet,
all this awakening is only semiconscious; but Ralph, though
he knows ". . . in a second that she had heard nothing" (319),
also sees that subconsciously she understands and agrees with
him.

Once having openly admitted his allegiance to the vision, Ralph begins to experience the fulfillment that union in love makes possible. Sitting alone at home, forcing himself to imagine Katharine as she really is, not as his dreams have created her, he is overwhelmed by a sense of her presence. "They seemed to pass in and out of each other's minds, questioning and answering. The utmost fullness of communion seemed to be theirs. Thus united, he felt himself raised to an eminence, exalted, and filled with a power of achievement such as he had never known in singleness" (409). Realizing that this sense of unity is love and that love is the force that can reconcile opposites, Ralph sees the Hilbery home as a symbol of this total vision.

> Lights burnt in the three long windows of the drawing-room.
> The space of the room behind became, in Ralph's vision,
> the centre of the dark, flying wilderness of the world; the
> justification for the welter of confusion surrounding it;
> the steady light which cast its beams, like those of a light-
> house, with searching composure over the trackless
> waste (418).

Almost from the beginning of their acquaintance Ralph has tried to convince Katharine of the validity of vision in any form, arguing that poetry is "the only thing worth doing . . . because . . . it keeps an ideal alive which might die otherwise" (152), then indicating that ideals and dreams make up the vision. If he helps Katharine to nurture the vision in her own soul, she insists on keeping the fact awake in his; and even after their friendship has grown to something greater she says:

> "You come and see me among flowers and pictures, and
> think me mysterious, romantic, and all the rest of it. Being.
> yourself very inexperienced and very emotional, you go
> home and invent a story about me, and now you can't
> separate me from the person you've imagined me to be. You
> call that, I suppose, being in love; as a matter of fact it's
> being in delusion. All romantic people are the same,"
> she added. "My mother spends her life in making stories

about the people she's fond of. But I won't have you do it about me, if I can help it" (404).

Yet Katharine in her own way makes up stories about Ralph and is as much in need of a counterbalance to her view of life as he is to his. If his love for her grows out of dreams more than reality, hers for him results from fact more than dream: "She wished he would go on for ever talking of plants, and showing her how science felt not quite blindly for the law that ruled their endless variations" (350). Yet love, when it appears, is vision for both of them. When Ralph first began to worship a dream of Katharine, his dream became absorbed into a line of trees against the sky, and those trees became symbolic of the vision. Now when Ralph's neatly presented facts bring order to her fragmented world, she looks up and sees that "The very trees and the green merging into the blue distance became symbols of the vast eternal world which recks so little of the happiness, of the marriages or deaths of individuals" (350).

It will take an encounter with the ugliest form of unyielding fact, however, before Katharine will be able to accept completely the marrying of fact and vision in love. While Mrs. Hilbery is away visiting Shakespeare's tomb, taking her vision with her, Katharine and her father are besieged by Katharine's aunt who has heard that William, while still engaged to Katharine, has been spending time with Cassandra. According to the social proprieties, Cassandra has committed a heinous sin, and the single-sighted Mrs. Milvain is incapable of seeing any extenuating circumstances. She is the woman, too, who stirred up anxiety about Cyril's misbehavior and, as Mrs. Hilbery says of her: " 'We're dreadfully afraid that she's going to lose the sight of one of her eyes, and I always feel that our physical ailments are so apt to turn into mental ailments" (517). Katharine, seeing how fact alone rules her aunt's life, realizes ". . . how infinitely repulsive the body of life is without its soul" (431) and determines that the woman will have no say in her own actions.

Leaving Cassandra to William, she sets about understanding her own relationship with Ralph, and soon recognizes her own state of mind as well as his, saying, " 'But my state is worse than yours, because it hasn't anything to do with facts. It's an hallucination, pure and simple—an intoxication. . . . One can be in love with pure reason?' she hazarded. 'Because if you're in love with a vision, I believe that's what I'm in love with'' (449). She sees that his vision and her fact have resulted in mutual vision in love; and the outcome of this new awareness is that each can give up something of his own position, thus allowing for a final balance between their two views of life. " 'No, you're right,' he said. 'I don't know you. I've never known you.' 'Yet perhaps you know me better than any one else,' she mused'' (446). In these two simple statements, Ralph admits the weakness in his factual knowledge and Katharine recognizes the truth in his vision. It is this newborn understanding that will bring their individual educations to completion in the dual world of love.

Having recognized the power of vision, Katharine, while her mother is away, grows so remarkably like Mrs. Hilbery in her mannerisms that Cassandra exclaims: " 'How like Aunt Maggie you look!' '' (460) and Katharine herself sees the resemblance:

> In truth, now that her mother was away, Katharine did feel
> less sensible than usual, but as she argued it to herself,
> there was much less need for sense. Secretly, she was a little
> shaken by the evidence which the morning had supplied
> of her immense capacity for—what could one call it?—
> rambling over an infinite variety of thoughts that were too
> foolish to be named (460).

Under the influence of love and a new perspective somewhat removed from her mother, Katharine can finally accept her visionary inheritance.

When Mrs. Hilbery returns, full of the spirit of Shakespeare and ready to straighten out the awkwardness created by her husband's factual treatment of Katharine's life, Katharine ". . . felt it to be amazingly appropriate that her mother should be there, thanking God emphatically for unknown blessings, and strewing the floor with flowers and leaves from Shakespeare's tomb" (508). Now that Katharine has entered her visionary world, Mrs. Hilbery can admit that she foresaw how things would be: " 'Nothing else matters in the world! . . . Names aren't anything; it's what we feel that's everything. I didn't want silly, kind, interfering letters. I didn't want your father to tell me. I knew it from the first. I prayed that it might be so' " (508). Katharine then turns to her mother and learns for the first time of the depths of her parents' own love as Mrs. Hilbery tells her: " 'It was life, it was death. The great sea was round us. It was the voyage for ever and ever' " (512). Free from the desire to escape her mother's approach to life, Katharine recognizes the power of this vision at last: "Once more she felt that instead of being a grown woman, used to advise and command, she was only a foot or two raised above the long grass and the little flowers and entirely dependent upon the figure of indefinite size whose head went up into the sky, whose hand was in hers, for guidance" (513–14).

Given free rein, Mrs. Hilbery guides indeed, bringing together the divided couples and then leaving them alone to work out their destinies. As Katharine and Ralph sit together, thinking of their relationship with each other, Ralph tries "to convey to her the possibility that although human beings are woefully ill-adapted for communication, still, such communion is the best we know" (515); while Katharine proves the validity of this communion by recognizing in his personal symbol of reality a kinship with her own view of life:

"I like your little dot with the flames round it," she said meditatively. . . . He was convinced that it could mean nothing to another, although somehow to him it conveyed not only Katharine herself but all those states of mind which had clustered round her since he first saw her pouring out tea on a Sunday afternoon. It represented by its circumference of smudges surrounding a central blot all that encircling glow which for him surrounded, inexplicably, so many of the objects of life. . . . She said simply, and in the same tone of reflection: "Yes, the world looks something like that to me too" (522).

Thus Ralph and Katharine have attained that world of unity in which fact and vision are joined, and Katharine "held in her hands for one brief moment the globe which we spend our lives in trying to shape, round, whole, and entire from the confusion of chaos" (533).

Night and Day ends before the lovers can experience those blows to vision that life in the real world invariably inflicts upon those who look for unity. But Virginia Woolf has succeeded in joining very delicately, if only for a moment, the conflicting realms of dream and reality, and thus has given balance and order to a seemingly divided world. In this novel we have again seen her employ symbolic figures of fact and vision as the angels of the action, but her central concern has been the uniting of these points of view in single individuals. Thus the novel hinges upon Katharine's ability to reconcile her love of clean abstractions with the visionary side of her nature and upon Ralph's coming to recognize the reality underlying his dreams. By uniting these two in love, Virginia Woolf completes the balance; for where Ralph lacks objectivity, Katharine supplies it, as he provides any vision lacking in her. In her next novel Virginia Woolf will make one last attempt within a realistic form to unite the two sides of life in a single person, a task comparable to concentrating *War and Peace* in the drawing-room world of *Emma*.

3

Jacob's Room

It is little wonder that the simple question "Who is Jacob?" that broods over *Jacob's Room* should have given the critics so much pause; for this novel is one of Virginia Woolf's most tangled works, and the question of Jacob's identity embraces all that is in the book. In *The Voyage out* and *Night and Day* Mrs. Woolf explored several different avenues leading to the ideal of a personality that combines existence in a factual world with the awareness that the self is only part of a great visionary whole embracing all times, places, and people. Death, with its ability to erase physical boundaries, love that unites solitary individuals in a personal vision, solid objects that suddenly reveal a pattern transcending objective limitations—all of these were presented as gateways to vision. Now in *Jacob's Room* Virginia Woolf attempts to combine her discoveries and present in Jacob that ideal factual/visionary being who lives in the world and at the same time permeates that world-like and all-pervasive mist.

Who is Jacob? Few critics who discuss this novel have a simple answer. The reason for this common bewilderment is summed up in Dorothy Brewster's statement about the work: "Jacob's 'room' is more vividly realized than Jacob. Presented chiefly through his surroundings and the often fleeting impressions he makes upon others, and doomed by an 'inexorable force' to a brief passage through time, Jacob escapes us."[1] Because it is a fact that the social world in which Jacob lives stands out more concretely than he, several critics have extracted from the novel a Jacob who is primarily a symbol of youth threatened by a war-torn society. Charles G. Hoffman, for example, says, "Jacob Flanders like Septimus Warren Smith after him is intended to represent a generation of young men whose destinies were suddenly changed, hopes and aspirations interrupted, lives destroyed, by the war."[2] A. D. Moody agrees with this point of view, saying, "Jacob's being killed in the War, and the fact that he has never emerged as a rounded and fully achieved character, enforce the point: his human nature had developed as far as his world allowed, and disappeared at the crisis of its history when its inhuman tendencies became dominant."[3] James Hafley does not limit these destructive forces to war, but feels that while Jacob "is fighting the fight against the materiality of the social structure around him, his own self is also exhausted and overcome."[4] It is true that Jacob dies in the war; it is also true that he has to put up with several awkward dinner parties; but neither of these events in his life receives so much attention that it should be deemed the central issue of the novel. And most critics look for more universal themes in the purposefully ill-defined picture of Jacob that Virginia Woolf gives us.

David Daiches sees the protracted presentation of Jacob's character as Virginia Woolf's attempt to provide an answer to various questions about human personality in general: "What is personality? How does it impinge on its environment? What is its relation to events in time? What is the nature of reality insofar as it is related to the mental and emotional world of men?"[5] Other critics have approached *Jacob's Room* from the same direction and have concentrated on one or more of these questions. William Troy, for example, sees the novel as "a poetic rendering of the dreams, desires, fantasies and enthusiasms which pass through"[6] Jacob's mind; while Floris Delattre feels that the reality of Jacob's spiritual life is being presented in the work through a succession of rapidly moving fragments, the emphasis being placed on this movement.[7] Delving a little deeper below the surface presentation of the events that make up Jacob's life, Ralph Freedman finds that the underlying scheme of the novel is provided by "the relation between being aware and being an object of awareness, between perceiving and being perceived."[8] Another critic who recognizes this fluctuation between subject and object is Jean Guiguet who sees that "the alternation between realistic descriptions and inward analyses gives way to a constant confrontation between impressions and the inaccessible, indescribable experience they conceal."[9] This interplay between inner and outer, and the accompanying fact that nothing can be known completely from its outward manifestations are studied by a number of other critics, among them Winifred Holtby and A. D. Moody. The former finds the personality question answered by the double truth that "we dwell in ourselves; we dwell in the mirror that lies in the eyes of our friends regarding us."[10] The latter looks at Jacob Flanders's chronicle as Virginia Woolf's search for a "form for the soul in the life of its world."[11] Melvin Friedman sees the presentation of Jacob's inner self as a process of self-discovery ending in death[12] and thus finds a parallel between Jacob's career and that of Rachel Vinrace in *The Voyage Out*. In spite of these explanations, however, many readers continue to find the obscurity of Jacob's personality very puzzling and would agree with J. K. Johnstone that "this is a serious weakness in the novel; for its centre, the character who might unite all the various scenes, is—not there."[13] Because the riddle of Jacob's incorporeality is still unsolved, a new approach, looking at *Jacob's Room* from the standpoint of fact and vision in human personality, though it may not satisfy those who like a novel with characters they can define, may throw some new light on the purpose behind Virginia Woolf's intentionally enigmatic presentation of her main character.

That Jacob was meant to be a puzzle is certain. Much of the general theme of the novel itself is stated as a mystery: "The strange thing about life is that though the nature of it must have been apparent to every one for hundreds of years, no one has left any adequate account of it."[14] Virginia Woolf demonstrates, in scenes such as the following, that the reason no one has been able to define life is that in the social realm every individual is a self-contained unit, showing only his cover to the outside world and seldom having the curiosity to look behind another's façade.

> The proximity of the omnibuses gave the outside passengers an opportunity to stare into each other's faces. Yet few took advantage of it. Each had his own business to think of. Each had his past shut in him like the leaves of a book known to him by heart; and his friends could only read the title, James Spalding, or Charles Budgeon, and the passengers going the opposite way could read nothing at all— save "a man with a red moustache," "a young man in grey smoking a pipe" (64–65).

Every now and again, however, someone asks the essential question, often without knowing its full import, and in this novel Virginia Woolf asks through Mrs. Plomer and others: "Does anybody know Mr. Flanders?" (33). The answer is always the same: "It is no use trying to sum people up. . . . One must follow hints, not exactly what is said, nor yet entirely what is done . . ." (31, 154). These hints are often supplied in *Jacob's Room* by other characters who encounter Jacob in passing. Each draws some conclusion about the young man, but every impression is only fragmentarily true at best. An old lady sits opposite him in a train, trying surreptitiously to discover what he is like. But "Nobody sees any one as he is, let alone an elderly lady sitting opposite a strange young man in a railway carriage. They see a whole—they see all sort of things —they see themselves . . ." (30–31). The charwoman for one of Jacob's friends listens to the two men talking in a nearby room: "Mr. Sanders was there again; Flanders she meant; and where an inquisitive old woman gets a name wrong, what chance is there that she will faithfully report an argument?" (102). Each of the many persons who comment upon Jacob's character has some particular bias, making it seem "that a profound, impartial, and absolutely just opinion of our fellow-creatures is utterly unknown" (71) so that ". . . however long these gossips sit, and however they stuff out their victims' characters till they are swollen and tender as the livers of

geese exposed to a hot fire, they never come to a decision"
(154–55).

Thus one attempt at presenting Jacob sends us "back to see
what the other side means—the men in clubs and Cabinets—
when they say that character-drawing is a frivolous fireside art,
a matter of pins and needles, exquisite outlines enclosing va-
cancy, flourishes, and mere scrawls" (155). The urge to understand another, however, cannot be quelled so easily: ". . . something is always impelling one to hum vibrating, like the hawk
moth, at the mouth of the cavern of mystery . . ." (73). So
after each attempt and failure we begin again from another
point of view—physical appearance, perhaps—to present a
person as he is: ". . . but surely," says Virginia Woolf, "of all
futile occupations this of cataloguing features is the worst. One
word is sufficient. But if one cannot find it?" (71). Because
Mrs. Woolf is aware that as author she could easily give us the
one word and so present more hints of Jacob than we could
objectively know, she takes special pains so qualify her own
statements about Jacob. For example, following a long passage
presenting the reader with Jacob's thoughts and actions, she
writes: "But though all this may very well be true . . . there
remains over something which can never be conveyed to a
second person save by Jacob himself. Moreover, part of this is
not Jacob but Richard Bonamy—the room; the market carts;
the hour; the very moment of history" (72–73). This sense that
Jacob's personality melts into everything around him is coun-
terbalanced by a realization of his ultimate reality, a contradiction that holds one key to *Jacob's Room*:

> In any case life is but a procession of shadows, and God
> knows why it is that we embrace them so eagerly, and see
> them depart with such anguish, being shadows. And why, if
> this and much more than this is true, why are we yet
> surprised in the window corner by a sudden vision that the
> young man in the chair is of all things in the world the most
> real, the most solid, the best known to us—why indeed? (72).

Jacob is shadow, yet he is solid; he is unreal, yet he is the greatest reality. He, like life, is apparent but unaccountable. How

reconcile the two? One answer may be this: Jacob, in his visionary self, is a part of every individual who crosses his path or the
path of anyone he knows. He is infused into every place, crosses
the barriers of every time, and encompasses so large a world
that he can no more be summed up than can the whole of life.
In his factual self, on the other hand, Jacob is defined, solid, a
totally objective almost inanimate being to those who see him,
a representative figure in a social world. When he assumes the
role of factual object, he has the power to spark momentary
vision in others, and, as I shall show later, to take on symbolic
significance like Rachel's tree or Katharine's equations. Thus
Jacob, by combining fact and vision in himself, is of necessity
an enigmatic figure.

In trying to make Jacob an inhabitant of the visionary world
while preserving his factual identity, Virginia Woolf employs
several of the paths to vision found in her earlier novels. In
The Voyage Out, for example, she had presented death as a
force that dissolves the factual limitations of the personality to
enable Rachel to become permanently united with both Terence and the world around her. In *Jacob's Room* death
becomes a constant cloud hanging over Jacob so persistently
that not only does his eventual physical death come as no
surprise, but the reader must feel that Jacob is part of the
boundless universality of death from his early childhood.
When Jacob's name is first sounded in the book, it comes as
a cry, echoing and reechoing with no answer: " 'Ja—cob! Ja—
cob!' " shouts Archer for the third time in two pages. "The
voice had an extraordinary sadness. Pure from all body, pure
from all passion, going out into the world, solitary, unan-
swered, breaking against rocks—so it sounded" (8–9). Jacob is
not here, but his disembodied name reverberates in his world;
and the cry sounds over and over again throughout the book,
gaining deeper significance each time it is repeated. " 'Jacob!
Jacob!' " thinks Clara (166), and at her party the reason for
Jacob's silence is reinforced symbolically. There another
couple like Jacob and Clara meet but do not unite; and soon
we hear that ". . . now Jimmy feeds crows in Flanders and
Helen visits hospitals" (97). Jacob Flanders, by his very name,

joins Jimmy's body on the fields of war. So by the time the cry rings out for the last time at the end of the novel, after Jacob has actually died, we have become so used to his not answering that Bonamy's " 'Jacob! Jacob!' " (176) seems no more or less final than any of the similar earlier cries. Jacob eludes us in life as thoroughly as he does in death.

Early in the novel Virginia Woolf explains indirectly her reason for surrounding Jacob with an atmosphere of death. Mrs. Flanders, Jacob's mother, is pondering the identity of her late husband and finds his personality difficult to isolate now that he is dead.

> Had he, then, been nothing? An unanswerable question, since even if it weren't the habit of the undertaker to close the eyes, the light so soon goes out of them. At first, part of herself; now one of a company, he had merged in the grass, the sloping hillside, the thousand white stones, some slanting, others upright, the decayed wreaths, the crosses of green tin, the narrow yellow paths, and the lilacs that drooped in April, with a scent like that of an invalid's bedroom, over the churchyard wall. Seabrook was now all that . . . (16).

Where Mr. Flanders, by dying physically, becomes merged with everything that surrounds him, Jacob, in his more visionary death in life, becomes a part of everything he relates to, and so emerges as a force for unity in his disjointed world.

If as a visionary personality Jacob must be too diffuse to be defined, he must also be enough detached from specific members of his personal universe to avoid becoming tied down or limited in any way. For example, as a small boy on the beach, while his brother is calling for him, Jacob is searching desperately for his nurse. "A large black woman was sitting on the sand. He ran towards her. 'Nanny! Nanny!' he cried, sobbing the words out on the crest of each gasping breath. The waves came round her. She was a rock. She was covered with the seaweed which pops when it is pressed. He was lost" (10). If he must lose the more binding relationships in his life, he is able to find comfort in less tangible alliances, in this case with a ram's skull that soon becomes a symbolic part of him. "He was about to roar when, lying among the black sticks and straw under the cliff, he saw a whole skull—perhaps a cow's skull, a skull, perhaps, with the teeth in it. Sobbing, but absent-mindedly, he ran farther and farther away until he held the skull in his arms" (10). Thus even as a child, Jacob has traded his old nurse for an old skull, a symbol of death, and must find in this emblem the solace others receive from more personal sources: mother love, marriage, children, and similar earthly ties. Like the rest of the death images that grow to symbolic proportions throughout the novel, this sheep's skull remains with Jacob, following him in this case to his actual death. For carved into the decorative woodwork of his last room is the skull of a ram.

That Jacob is especially marked out by death is emphasized by another childhood association that takes on greater and greater visionary significance as it is reiterated. Jacob collects butterflies. As in the case of the moths in *The Voyage Out,* these insects function as more than casual bits of beauty, fluttering about a room or garden. "The stag-beetle dies slowly (it was John who collected the beetles). Even on the second day its legs were supple. But the butterflies were dead. A whiff of rotten eggs had vanquished the pale clouded yellow which came pelting across the orchard and up Dods Hill and away on the moor . . ." (23). This connection between butterflies and death is repeated frequently and linked decisively to Jacob. The blues he stalks "settled on little bones lying on the turf with the sun beating on them, and the painted ladies and the peacocks feasted upon bloody entrails dropped by a hawk" (24). Rebecca catches a death's-head moth for him in the kitchen (23). One moth in his collection takes on a special meaning because "The tree had fallen the night he caught it. There had been a volley of pistol-shots suddenly in the depths of the wood" (23). This moth and the "terrifying volley of pistol-shots" and "death in the forest" (32) recur several times as images during the course of the novel, weaving together moths, guns, and death to make an image-shroud for Jacob. Bernard Blackstone, noticing the sheep's jaw, the butterfly, the falling tree, says that these images "are not allowed to stiffen into symbols";[15] but the purpose they serve in the novel is closer to symbol than to decoration, for all these objects surround Jacob with an aura of death that never leaves him.

Jacob's association with death is not, however, restricted to the use of suggestive imagery. Time and again authorial comment or the thoughts of his friends call up foreshadowings of early death. The young men at Cambridge, Jacob among them, sit reading in their rooms. "Simple young men, these," says the voice of the author, "who would—but there is no need to think of them grown old . . . (43). Then Jacob's closest friend, Richard Bonamy, sits tearing old newspapers unconsciously into shreds, "eager and contented no more, but almost fierce. Why? Only perhaps that Keats died young—one wants to write poetry too and to love—oh, the brutes!" (44). Next a young girl in love with Jacob watches him lean over the railing of a bridge, the smoke from his cigarette hanging about him like a personal cloud. "And for ever the beauty of young men seems to be set in smoke," she thinks, "however lustily they chase footballs, or drive cricket balls, dance, run, or stride along roads. Possibly they are soon to lose it" (117). The presentiments are true. Jacob is soon to lose his beauty and his life, dying young like Keats, and never living to grow old with his classmates at Cambridge.

Virginia Woolf makes it clear that Jacob, by being so frequently associated with death, is already an inhabitant of the infinite incorporeal world, when, in presenting a moment of vision, she writes that "if the exaltation lasted we should be blown like foam into the air. The stars would shine through us. We should go down the gale in salt drops—as sometimes happens" (120). Jacob's character is so insubstantial in its unity with death that the stars do seem to shine through him. His inevitable end must be an actual dying that is perfectly consistent with his life. This ghostly side of Jacob often haunts his rooms when his physical body is absent. "Jacob's rooms . . . were in Neville's Court; at the top; so that reaching his door one went in a little out of breath; but he wasn't there" (38). Though his rooms may be unexpectedly empty, the missing

Jacob makes his presence felt as though his spirit hovers there. "Listless in the air in an empty room, just swelling the curtain; the flowers in the jar shift. One fibre in the wicker arm-chair creaks, though no one sits there" (39). When Virginia Woolf includes this passage, word for word, in the final chapter, presenting his room after his death, the point is solidified. Jacob has always been a phantom. His death changes nothing. His rooms in his absence contain his ghost in life and in death, in the creaking arm-chair and in the ram's skull carved in the wood (70, 176). Implicit in Jacob's surroundings is a continuity that is uninterrupted by his dying.

If Jacob's individual living quarters absorb and give off the essence of his being, so does the greater "room" of the world in which he lives. At times, as in his trip to the Scilly Isles, the landscape reacts to his presence by a symbolic sympathetic fallacy. Here the peaceful coastline assumes a special character as he sails past: ". . . imperceptibly the cottage smoke droops, has the look of a mourning emblem, a flag floating its caress over a grave. The gulls, making their broad flight and then riding at peace, seem to mark the grave" (49). But this association of the environment with Jacob's personal death is unusual. What is more common is the infusing of universal significance that transcends spatial boundaries into each place in which Jacob lives or travels. Dods Hill, his childhood home, is the first to be described in these visionary terms.

> No words can exaggerate the importance of Dods Hill. It was the earth; the world against the sky; the horizon of how many glances can best be computed by those who have lived all their lives in the same village, only leaving it once to fight in the Crimea, like old George Garfit, leaning over his garden gate smoking his pipe. The progress of the sun was measured by it; the tint of the day laid against it to be judged (17).

This universality on a personal scale is expanded in Jacob's Cambridge "room" that creates vision within vision.

> They say the sky is the same everywhere. Travellers, the shipwrecked, exiles, and the dying draw comfort from

the thought, and no doubt if you are of a mystical tendency, consolation, and even explanation, shower down from the unbroken surface. But above Cambridge—anyhow above the roof of King's College Chapel—there is a difference. Out at sea a great city will cast a brightness into the night. Is it fanciful to suppose the sky, washed into the crevices of King's College Chapel, lighter, thinner, more sparkling than the sky elsewhere? Does Cambridge burn not only into the night, but into the day? (31–32).

As this picture is being presented, Jacob is sitting in King's College Chapel. As one of the "dying" he is associated with the greater sky that unites everyone and everything under its canopy; but as one of the insubstantial dead, sitting among the living, he becomes part of the pervasive brightness in the Cambridge sky that burns like a signal beacon for the soul by day and by night.

It is not surprising that, as a representative of the infinite universe, Jacob influences his world temporally as well as spatially, for one of the important elements of the vision is that it transcends time. If Dods Hill and Cambridge become the universe while he lives in these places, they also absorb all time into themselves while he is there. A young man (who seems to be Jacob, for chronology in this novel is extremely fluid) stands on the pier in a small town at the foot of Dods Hill and surveys the busy scene before him.

But there was a time when none of this had any existence (thought the young man leaning against the railings). Fix your eyes upon the lady's skirt; the grey one will do— above the pink silk stockings. It changes; drapes her ankles— the nineties; then it amplifies—the seventies; now it's burnished red and stretched above a crinoline—the sixties; a tiny black foot wearing a white cotton stocking peeps out. Still sitting there? Yes—she's still on the pier. The silk is now sprigged with roses, but somehow one no longer sees so clearly. There's no pier beneath us. The heavy chariot may swing along the turnpike road, but there's no

pier for it to stop at, and how grey and turbulent the sea
is in the seventeenth century! (19).

Back he goes, discovering the whole of English history from
the Romans to the moment he lives in, and somehow uniting
them in the present moment. Even more explicit is the rolling
back of time at Cambridge:

> The stroke of the clock even was muffled; as if intoned by
> somebody reverent from a pulpit; as if generations of
> learned men heard the last hour go rolling through their
> ranks and issued it, already smooth and time-worn, with
> their blessing, for the use of the living.
>   Was it to receive this gift from the past that the young
> man came to the window and stood there, looking out
> across the court? It was Jacob (45).

No matter where he goes, Jacob in his very boundlessness carries with him the ability to draw together all time in his own
existence, the ultimate test of the visionary personality. When
he reads at the British Museum, the dome of that building
becomes a great skull, lying "cool over the visions and heat of
the brain" (109) and that brain is not only Jacob's but Plato's
and Shakespeare's, the brain of the ancient potter, the brain
of the jeweler, a brain that has "crossed the river of death this
way and that incessantly" (109) for all time and in all countries,
uniting every place and every age through death in this one
room where Jacob sits. When Jacob visits Athens and lady
tourists compare his beauty to that of the Greek statues, the
Parthenon stands apart from all the muddy sentiments of
individuals; "and if you consider how it has stood out all night,
for centuries, you begin to connect the blaze (at midday the
glare is dazzling and the frieze almost invisible) with the idea
that perhaps it is beauty alone that is immortal" (148). So
Jacob joins the immortality of the Parthenon in his Attic
beauty—death does not contradict his living—and is capable of
suffusing his surroundings with the same deathless quality.
    As the novel flows smoothly along in a sort of timeless world
suspended in the visionary stuff of Jacob's being, all the

boundaries of time begin to disintegrate through lack of use until at one point the authorial voice intrudes to ask: "But what century have we reached? Has this procession from the Surrey side to the Strand gone on for ever? That old man has been crossing the Bridge these six hundred years, with the rabble of little boys at his heels . . ." (113). Yet "No one stands still. It seems as if we marched to the sound of music; perhaps the wind and the river; perhaps these same drums and trumpets—the ecstasy and hubbub of the soul" (113). It is Jacob's soul that stretches wide enough to include all this movement, all this time without seeming to move itself. Like the vision, he is larger than time, larger than space, encompassing everything. This illusion of movement without change that pervades Jacob, Jacob who never seems to develop from the first crying out of his name to the last, spills over into the form of the book. For although the action, such as it is, begins with Jacob's early childhood, follows him through school and the university to work and finally to death—a span of nearly twenty years—the structure of the novel contains everything within a little more than a year. The first episode begins in early September, the last ends at the very end of the summer, circling from the season of dying to death itself. In between, each episode follows the next in careful seasonal succession: April, May, July, October, November, December, January, February, April, then summer, and the cycle, we may assume, begins again. Thus by taking on the all-inclusive aspects of death that ignores spatial and temporal barriers, Jacob becomes one with the vision, embracing a world that extends beyond the individual life to include all people in all ages.

But it is not through death alone that Jacob conveys a message of unbounded human unity; for death in the world of human relationships unites people only in a very abstract sense. Thus in order that Jacob may embody a vision that is not incompatible with life in society, Virginia Woolf provides two groups of characters who, in their association with Jacob, either define his visionary qualities or serve as emissaries to carry his vision into the world. The first group, made up primarily of older women, clarifies by contrast or kinship that side of Jacob that is unbounded and extends into other times, lives, and places. Those who compose the second group, the men and women who love Jacob or are loved by him, experience the vision in their daily lives, thus widening Jacob's existence by uniting him through love not only to themselves but to all the facts and people who touch their lives.

The first woman of any importance in Jacob's life belongs to the first group and is, as might be expected, his mother. She serves not as a model of love and vision to be emulated, but as an example of limited cruelty and unyielding fact to be rejected. She spurns the honest love of Mr. Floyd, her sons' tutor, and expresses her contempt for him by gelding the cat he gives her youngest child. Her choice of male companion runs instead to Captain Barfoot, a married man who neglects his wife and prides himself upon his sense of order and law, displaying the short-sighted view of life that denies the soul (23). Therefore Jacob becomes defined as his mother's opposite and is "the only one of her sons who never obeyed her . . ." (23). Although Mrs. Flanders is herself totally limited to the factual world, she partakes of eternity through her relationship with her son, symbolized by a garnet brooch, his gift to her, which she once lost on the moors. Not long before Jacob dies, his mother sits in a hollow where the lost bit of jewelry mingles with the bones of ancient Romans lying buried beneath the hills. "Did the bones stir, or the rusty swords? Was Mrs. Flanders' twopenny-halfpenny brooch for ever part of the rich accumulation? and if all the ghosts flocked thick and rubbed shoulders with Mrs. Flanders in the circle, would she not have seemed perfectly in her place, a live English matron, growing stout?" (132). Because Betty Flanders refuses love and can never feel close to Jacob personally, she is included in his visionary being only as a fragment of the great pattern of space and time defined by the unifying power of his death. Yet the very fact of her being included serves as proof that the vision can embrace even the most limited aspects of human existence.

If Mrs. Flanders cannot understand or grow fond of her son and serves primarily to bring out his infinite scope in contrast to her own limitations, Mrs. Jarvis, another woman in Jacob's childhood life, emphasizes his vision by demonstrating her sympathy with it. Mrs. Jarvis likes Jacob best of all the Flanders boys, and her affection for him is explained by her emotional kinship with him. She is the sort of woman "to confound her God with the universal . . ." (27), to read poetry, and to search for a meaning behind the outward confusion of life. After reading one of Jacob's last letters to his mother, she expresses a sense of closeness to the dead that Mrs. Flanders, making a great noise with her scissors, of course does not hear.

A third woman who will observe and define Jacob from without is Julia Eliot, a prototype of Lily Briscoe in *To the Lighthouse* both in her painting and in her desire to contemplate life rather than to assume a central role in it herself. (" 'Please,' said Julia Eliot, taking up her position by the curtain almost opposite the door, 'don't introduce me. I like to look on' " [85].) Yet the extent to which Miss Eliot does involve herself in the sorrows of others enables her to develop an instinct for tragedy which allows her to see that Jacob is somehow not of this world. "The silent young man" (59), she calls him. Like many of the women who sense death hovering about Jacob, she connects this aura with his beauty and his kinship to the ancients.

> . . . five minutes after she had passed the statue of Achilles she had the rapt look of one brushing through crowds on a summer's afternoon, when the trees are rustling, the wheels churning yellow, and the tumult of the present seems like an elegy for past youth and past summers, and there rose in her mind a curious sadness, as if time and eternity showed through skirts and waistcoats, and she saw people passing tragically to destruction (168).

Because Jacob in his visionary capacity must be able to envelop everyone in the novel and so give it unity by his presence, every person who steps through the pages of *Jacob's Room* reflects some measure of the light from his personality. Yet those who seem to absorb this light and then shed it again over their own small worlds are those connected to Jacob by love. In both *The Voyage Out* and *Night and Day* Virginia

Woolf explored the possibilities of love as a unifying force
that might lead to the greater unity of vision. Here by joining
more than two people in love she attempts to extend this form
of vision to its widest range, holding together a number of
disparate worlds by this single strand.

The first girl who falls in love with Jacob is Clara Durrant, a
girl enough like Katharine Hilbery to be her sister, and so a
link between Jacob and the world of intellectual upper-middle-
class society. "Alas, women lie!" remarks the authorial voice,
"But not Clara Durrant. A flawless mind; a candid nature; a
virgin chained to a rock (somewhere off Lowndes Square)
eternally pouring out tea for old men in white waistcoats,
blue-eyed, looking you straight in the face, playing Bach"
(123). Like Katharine, Clara is overshadowed by a mother
whose mind skims leagues and centuries while her body seems
nearly transparent in her lack of attachment to earthly things
(56). Like Katharine, too, Clara has difficulty reconciling herself with her mother's style of life and reacts by clinging to
silence as an escape from the verbal soul-searching and out-
bursts of emotion in which Mrs. Durrant indulges. Clara's
daily life is enmeshed in the trappings of social protocol that
seem to offer her no escape. "Clara Durrant procured the
stockings, played the sonata, filled the vases, fetched the pudding, left the cards, and when the great invention of paper
flowers to swim in finger-bowls was discovered, was one of
those who most marvelled at their brief lives" (84). Yet when
Jacob enters her life, Clara takes on the transparent qualities of
her mother, seeming to catch the sense of unworldliness from
him. He comes to dinner and sees opposite him "hazy, semi-
transparent shapes of yellow and blues" (57). Then "'Oh,
Clara, Clara!' exclaimed Mrs. Durrant, and Timothy Durrant
adding, 'Clara, Clara,' Jacob named the shape in yellow gauze
Timothy's sister, Clara. The girl sat smiling and flushed. With
her brother's dark eyes, she was vaguer and softer than he
was" (57). It is as if the double calling of her name unites her
with Jacob whom we have learned to associate with the repeated call. Whenever she is with him after this during their
unstated courtship, she assumes the same unbounded char-

acter and seems, like Jacob, to melt into the world around her. "She looked semi-transparent, pale, wonderfully beautiful up there among the vine leaves and the yellow and purple bunches, the lights swimming over her in coloured islands" (62). So Clara, who loves Jacob, loses the definite outlines that define her as a sharp-minded, dutiful, society daughter and with him seems to spill over into the light that shines on her world, thus extending his influence into her social sphere. But Clara is not to keep Jacob's love, as she herself realizes when, one night at the opera, she "said farewell to Jacob Flanders, and tasted the sweetness of death in effigy . . ." (68). Because Jacob is in most respects a symbolic figure, he is not meant to follow love through the ordinary channels of engagement, marriage, and a family. Instead he serves only to kindle love in a number of people, thus extending his existence and uniting his incorporeal self with more and more of the world around him. Clara sums up this side of Jacob when she writes simply in her diary: "I like Jacob Flanders. . . . He is so unworldly" (71).

The next girl who flickers across the surface of Jacob's life never seems to settle completely into the factual world of solid bodies and clearly defined identities. Her insubstantiality is emphasized from the moment she appears with Jacob at the Guy Fawkes bonfire.

> Of the faces which came out fresh and vivid as though painted in yellow and red, the most prominent was a girl's face. By a trick of the firelight she seemed to have no body. The oval of the face and hair hung beside the fire with a dark vacuum for background. As if dazed by the glare, her green-blue eyes stared at the flames. Every muscle of her face was taut. There was something tragic in her thus staring . . . (74).

Like a foreboding ghost, Florinda hovers beside Jacob in the light of the flames, her face predicting his death, her lack of physical outline uniting her to Jacob's deathly qualities. In the broad daylight, too, she remains ill-defined, and even her name is not her own.

> As for Florinda's story, her name had been bestowed upon
> her by a painter who had wished it to signify that the flower
> of her maidenhood was still unplucked. Be that as it may,
> she was without a surname, and for parents had only the
> photograph of a tombstone beneath which, she said, her
> father lay buried. Sometimes she would dwell upon the size
> of it, and rumour had it that Florinda's father had died
> from the growth of his bones which nothing could
> stop . . . (77).

Even in her parentage Florinda is associated with death, so it
is significant that it is with her that Jacob enjoys his greatest
physical love. By uniting his body with a girl who has no real
body of her own, he seems to bring together the two paths to
visionary unity: love and death. At the same time, since their
relationship is all physical with no interplay of minds, Jacob
succeeds in joining himself to the physical world without as
a result becoming trapped in its limitations.

Almost without exception the girls whom Jacob loves or
who love him take on some aspect of visionary incorporeality.
Clara becomes semi-transparent with Jacob; the mindless Florinda gives him a body that is no body; and Fanny Elmer, a
girl who loves him in silence, joins these two in her own association with various roads to vision. She enters the scene
"Through the disused graveyard in the parish of St. Pancras
. . ." and strays "between the white tombs which lean against
the wall, crossing the grass to read a name, hurrying on when
the grave-keeper approached . . ." (114). Besides being close to
death here and in a long illness during her brief connection
with Jacob, Fanny touches vision, like Jacob, in her beauty.
Beauty has none of the fixity of other factual attributes, according to Virginia Woolf, but rather is something that hovers
about a person, uniting him to all the beauty that has ever
existed and shedding a light that shows others a flash of this
visionary unity.

> As for the beauty of women, it is like the light on the sea,
> never constant to a single wave. They all have it; they
> all lose it. Now she is dull and thick as bacon; now trans-

parent as a hanging glass. . . . Then, at a top-floor window,
leaning out, looking down, you see beauty itself; or in
the corner of an omnibus; or squatted in a ditch—beauty
glowing, suddenly expressive, withdrawn the moment
after. No one can count on it or seize it or have it wrapped
in paper. . . . Thus if you talk of a beautiful woman you
mean only something flying fast which for a second uses the
eyes, lips, or cheeks of Fanny Elmer, for example,
to glow through (115).

Fanny recognizes the immortal beauty in Jacob as she sees him
in the Ulysses at the British Museum (170). So in their mutual
beauty and in their closeness to death, Jacob and Fanny experience the vision together. Love, like death and beauty, unites
people on a plane beyond that limited by time and space; and
Fanny's love for Jacob, though it is never returned, acts as a
thread to tie her world to him. Thus merely by leaving her
umbrella in a shop, she brings the people there under the great
umbrella of unity that Jacob creates.

In the last woman to whom Jacob is linked by love, the vision
is made explicit. She enters the novel with the words:

"I am full of love for every one . . . for the poor most of
all—for the peasants coming back in the evening with
their burdens. And everything is soft and vague and very
sad. It is sad, it is sad. But everything has meaning," thought
Sandra Wentworth Williams, raising her head a little and
looking very beautiful, tragic, and exalted. "One must
love everything" (141).

Universal love. This is the message of many of Woolf's visionaries; for universal love could accomplish the total conjunction
of all the disparate elements in life to realize the vision in a
factual world. In *Jacob's Room* Jacob goes as far as one man,
even a symbolic man, can go to lead the world to this ideal
union. And Sandra Wentworth Williams, when she compares
his head with the head of the Hermes of Praxiteles and finds
the comparison all in Jacob's favor, recognizes that he stands
for beauty and love greater than the love of any one man for
any one woman.

If Jacob inspired only women with a vision of love and beauty, he could not serve as a universal ordering force. Thus Richard Bonamy, "who couldn't love a woman and never read a foolish book" (140), perfects Jacob's interwoven world by bringing into it, through his love for his friend, the element of fact-loving masculine intellect. He likes "sentences that don't budge though armies cross them" (140) and hard, concise facts, but recognizes that Jacob is "not at all of his own way of thinking . . ." (140). In his clear-sighted way, Bonamy understands that Jacob "was not much given to analysis, but was horribly romantic . . ." (139–40), thus seeing both the factual and visionary sides of Jacob's nature.

Jacob has a strong factual side, a necessary attribute if he is to combine in himself the all-embracing world of vision and the precise, defining world of fact. Yet this concrete self is very strange, for it either manifests itself in material objects that surround him or becomes solidified so that at moments Jacob seems to be himself an inanimate object, a statue. The reason for this peculiar existence is explained if we realize that a Jacob who took on the individual idiosyncracies of other men could never assume true symbolic proportion but would instead be reduced to the level of any other person living in a bounded world. Thus when we approach him from outside we must find in his personality an equal balance of the mystical and the concrete.

When we first encounter him at Cambridge, where, as a young man he has presumably assumed a mature identity, he appears simply as one of the many students hurrying to chapel. "Look, as they pass into service, how airily the gowns blow out, as though nothing dense and corporeal were within. What sculptured faces, what certainty, authority controlled by piety, although great boots march under the gowns" (32). Here the concrete side of Jacob is presented by his boots and mask-like face, while the rest of his selfhood blows about as insubstantial as the wind. And it is noteworthy that here, as in countless other places, Jacob does not stand out as an individual, but seems to merge with those around him to become a universal type. He is often not "Jacob" but "the young man."

It is not surprising then that we should discover most about his substantial self from the objects in his room. Like his chambermaid in Greece, we must conclude by "fingering keys, studs, pencils, and bottles of tabloids strewn on the dressing-table" that "he had grown to be a man" (139). His intellectual precision, then, is shown to us in the corrections he makes in the margins of his books with his very fine pen (23); or in the essay lying on the table, "Does History consist of the Biographies of Great Men?" (39). His whole factual self seems to be contained in a black wooden box in which he keeps his rejected essays, "his mother's letters, his old flannel trousers, and a note or two with the Cornish postmark." (70) And, when he closes this box, "The lid shut upon the truth" (70). The limits of this definable self are best represented by the letters that Jacob sends and receives and to which Virginia Woolf as author devotes particular attention, saying, "Let us consider letters—how they come at breakfast, and at night, with their yellow stamps and their green stamps, immortalized by the postmark—for to see one's own envelope on another's table is to realize how soon deeds sever and become alien" (92). Letters attempt to communicate the self but always manage to include only a fragment, and that fragment outdated by the time it reaches its destination.

If letters sent and received make up a large portion of Jacob's solid self, clothing composes an equally important segment. When we enter his room we find his slippers, "incredibly shabby, like boats burnt in the water's rim" (39), and remember Miss Allan's statement in *The Voyage Out* to the effect that people are so like their boots. After Jacob's death the letters, papers, and the boots will remain; and, since they comprise most of his identity, he can scarcely be said to have died at all. This use of clothing to give shape to the self in the world is explained explicitly on Jacob's voyage to the Scilly Isles. While out on the water, he goes naked and lets himself become a part of the wind and the waves. Here the "discreet black object" that is his dinner jacket "had made its appearance now and then in the boat among tins, pickles, preserved meats, and as the voyage went on had become more and more irrelevant, hardly to be believed in" (57). Once on shore, however, and "the world being stable, lit by candle-light, the dinner jacket alone preserved him" (57).

If, in general, Jacob is defined by the objects that surround him, at times he seems to assume the singleness and solid form of an object himself, becoming a fact in the factual world. For example, having drifted almost entirely into the insubstantial realm in his affair with the formless Florinda, he swings back into objective reality in a moment of startling clarity when she leaves him for another. "The light drenched Jacob from head to toe. You could see the pattern on his trousers; the old thorns on his stick; his shoe laces; bare hands, and face" (94). To restore the balance between unity and individuality that his liaison with Florinda almost destroyed, he must first recapture his definable self completely.

What usually stands out when Jacob assumes this statuesque immobility is his beauty. As a result, he becomes a representative figure of all beauty and, like other solid objects that engender awareness of vision in Virginia Woolf's novels, becomes one with all beauty in every age and place. Percival in *The Waves* will assume this same function, acting as the objective reality from which poets leap to vision, the definable one who comes to represent the indefinable whole. In *Jacob's Room* one notable instance of Jacob's becoming this symbolic statue occurs at the Guy Fawkes ball.

> "We think," said two of the dancers, breaking off from the rest, and bowing profoundly before him, "that you are the most beautiful man we have ever seen."
>
> So they wreathed his head with paper flowers. Then somebody brought out a white and gilt chair and made him sit on it. As they passed, people hung glass grapes on his shoulders, until he looked like the figure-head of a wrecked ship (75).

Here Jacob becomes both statue and god of beauty, an object, but an object with a symbolic significance far greater than one physical form can contain.

At times then, Jacob can be an objective personality defined by his boots and his books; at others he can be an object of worship, but an object all the same. At still others, Jacob incorporates the factual world into himself, as has been noted above, by suddenly becoming the representative figure for an entire social group. At Cambridge,

> . . . Jacob moved. He murmured good-night. He went out into the court. He buttoned his jacket across his chest. He went back to his rooms, and being the only man who walked at that moment back to his rooms, his footsteps rang out, his figure loomed large. Back from the Chapel, back from the Hall, back from the Library, came the sound of his footsteps, as if the old stone echoed with magisterial authority: "The young man—the young man—the young man—back to his rooms" (46).

Or, as one of innumerable clerks and office workers, he melts into this crowd: "Innumerable overcoats of the quality prescribed hung empty all day in the corridors, but as the clock struck six each was exactly filled, and the little figures, split apart into trousers or moulded into a single thickness, jerked rapidly with angular forward motion along the pavement; then dropped into darkness" (66–67).

As a visionary being, Jacob has absorbed into himself all of the people and places of *Jacob's Room;* as a factual being he has collected memorabilia, represented the social actions of students, workers, partygoers, and other inhabitants of the world of limited time and space, and has served as a tangible symbol for an intangible meaning behind the objective surface of life. So, after his death, what has been lost? His room remains the same with its creaking chair, flowers, carved ram's head, and roses. His wooden box still holds his letters and papers. The types he has represented still flourish in university and office. Thus when Mrs. Flanders holds out a pair of Jacob's old shoes and asks, " 'What am I to do with these, Mr. Bonamy?' " (176), she is in essence holding the whole of the factual Jacob in her hands. The visionary Jacob lived consistently in the world of death and so has not changed. So Jacob, by flowing from childhood through death without rippling the waters of the world around him, is actually absorbed into that world, thereby combining literally the fact and vision that Rachel and Terence, Katharine and Ralph, tried to join on a limited scale in their own lives.

Because *Jacob's Room* is meant to contain all of life, it is not surprising that in one form or another it includes the fruit or the seeds of Virginia Woolf's other novels concealed in its pages. I have already mentioned in passing several similarities between this book and her first two works. But there are countless other echoes from her later novels as well. In fact, after returning to *Jacob's Room* having read all of Mrs. Woolf's novels, it is almost eerie to find surprising fragments of most of them here, some direct, some only suggested. For example, Mr. Bowley who loves Clara and walks her dog for her appears by name among the minor characters of *Mrs. Dalloway,* again walking a dog. Clara and Mrs. Durrant attend the Dalloway party. And can it be coincidence that the Durrant mother and daughter who have such problems communicating should be named Elizabeth and Clara while the names of the similar pair in *Mrs. Dalloway* are Clarissa and Elizabeth? Then Bonamy's relationship to Jacob as he would "play round him like an affectionate spaniel" (165) is mirrored in kind and in image in Septimus Warren Smith's doglike devotion to Evans, again in *Mrs. Dalloway*. Perhaps it is to be expected that some of *Jacob's Room* would wash into the novel that followed it so closely. But there are an equal number of foreshadowings of *To the Lighthouse* in the earlier book. The Durrants' home in the Scilly Isles is inhabited by the visionary Mrs. Durrant, who, like the visionary Mrs. Ramsay, spends much of her time knitting; Miss Julia Eliot, who, like Lily Briscoe, sets up her easel on the lawn and paints; Mr. Clutterbuck, who might even be Mr. Carmichael in disguise: a man who lives with the Durrants because of an unhappy relationship with his wife, who even maintains the same eating habits, going on with his food long after others have finished (see pp. 58 and 88). Then like Bernard and Neville in *The Waves,* Jacob and Timmy sit talking and rocking in a boat on the river near Cambridge, consuming fruit like the imitator of Percival in that later book.

And the unsympathetic Captain Barfoot, with his two missing fingers, leaves his sick wife to visit another woman just as will the similarly deformed Colonel Pargiter in *The Years*. So *Jacob's Room* contains past, present, and future in more ways than one and stands as a symbol of infinite unification more completely than perhaps even its author was aware.

So technically, *Jacob's Room* manages to cram into its few pages practically every aspect of fact and vision in the everyday world. But it is a slight book to carry so great a burden, and it suffers from being overly full. Jacob himself, while succeeding as a symbol of reconciled fact and vision, is so weighted down with significance that he can barely move through his life at all. Because he is unable, in his symbolic capacity, to assume the quirks of a complex human being or even the clear-cut proportions of a typically two-dimensional character, he cannot fail to oppress the mind of the reader and lose his impact in the process.

In *Mrs. Dalloway* Virginia Woolf will give up trying to present the total unity of fact and vision in a single "realistic," symbolic figure. Instead she will begin to concentrate on defining the various aspects of these dual realms by assigning only one or two attributes of each to a single character.

4

Mrs. Dalloway

WHEN Virginia Woolf discusses her next novel in her diary, she gives the eager critic any number of ways to attack and dissect *Mrs. Dalloway*. "I want to give life and death, sanity and insanity," she writes. "I want to criticize the social system, and to show it at work, at its most intense."[1] This and similar clues have sent her commentators off in all directions. Some, like Joseph Warren Beach, have chosen to see the novel's subject as "what life seems like on a fine day in London."[2] Others, following this social path, have turned upon the story's heroine as "a sentimental, worldly sort of average sensual woman . . . the trivialities of her pointless, sensational life inflated to universal proportions";[3] or have seen her as a symbol of narrow, mechanical society;[4] or, with less ferocity, have looked at her as one individual whose soul has withered in the glaring sun of her social world.[5] Those who focus on Woolf's criticism of society tend, like Harvena Richter, to concentrate on Clarissa's snobbishness[6] and the shallower aspects of her role as hostess. But it should be evident, not only from the novel itself but also from Virginia Woolf's statement about it, that the negative social element is only a fragment of the whole, and that to overstress this theme is to warp the full meaning of the work. So critics like Ralph Freedman come closer to apprehending the full scope of Virginia Woolf's intention when they find the substance of *Mrs. Dalloway* to lie "in the opposition of an external world of manners and an internal symbolic world."[7]

Because the complementary and opposing themes of this novel are so tightly woven into its form, many critics have concentrated on method more than meaning. Bernard Blackstone, for example, sees *Mrs. Dalloway* as "an experiment with time and point of view";[8] while David Daiches constructs a brilliant plot of spatial and temporal structuring in the novel.[9] Those who attempt to elucidate the main themes often approach *Mrs. Dalloway* with Jean Guiguet through another form of diagramming, examining the characters as they represent various adaptations to life in society.[10] In spite of the fact, however, that several critics have focused on the various men and women in *Mrs. Dalloway* individually, none has associated these figures with Virginia Woolf's major concern with the duality of fact and vision. This method is naturally suited to the novel; for here, for the first time, Virginia Woolf attempts to define the different aspects of fact and vision that compose the human universe, displaying each individual element or possible combination in separate symbolic characters.

Beginning with the most limited and constricting aspect of factual life, Mrs. Woolf presents us with Sir William Bradshaw, who demonstrates "the peculiar repulsiveness of those who dabble their fingers self-approvingly in the stuff of others' souls."[11] As she indicated in *The Voyage Out* with Rachel's need to discover herself before launching into comprehensible vision, Virginia Woolf feels that one of the prerequisites for successful vision is an awareness and maintenance of a private soul that can separate itself from the world around it and so gain a perspective that discovers a larger unity in the seeming discontinuity of life. Thus the most destructive element in the factual world is the desire of one man to impose inflexible laws and boundaries on others, to possess their individual souls and make them conform to his own. Sir William Bradshaw in his successful Harley Street psychiatric practice embodies all of this antivision.

Worshipping proportion, Sir William not only prospered himself but made England prosper, secluded her lunatics,

forbade childbirth, penalised despair, made it impossible
for the unfit to propagate their views until they, too,
shared his sense of proportion . . .[12]

On a limited scale proportion is not necessarily a negative
force, for ideally it could recognize that a balance exists between fact and vision that no event can upset. For Sir William,
however, vision does not exist. He has no inner sense of unity
but only a very efficient mechanical view of normalcy, which
completely denies all creativity and individuality, let alone the
merging of souls. Each person, according to his theory, has his
pigeonhole; and the good doctor not only believes this theory,
but demands that the world conform to it.

> . . . Proportion has a sister, less smiling, more formidable.
> . . . Conversion is her name and she feasts on the wills of the
> weakly, loving to impress, to impose, adoring her own
> features stamped on the face of the populace. At Hyde Park
> Corner on a tub she stands preaching; shrouds herself in
> white and walks penitentially disguised as brotherly love
> through factories and parliaments; offers help, but desires
> power; smites out of her way roughly the dissentient, or
> dissatisfied; bestows her blessing on those who, looking
> upward, catch submissively from her eyes the light of their
> own. This lady too . . . had her dwelling in Sir William's
> heart, though concealed, as she mostly is, under some
> plausible disguise; some venerable name; love, duty,
> self sacrifice (151–52).

Thus when the intuitive Clarissa hears that one of Sir William's patients has committed suicide, she thinks:

> . . . there were the poets and thinkers. Suppose he had had
> that passion, and had gone to Sir William Bradshaw, a great
> doctor yet to her obscurely evil, without sex or lust,
> extremely polite to women, but capable of some indescrib-
> able outrage—forcing your soul, that was it—if this young
> man had gone to him, and Sir William had impressed
> him, like that, with his power, might he not then have said

(indeed she felt it now), Life is made intolerable; they
make life intolerable, men like that? (281).

Doris Kilman, as her name suggests, is another disciple of
the goddess Conversion, and her physical habits and appearance reflect her lack of vision. In the first place she is painfully
homely; and beauty, as we have seen in *Jacob's Room,* is often
a path to unity. Music, too, as it brings together individual
notes to form a sense of pattern and harmony, can realize the
vision as it does for Rachel Vinrace. But Miss Kilman, though
she finds comfort in the evenings with her violin, produces ex-
cruciating sounds, for "she had no ear" (188). Her insensitivity
to the vision is presented not only in symbolic allusion, but
also in action; and her need to overcome others makes her the
factual sister of Sir William Bradshaw. Where Sir William acts
on principle and is thus universally dangerous, making his will
seem indisputable law to those who consult him, Miss Kilman
acts from passion on a more limited personal scale. But both
these destructive individuals mask their spiritual cannibalism
with some respectable disguise—a sense of proportion in the
case of Sir William, devotion to religion in the case of Miss
Kilman. "She had seen the light two years and three months
ago. Now she did not envy women like Clarissa Dalloway; she
pitied them. She pitied and despised them from the bottom of
her heart . . ." (187–88). With religion as her shield, Miss Kilman can determine to bring her superiors down to her own
restricted level without seeming to be acting from envy. So
when she faces Mrs. Dalloway,

> . . . there rose in her an overmastering desire to overcome
> her; to unmask her. If she could have felled her it would
> have eased her. But it was not the body; it was the soul
> and its mockery that she wished to subdue; make feel her
> mastery. If only she could make her weep; could ruin her;
> humiliate her; bring her to her knees crying, You are
> right! But this was God's will, not Miss Kilman's. It was
> to be a religious victory (189).

If Doris Kilman translates religion as the personal power of conversion, she also demonstrates the negative possibilities of love on the factual plane. Miss Kilman loves Elizabeth Dalloway with her whole being, but her love seeks fulfillment not in communication and visionary unity, but in possession. "If she could grasp her, if she could clasp her, if she could make her hers absolutely and forever and then die; that was all she wanted" (199–200). As an entryway to vision, love, as we have seen in all of Virginia Woolf's earlier novels, exemplifies in the factual world the unity that embraces all people at the level of vision. But when limited to the world of fact exclusively, it becomes a desire to possess, restrict, imprison others as though they were inanimate objects to be locked away in a personal safe. So Clarissa, when faced with the unspoken animosity of her daughter's teacher, thinks: "Love and religon! . . . How detestable, how detestable they are!" (191). Yet she recognizes that it is not the pathetic Miss Kilman she finds so repugnant, but all that the insensitive woman stands for. "For it was not her one hated but the idea of her, which undoubtedly had gathered in to itself a great deal that was not Miss Kilman; had become one of those spectres with which one battles in the night; one of those spectres who stand astride us and suck up half our life-blood, dominators and tyrants . . ." (16–17) Miss Kilman, like Sir William Bradshaw, comes to represent more than a single individual's limited insight. She is a symbol of the person who constructs inflexible categories in the factual world and then attempts to force each new experience into one of these limited molds.

Sir William Bradshaw and Doris Kilman, then, lie at the negative pole in the dual world of vision and fact, assigned there for their denial of the unbounded soul and their attempts to impose this view on others. Barely above them in the factual scale stands the empty man, Hugh Whitbread. As David Daiches has pointed out, Hugh "has almost lost his real personality in fulfilling his social function."[13] He may not forcibly attempt to destroy the vision in others, but he certainly possesses none of it himself, for he has literally become a part of the factual world, being defined completely by his social actions. Throughout the novel, Hugh Whitbread is portrayed as the mere husk of the perfect British gentleman without even the driest kernel of a soul rattling about inside. When he meets Clarissa in the park, both his conversation and appearance make manifest his exclusively factual character:

> Was Evelyn ill again? Evelyn was a good deal out of sorts, said Hugh, intimating by a kind of pout or swell of his very well-covered, manly, extremely handsome, perfectly up-holstered body (he was almost too well dressed always, but presumably had to be, with his little job at Court) that his wife had some internal ailment, nothing serious, which, as an old friend, Clarissa Dalloway would quite understand without requiring him to specify (7).

Hugh has about as much inner life as a sofa and he finds any internal problem, even in his wife, something unmentionable. "He did not go deeply. He brushed surfaces . . ." (155). As a result, he is a master at writing meaningless but proper letters to the *Times,* "drafting sentiments in alphabetical order of the highest nobility . . ." (167). So at Clarissa's party, where people seem to become their fullest selves, Hugh goes "strolling past in his white waistcoat, dim, fat, blind, past everything he looked, except self-esteem and comfort" (288). He is the perfect embodiment of society in its purely factual aspects, going through the motions of life mechanically, hardly aware of himself and totally unaware of the vital existence of others. Peter Walsh, whose uncompromising devotion to factual truth isolates him from the often hypocritical social world, sees that Hugh has "no heart, no brain, nothing but the manners and breeding of an English gentleman . . ." (8). But Clarissa, who sees the need for a balance between the vision and social fact, admires Hugh for his faultless performance of the less selfish social actions: "When his old mother wanted him to give up shooting or take her to Bath he did it, without a word . . ." (8).

Richard Dalloway, though akin to Hugh in being a minor government official, concerned with social protocol, is not restricted entirely to factual existence. He may, to be sure, get seriously and solemnly "on his hind legs" and say "that no decent man ought to read Shakespeare's sonnets because it was like listening at keyholes . . ." (113). But in his own love for his wife, his delight in continuity (177), and his instinctive aversion to Sir William Bradshaw (278–79), Mr. Dalloway approaches the world of vision, at least on a limited scale. As we have seen in all of Woolf's novels, love can create an almost mystical sense of revelation in an individual. At Lady Bruton's luncheon party, while Hugh is alternately stuffing himself and playing with empty phrases, Richard is suddenly overwhelmed by a feeling of love for Clarissa that grows to visionary proportions during the next few hours. "It was a miracle. Here he was walking across London to say to Clarissa in so many words that he loved her. Which one never does say, he thought" (174). Love, in its fullest sense, is too boundless to be articulated and must be expressed by the more comprehensive message of symbol. "He wanted to come in holding something. Flowers? Yes, flowers . . . any number of flowers, roses, orchids, to celebrate what was, reckoning things as you will, an event; this feeling about her when they spoke of Peter Walsh at luncheon . . ." (174). Barbara Seward recognizes that in Virginia Woolf's fiction "the flower appears in intense moments during which her characters realize the ineffable meanings of their lives. The moments are moments of true vision expressing Mrs. Woolf's own conviction that ecstasy, solitude, love, and death are interchangeable aspects of life."[14] Here and at several other important points in *Mrs. Dalloway* flowers serve just this purpose, and Clarissa, receiving the roses from her husband, immediately recognizes their significance: "But how lovely, she said, taking his flowers. She understood; she understood without his speaking . . ." (179). The relationship between the Dalloways at its most ideal moments captures the perfect unity of vision in which each retains his own distinct identity while maintaining an unspoken spiritual bond.

In Sir William Bradshaw, Doris Kilman, Hugh Whitbread, and Richard Dalloway we have seen examples of individuals existing primarily at the social level of fact and presenting us with fairly one-sided personalities. With Peter Walsh, however, we encounter new complexities, and it is not surprising that he has been diversely interpreted by those critics who choose to examine him. Some set him among the destroyers of the privacy of the soul along with Sir William and Miss Kilman.[15] Others see him as "the average man" who is too attached to his identity to escape to vision.[16] Still others interpret him as the path to freedom that Clarissa failed to take.[17] Perhaps the best way to understand what Peter represents is to set him beside St. John Hirst of *The Voyage Out*. For Peter, like the younger man, is so unflaggingly devoted to truth that he cannot bring himself to accept the compromise that life in an insincere society offers him. Yet he is too honest to see his own observations as the only truth and so can comprehend the importance of vision. Peter Walsh comes even closer to an awareness of visionary unity than did St. John Hirst, however, for Peter can fall in love, and can receive brief moments of revelation created by this love, even if he is unable to reconcile them with fidelity to abstract principles.

Perhaps the reason that Peter cannot maintain the revelatory aspect of love is that, too often for him, love becomes a passion that dominates the body rather than the soul. So a passing pretty woman can easily appear to be "the very woman he had always had in mind" (79), a woman he can follow through the street, build fantasy adventures and seductions around, and then abandon in sudden deflating realization that ". . . it was smashed to atoms—his fun, for it was half made up, as he knew very well . . ." (81). Even his Daisy, the girl in India he plans to marry, keeps his love alive only through jealousy; and although this love takes on visionary proportions when he confesses it to Clarissa, in the everyday world his determined honesty makes him admit that "for hours and days he never thought of Daisy" (120). As the novel progresses, it becomes clear that Peter's love for Clarissa came closest to real vision for him, but that even there "His demands upon [her] (he could see it now) were absurd. He asked impossible things" (95). Because he is forever demanding absolutes, he discovers himself always left with compromises.

The essential concern with important abstract truths that lies at the core of Peter's character is symbolized by his continually opening and closing his jackknife: "What an extraordinary habit that was, Clarissa thought; always playing with a knife. Always making one feel, too, frivolous; empty-minded; a mere silly chatterbox, as he used" (65). This association with knives and intellectual honesty reappears in *The Waves* with Neville's pride in his knife, a recurrence noted by N. C. Thakur in *The Symbolism of Virginia Woolf*.[18] In his capacity of unflinching truth-seeker, Peter Walsh has no mercy (263), no tact. He refuses to cover the facts with facile social lies and points sternly to Clarissa's frequent insincerities as well as to the superficiality of others. Of course such behavior, such insistence on outspoken truth, leads to social disgrace, a fact that Peter readily admits. "He had been sent down from Oxford—true. He had been a Socialist, in some sense a failure—true. Still the future of civilisation lies, he thought, in the hands of young men like that; of young men such as he was, thirty years ago; with their love of abstract principles . . ." (75). Like other truth-driven men before and after him in Virginia Woolf's novels, Peter Walsh misses much of the individual beauties in life while attending to larger issues.

> But Peter—however beautiful the day might be, and the trees and the grass, and the little girl in pink—Peter never saw a thing of all that. He would put on his spectacles, if she [Clarissa] told him to; he would look. It was the state of the world that interested him; Wagner, Pope's poetry, people's characters eternally, and the defects of her own soul (9).

Yet for all his concern with great truths and abstractions, Peter recognizes the need in every man for contact with the surrounding world, and even admits to himself with surprise that "there were moments when civilisation . . . seemed dear to him as a personal possession; moments of pride in England; in butlers; chow dogs; girls in their security. Ridiculous enough, still there it is, he thought" (82). The fact that he can, at times, understand Clarissa's fascination with externals allows Peter to confess that his devotion to principle and abstraction is not the whole of life. "For this is the truth about our soul, he thought, our self, who fish-like inhabits deep seas and plies

among obscurities threading her way between the boles of
giant weeds, over sun-flickered spaces and on and on into
gloom, cold, deep, inscrutable; suddenly she shoots to the
surface and sports on the wind-wrinkled waves; that is, has a
positive need to brush, scrape, kindle herself, gossiping" (244).
The person who serves as a flame to kindle another side of
Peter is Clarissa. Although he sees objectively her social shal-
lowness and openly criticizes her for it, yet "She had influenced
him more than any person he had ever known" (232–33). He
recognizes, then, that somehow, below the surface superficiality
of the hostess Clarissa, there lies an all-seeing soul; so he offers
up his own visions to this deeper Clarissa as the proper recipient of those most important truths. " 'I am in love,' he said,
not to her however, but to some one raised up in the dark so
that you could not touch her but must lay your garland down
on the grass in the dark" (66).

Because Peter cannot overlook Clarissa's social side, he must
often wait until he has left her physical presence before her
creative powers can light in him the awareness of universal
vision. His most significant glimpse of this all-embracing
world, for example, comes to him during a mid-morning nap
soon after he leaves Clarissa preparing for her party. In his
dream he can assume a symbolic self as "the solitary traveller"
and encounter the visionary Clarissa, who assumes the proportions of a goddess:

> By conviction an atheist perhaps, he is taken by surprise
> with moments of extraordinary exaltation . . . advancing
> down the path with his eyes upon the sky and branches
> he rapidly endows them with womanhood; sees with
> amazement how grave they become; how majestically, as the
> breeze stirs them, they dispense with a dark flutter of the
> leaves charity, comprehension, absolution . . . (85–86).

That this tree woman who metamorphoses into a siren "lollop-
ing away on the green sea waves" (86) is Clarissa is made clear
at her party, where she wears a "silver-green mermaid's dress"
and "lollops" on the waves (264).

Such are the visions which ceaselessly float up, pace beside, put their faces in front of, the actual thing; often over-powering the solitary traveller and taking away from him the sense of the earth, the wish to return, and giving him for substitute a general peace, as if . . . all this fever of living were simplicity itself; and myriads of things merged in one thing; and this figure, made of sky and branches it is, had risen from the troubled sea . . . as a shape might be sucked up out of the waves to shower down from her magnificent hands compassion, comprehension, absolution (86).

Here, with Clarissa's help, Peter experiences Woolf's central vision of a universal merging and peace. Like Rachel's vision in *The Voyage Out* and the mutual visions of Katharine and Ralph in *Night and Day,* this momentary revelation presents a melting of man into trees and sky.

The dream of the solitary traveler is not the only glimpse Peter gains of vision. There is at least one other important moment, before his final revelation at the party, when he dis-covers a sudden sense of unity in life. Walking through London on the afternoon of Clarissa's entertainment, Peter is passed by an ambulance carrying the mangled remains of Septimus Warren Smith; and all at once he feels "really it took one's breath away, these moments; there coming to him by the pillar-box opposite the British Museum one of them, a mo-ment, in which things came together; this ambulance; and life and death" (230). What makes this fleeting vision of unity espe-cially significant is that it provides a link between Septimus's death and Clarissa's life. Both the young man in the ambulance and the woman at her party are vision makers, and will grad-ually be revealed to be doubles as well.

All of the characters discussed thus far have dwelled pri-marily in the realm of fact, some experiencing moments of unity, but none providing an unadulterated representation of the purely visionary world. The man in this novel who does stand for total vision is Septimus Warren Smith, and, signifi-cantly, he is "mad." One of the first symptoms of this madness is his "attaching meanings to words of a symbolical kind" (145), thus refusing to recognize definable limits to either objects or communication. A second symptom of his madness is the fact that "he could not taste, he could not feel." (132). Although he himself associates this lack of feeling with an emotional vacuum, it is equally, and perhaps more accurately, an inability to achieve any concrete subject-object relationship: his sense of a definable self is missing, so that instead of coming into contact with the external world, he literally feels himself one with it.

What "disease" can be recognized by this inability to sense boundaries and the resulting tendency to merge completely with the universe? In ideal terms it is not a disease at all but a total realization of vision, vision that reveals the unity of man and world. Each new phase of Septimus's madness, then, must be seen not through the short-sighted eyes of the fact-bound Sir William Bradshaw but through eyes sensitive to vision. When we first encounter Septimus on the verge of joyful tears brought on by the sight of the ephemeral skywriting that draws the attention of crowds of Londoners, we understand that, true to his vision, he is recognizing "unimaginable beauty" (31). If love of beauty is characteristic of the visionary, so is aware-ness of the unreality of death. Thus the birds who bring their secret message to Septimus sing "how there is no death" (36). Rachel, Katharine, Ralph, and even Peter Walsh experience an almost mystical feeling of convergence and meaning at the sight of a tree; and trees continually work themselves into Septimus's visions. "A marvellous discovery indeed," he thinks, "—that the human voice in certain atmospheric conditions (for one must be scientific, above all scientific) can quicken trees into life!" (32). So when his great message is ready to be presented "to the Prime Minister," it states "first that trees are alive; next there is no crime; next love, universal love . . ." (102). All of Septimus's fantasies carry with them the meaning of vision that Virginia Woolf is intent upon presenting in all her novels.

It is not only the meaning of vision, however, but its literal enactment that we see in Septimus. In the visionary moments experienced by Virginia Woolf's most perceptive characters, there is a sense of spiritual merging with all people, places, and things. So Septimus, watching the branches of an elm tree rise and fall, feels that "the leaves being connected by millions of fibres with his own body, there on the seat, fanned it up and down; when the branch stretched he, too, made that statement. The sparrows fluttering, rising, and falling in jagged fountains were part of the pattern . . ." (32–33). When he lies on the grass of a city park, "He lay very high, on the back of the world. The earth thrilled beneath him. Red flowers grew through his flesh; their stiff leaves rustled by his head" (103). This uncompromising vision, this continual experiencing of total unity, this lack of definable, separate selfhood—all are incompatible with life in the factual world. So for the first time we recognize that vision without fact, like fact without vision, marks an incomplete existence. There is no doubt, however, that total vision, in Virginia Woolf's view, is not to be censured as a negative force. It is only because of the inescapable presence of limited fact in life that the total visionary cannot exist in society. So Septimus must become an unwilling martyr to the purity of his vision:

> Look the unseen bade him, the voice which now communicated with him who was the greatest of mankind, Septimus, lately taken from life to death, the Lord who had come to renew society, who lay like a coverlet, a snow blanket smitten only by the sun, for ever unwasted, suffering for ever, the scapegoat, the eternal sufferer, but he did not want it, he moaned, putting from him with a wave of his hand that eternal suffering, that eternal loneliness (37).

In a world dominated by the narrow dictates of Sir William Bradshaw and his kind, total vision must be victimized. That the eminent doctor will prove to be Septimus's executioner is then inevitable. But Septimus does not die for his vision in vain; for before the novel ends, it becomes clear that he has died to preserve not only his own vision, but that of Mrs. Dalloway, a woman whose activities in the limited world demand some sacrifice to purify her own sense of unity from insincerity or social lies.

From *The Voyage Out* to *Jacob's Room* Virginia Woolf has attempted to present an effective joining of the seemingly contradictory worlds of fact and vision. In *Mrs. Dalloway* she lets the secondary characters demonstrate the varying deficiencies in lives that fail to achieve this balance and in Clarissa herself presents a woman who comes as close as possible, with the help of others, to achieving a life in which fact and vision are delicately harmonized. Thus of all the men and women in this novel, Clarissa is the most complex; for she must contain a successful social identity as well as a visionary sensitivity that can function in the public world.

Because Clarissa is an integrated member of a society that is partially composed of Sir William Bradshaws and Hugh Whitbreads, she of necessity reflects many of the insincerities of her community. As Peter recognizes, "The obvious thing to say of her was that she was worldly; cared too much for rank and society and getting on in the world—which was true in a sense; she had admitted it to him" (115). In moments of weakness, too, she brushes close to the possessiveness of the least attractive of her acquaintances, a fact Peter also notices: "The way she said "Here is my Elizabeth!'—that annoyed him. Why not 'Here's Elizabeth' simply? It was insincere" (73). But Clarissa does not condone her own weakness. When she catches herself at such moments she admits her shortcomings and berates herself. "How much she wanted it—that people should look pleased as she came in, Clarissa thought and turned and walked back towards Bond Street, annoyed, because it was silly to have other reasons for doing things" (13). She recognizes that living as she does in the social world the demons of hatred and hypocrisy are for ever lurking, ready to usurp the throne of her soul:

> It rasped her . . . to have stirring about in her this brutal monster! to hear twigs cracking and feel hooves planted down in the depths of that leaf-encumbered forest, the soul; never to be content quite, or quite secure, for at any moment the brute would be stirring, this hatred, which, especially since her illness, had the power to make her feel

scraped, hurt in her spine; gave her physical pain, and made all pleasure in beauty, in friendship, in being well, in being loved and making her home delightful rock, quiver, and bend as if indeed there were a monster grubbing at the roots, as if the whole panoply of content were nothing but self love! (17).

In her essay on Montaigne in *The Common Reader,* Virginia Woolf writes, "This soul, or life within us, by no means agrees with the life outside us."[19] So Clarissa's limited external self, though it serves an important purpose as we shall see later, is only a flimsy veil thrown over the boundlessness of her soul. "She knew nothing; no language, no history; she scarcely read a book now, except memoirs in bed; and yet to her it was absolutely absorbing; all this; the cabs passing; and she would not say of Peter, she would not say of herself, I am this, I am that" (11). "Absorbing." The word is almost a pun. For Clarissa's visionary self drinks in all of life through love, and at moments through the vision itself. The facts—languages, history—are not to be singled out for their own sakes, but to be absorbed in a general embracing of life. "For Heaven only knows," she thinks, "why one loves it so, how one sees it so, making it up, building it round one, tumbling it, creating it every moment afresh . . ." (5).

If love allows Mrs. Dalloway to embrace the world, it is not the kind of love that joins a woman to a man through passion, for she is not strong enough to give herself entirely to one person and still be able to serve as a force to bring others together in the unity of vision. She recognizes that "there is a dignity in people; a solitude; even between husband and wife a gulf; and that one must respect . . . for one would not part with it oneself, or take it, against his will, from one's husband, without losing one's independence, one's self-respect—something, after all, priceless" (181). So she marries Richard Dalloway, who allows her this individual license, sacrificing what would have been a more intimate relationship with Peter Walsh, recognizing that "with Peter everything had to be shared; everything gone into. And it was intolerable, and when it came to that scene in the little garden by the fountain, she had to break with him or they would have been destroyed, both of them ruined . . ." (10). Even after she is safely middle-aged, almost old in fact, she reacts defensively when Peter comes to visit. "She made to hide her dress, like a virgin protecting chastity, respecting privacy" (59). And she sees that this scruple against physical passion was "sent by Nature (who is invariably wise)" (46).

If Clarissa cannot dispel a kind of perpetual virginity in herself, lacks "something central which permeated; something warm which broke up surfaces and rippled the cold contact of man and woman, or of women together," she can catch a glimpse of the vision possible in passionate love when she yields "to the charm of a woman, not a girl, or a woman confessing, as to her they often did, some scrape, some folly" (46). To love a woman is safe for Clarissa, since in her world such love never takes on the demanding aspects of male/female passion. So she can enjoy the sensation without experiencing any threat to the freedom of her selfhood, or to the chosen purpose of her life. When Sally Seton, whom she loved as a girl, kissed her on the lips, Clarissa felt the rest of the world disappear; but, because of the nature of love between women, this dangerous moment of separation (dangerous for one whose mission is to unite the world) was just one instant of her life, made pure by the "presentiment of something that was bound to part them . . ." (50). At such moments, when she understands what men feel, she pervades all of life and apprehends, fleetingly, a force that unites the entire world beneath the splintered factual surface, a force that she can use on a more universal plane to bring all of life together in her parties.

It was a sudden revelation, a tinge like a blush which one tried to check and then, as it spread, one yielded to its expansion, and rushed to the farthest verge and there quivered and felt the world come closer, swollen with some astonishing significance, some pressure of rapture, which split its thin skin and gushed and poured with an extraordinary alleviation over the cracks and sores! Then, for that

moment, she had seen an illumination; a match burning
in a crocus; an inner meaning almost expressed (47).

The vision never passes through an individual's life without
leaving its mark, as we have seen in each of Virgina Woolf's
early novels. For Mrs. Dalloway, too, then, "moments like this
are buds on the tree of life, flowers of darkness they are . . . not
for a moment did she believe in God; but all the more, she
thought . . . must one repay in daily life to servants, yes, to dogs
and canaries, above all to Richard her husband" (43). Ecstasy,
love, and revelation must be shared, must overflow into the
factual world. Thus Clarissa determines never to bow to the
laws of limitation set up in society, but instead to carry a sense
of freedom and love into her world. "Had she ever tried to
convert any one herself?" (191) she asks. "She would not say of
any one in the world now that they were this or were that" (11).

Since Clarissa Dalloway realizes that to define a person is to
limit his existence, it is not surprising that at times her own factual limitations seem to dissolve: ". . . often now this body she
wore...this body, with all its capacities, seemed nothing—nothing at all. She had the oddest sense of being herself invisible;
unseen; unknown..." (14). This total dissolution of the limited
self, as we have seen in both *The Voyage Out* and *Jacob's
Room,* is fully and permanently achieved only at death, and in
Mrs. Dalloway death takes on a complexity of significance far
greater than in Virginia Woolf's earlier work. As might be
expected, Clarissa, as representative of the vision, is shrouded
with allusions to death, allusions whose meanings are concentrated into a phrase from Shakespeare's *Cymbeline:* "Fear no
more the heat o' the sun/Nor the furious winter's rages" (13).
From the moment early in the novel when Mrs. Dalloway
reads this quotation in a bookstore window, the lines begin to
take on more and more expansive connotations through repetition. At first they seem to embody death itself; for not only
are they taken from a funeral dirge in the Shakespeare play,
but Clarissa herself also connects them with the rapid movement of time toward her personal end. " 'Fear no more,' said
Clarissa. Fear no more the heat o' the sun. . . . But she feared

time itself, and read on Lady Bruton's face, as if it had been a
dial cut in impassive stone, the dwindling of life; how year by
year her share was sliced; how little the margin that remained
was capable any longer of stretching, of absorbing . . ." (44).
Thus begin a series of images and foreshadowings that seem
to point inevitably to Clarissa's dying before the book is finished. "Narrower and narrower would her bed be. The candle
was half burnt down and she had read deep in Baron Marbot's
Memoirs" (45–46), writes Virginia Woolf about Clarissa; and
then, more explicitly, "if ever I have a moment, thought Clarissa (but never would she have a moment any more), I shall
go and see her [her old dressmaker] at Ealing" (58). Peter, too,
has a sudden vivid premonition of her death: "It was her heart,
he remembered; and the sudden loudness of the final stroke
tolled for death that surprised in the midst of life, Clarissa
falling where she stood, in her drawing-room. No! No! he
cried. She is not dead!" (75)

So at first the phrase "Fear no more" calls up terrifying
images of destruction and cessation. But there is a deeper tone
which sounds below this shrill and fearful note. For death,
though it is in one sense an ending, is in another sense a
greater beginning in the visionary unity that succeeds it. Now
the somber verse takes on more hopeful meaning and pro-
claims that there is no need to fear death.

> Did it matter then, she asked herself, walking towards Bond
> Street, did it matter that she must inevitably cease com-
> pletely; all this must go on without her; did she resent it;
> or did it not become consoling to believe that death ended
> absolutely? but that somehow in the streets of London, on
> the ebb and flow of things, here, there, she survived, Peter
> survived, lived in each other, she being part, she was
> positive, of the trees at home; of the house there, ugly,
> rambling all to bits and pieces as it was; part of people she
> had never met; being laid out like a mist between the
> people she knew best, who lifted her on their branches as
> she has seen the trees lift the mist, but it spread ever
> so far, her life, herself (12).

And from this sense of immortal unity grows up another possibility. Clarissa may not die as soon as we expect (as indeed she does not). The predictions may be false. It must be remembered, after all, that Shakespearean dirge was sung for a girl who was not dead but only seemed to be so. Do the foreshadowings of death, then, lead us nowhere? The answer seems to lie in another vision of unity that surrounds and explains Clarissa: "she felt herself everywhere; not 'here, here, here'; and she tapped the back of the seat; but everywhere. . . . So that to know her, or any one, one must seek out the people who completed them . . ." (231).

Septimus, as Virginia Woolf admitted and as imagery in the novel makes plain, is Clarissa's double, one of the people who complete her. His death, then, may fulfill the warnings that surround her throughout the novel and so prove the tentative thesis that Clarissa herself submits for consideration: ". . . since our apparitions, the part of us which appears, are so momentary compared with the other, the unseen part of us, which spreads wide, the unseen might survive, be recovered somehow attached to this person or that, or even haunting certain places after death . . . [suspension points are Virginia Woolf's] perhaps—perhaps" (232).

With this third possibility beginning to shed its light on the symbolic phrase, "Fear no more" can hover like a protective aura over Mrs. Dalloway:

> Quiet descended on her, calm, content, as her needle, drawing the silk smoothly to its gentle pause, collected the green folds together and attached them, very lightly, to the belt. So on a summer's day waves collect, overbalance, and fall; collect and fall; and the whole world seems to be saying "that is all" more and more ponderously, until even the heart in the body which lies in the sun on the beach says too, That is all. Fear no more, says the heart. Fear no more, says the heart, committing its burden to some sea, which sighs collectively for all sorrows, and renews, begins, collects, lets fall. And the body alone listens to the passing

bee; the wave breaking; the dog barking, far away
barking and barking (58–59).

Then, just as Clarissa's needle gathers up the separated folds
of her dress, Virginia Woolf will gather up the individual
fragments of her story to weave irrevocably together Septimus
and Clarissa. We have already seen a similarity between Septimus's revelations of universal love and unity and Clarissa's
less extreme but similar belief—their kinship as visionaries is
undeniable. Now there remains only to establish some more
delicate ties and the full extent of their relationship will be
clear. This Virginia Woolf accomplishes by linking them
through similar experiences and associated images. Richard
brought Clarissa roses, giving husband and wife their deepest
moment of communion in the book. Rezia, Septimus's wife,
brings roses to her husband, and seeing them he thinks,
"Communication is health; communication is happiness, communication——" (141). Then later, just before his suicide, as
Rezia sits sewing peacefully, Septimus hears the sound of water
in the room. "Every power poured its treasures on his head,
and his hand lay there on the back of the sofa, as he had seen
his hand lie when he was bathing, floating, on the top of the
waves, while far away on shore he heard dogs barking and
barking far away. Fear no more, says the heart in the body;
fear no more" (211). The waves, the dogs, the words from
Shakespeare, even the peaceful motion of the needle serve to
weave two unacquainted persons so closely together that they
seem to become one. Thus when Septimus leaps into the warm
sunshine from his window to his death and, seeing an old man
coming down the staircase opposite, cries " 'I'll give it you!' "
(226) we feel that the offering will be relayed to Clarissa, its
proper recipient, before the day is through. So, too when Rezia,
after her husband's death, feels that she is stepping through
long windows into a peaceful garden, we wonder if this garden
is not outside the French windows at Bourton, and whether in
this interchange of offerings Clarissa has not given her own
special gift to Septimus through his wife.

When Septimus dies, he in effect enables Clarissa to carry the vision into her fact-bound social world without becoming completely entangled in that world's limitations. But as we have seen in Septimus's own case, this vision cannot be presented to society in its purest essence without being received as mere madness. Instead it must be demonstrated in factual terms. Thus Clarissa, before giving her party, must be able to assemble her own complete, objective self, that will then serve as catalyst for the unifying of the many disparate individuals gathered together in her drawing-room.

> . . . Clarissa (crossing to the dressing-table) plunged into the very heart of the moment, transfixed it, there—the moment of this June morning on which was the pressure of all the other mornings, seeing the glass, the dressing-table, and all the bottles afresh, collecting the whole of her at one point(as she looked into the glass), seeing the delicate pink face of the woman who was that very night to give a party; of Clarissa Dalloway; of herself (54).

Even as she composes this being, she recognizes both the advantages and the limitations of a dartlike, definite self. "That was her self when some effort, some call on her to be her self, drew the parts together, she alone knew how different, how incompatible and composed so for the world only into one centre, one diamond, one woman who sat in her drawing-room and made a meeting-point, a radiancy . . ." (55). Of course in some respects this factual self is a half-truth, a compromise in the face of society's restrictions; but what a man like Peter Walsh does not realize is that Clarissa's "extraordinary gift, that woman's gift, of making a world of her own wherever she happened to be" (114) depends entirely on her being able to present her vision on society's own terms. By concentrating her boundless self within the hostess Mrs. Dalloway, Clarissa "filled the room she entered" (44). Jean Guiguet, without going into the source of Clarissa's powers, recognizes their results, saying, "certain people carry within them a sort of power that renders them sensitive to the beauty of life and at the same time makes them mediums through whom other people are sensitized in their turn. Clarissa is one of these, despite her faults, her failings and lapses."[20] What he, like Peter, fails to see is that it is impossible to reconcile fact and vision in daily life without the compromises that stand out as weaknesses in an ideal world. Clarissa, then, "to kindle and illuminate" (6), must give her party.

It is clear from the very beginning that this party is to be not merely a typical social entertainment but the culmination and climax of the entire novel, a symbol of Mrs. Dalloway herself. Challenged to explain the reason behind her party-giving, Clarissa says

> Here was So-and-so in South Kensington; some one up in Bayswater; and somebody else, say, in Mayfair. And she felt quite continuously a sense of their existence; and she felt what a waste; and she felt what a pity; and she felt if only they could be brought together; so she did it. And it was an offering; to combine, to create; but to whom?
>
> An offering for the sake of offering, perhaps. Anyhow, it was her gift (184–85).

So at the level of society, where people are limited and isolated by their factual selves, Clarissa's party provides the uniting force, provides the vision. Even as she sits mending her sea-green dress in the morning, the first signs of the importance of the evening to come begin to appear. "By artificial light the green shone, but lost its colour now in the sun" (55). Green, the color of trees, grows to symbolize the vision. Not until her party will Clarissa's dress take on its deepest shade. Then, as we have seen in Peter's vision of the solitary traveler, she becomes the silver-green siren who can "sum it all up in the moment as she passed . . ." (264).

To sum it all up, to create this vision, this is why the party must be given. In order, then, that this uniting of the factual and visionary worlds may be complete, the final scenes must include representatives of as many forms of life as possible. So Mrs. Dalloway's guest list is composed of an interesting assortment of persons taken not only from the society of this novel, but from others as well, thus making the illusion of total unity all the more complete. Mrs. Durrant and Clara from *Jacob's Room* attend. Then "up came that wandering will-o'-the-wisp, that vagulous phosphorescence, old Mrs. Hilbery" (267) from *Night and Day*. Being a visionary herself, Mrs. Hilbery can see the enchantment that Clarissa is working. "Did they know, she asked, that they were surrounded by an enchanted garden? Lights and trees and wonderful gleaming lakes and the sky. Just a few fairy lamps, Clarissa Dalloway had said, in the back garden! But she was a magician!" (291). Phantoms from Clarissa's own past are here, too, with a suggestion that even the dead may be attending. For example, before coming to the party, Peter remembers Clarissa's Aunt Helena and thinks, "She was dead now" (246). But when he arrives, "There was old Aunt Helena in her shawl. . . . For Miss Helena Parry was not dead . . ." (271). And even Sally Seton turns up unexpectedly. Of course representatives of the daily social world must attend, from the little seamstress Ellie Henderson to Hugh Whitbread, stuffed and polished as ever, to Lady Bruton at whose luncheon Richard experienced his vision of love, to any number of stray scholars, students, and lovers, and finally to the Prime Minister himself, the perfect symbol of the factual world of society. "One couldn't laugh at him. He looked so ordinary. You might have stood him behind a counter and bought biscuits—poor chap, all rigged up in gold lace" (261). Yet even this unimpressive emblem of society has his role in creating a continuity that grows into the visionary pattern, becoming "the enduring symbol of the state which will be known to curious antiquaries, sifting the ruins of time, when London is a grass-grown path and all those hurrying along the pavement . . . are but bones with a few wedding rings mixed up in their dust . . ." (23).

The only essential figure who is missing after the party is well under way is Septimus. Sir William Bradshaw, for all his blindness, serves as the vision-maker's unwitting messenger as he tells Mrs. Dalloway of the afternoon suicide. "Oh! thought Clarissa, in the middle of my party, here's death, she thought" (279). Now, with the vision surrounding her and the disparate fragments of life united in her drawing-room, she is ready to become joined to Septimus and to understand the full significance of his sacrifice.

> She had once thrown a shilling into the Serpentine, never
> anything more. But he had flung it away. They went on
> living (she would have to go back; the rooms were still
> crowded; people kept on coming). They . . . they would
> grow old. A thing there was that mattered; a thing, wreathed
> about with chatter, defaced, obscured in her own life, let
> drop every day in corruption, lies, chatter. This he had
> preserved. Death was defiance. Death was an attempt to
> communicate; people feeling the impossibility of reaching
> the centre which, mysteriously, evaded them; closeness
> drew apart; rapture faded, one was alone. There was
> an embrace in death (280–81).

Somehow Septimus by his death has purged the corruption from Clarissa's life, has offered her communication. So, with a new sense of joy surrounding her, she walks to her window to receive the gift. And there, "but how surprising!—in the room opposite the old lady stared straight at her!" (283). This old lady, whom Clarissa has watched daily climbing and descending her stairs, living her own essential, private life, suddenly has linked herself to Clarissa as if the old man on the stair to whom Septimus had tossed his life had relayed it through the old woman to Septimus's visionary double. Standing by the window, Clarissa "felt somehow very like him—the young man who had killed himself. She felt glad that he had done it; thrown it away. The clock was striking. The leaden circles dissolved in the air. He made her feel the beauty; made her feel the fun. But she must go back. She must assemble" (283–84). Now that her need for the purification of death has been fulfilled through her double, Clarissa is ready to return to her party and complete the vision for others. Peter Walsh sits outside in the drawing-room, waiting; and as Clarissa reenters her party world, "What is this terror? what is this ecstasy? he thought to himself. What is it that fills me with extraordinary excitement? It is Clarissa, he said. For there she was" (296). At last the vision is fully realized.

This fullness of being, this combining of both fact and vision at her greatest moments, makes Clarissa Dalloway the uniting force of the novel. But Virginia Woolf, through her use of imagery, gives us other glimpses of the two worlds united. For example, there are the clocks, whose chimes, as Daiches and others have pointed out, both divide the day and unite the action in *Mrs. Dalloway*. "There! Out it boomed. First a warning, musical; then the hour, irrevocable. The leaden circles dissolved in the air" (5). Time can either be forged out of metal, cutting lives into precise factual slices, or it can dissolve to spread an unseen wash of consistency and pattern over life. The factual side of clock time is emphasized, quite appropriately, outside the offices of the inflexible Sir William Bradshaw: "Shredding and slicing, dividing and subdividing, the clocks of Harley Street nibbled at the June day, counselled submission, upheld authority, and pointed out in chorus the supreme advantages of a sense of proportion . . ." (154–55). Clarissa's clock on the other hand, St. Margaret's, serves to unite all time as well as to state a precise hour:

> Ah, said St. Margaret's, like a hostess who comes into her drawing-room on the very stroke of the hour and finds her guests there already. I am not late. No, it is precisely half-past eleven, she says. Yet, though she is perfectly right, her voice, being the voice of the hostess, is reluctant to inflict its individuality. Some grief for the past holds it back; some concern for the present. It is half-past eleven, she says, and the sound of St. Margaret's glides into the recesses of the heart and buries itself in ring after ring of sound, like something alive which wants to confide itself, to disperse itself, to be, with a tremor of delight, at rest— like Clarissa herself . . . (74).

Other symbols, too, seem to unite the factual world with more visionary truth: the airplane that becomes "an aspiration; a concentration; a symbol . . . of man's soul" (41); a cross, "the symbol of something which has soared beyond seeking and questing and knocking of words together and has become all spirit" (42); even the old woman singing in the street who brings comfort to Rezia and unites all time and space in her body. Her wordless song is embodied in a

> voice of no age or sex, the voice of an ancient spring
> spouting from the earth; which issued, just opposite Regent's
> Park Tube station from a tall quivering shape, like a
> funnel, like a rusty pump, like a wind-beaten tree for ever
> barren of leaves which lets the wind run up and down
> its branches singing
>
> > ee um fah um so
> > foo swee too eem oo
>
> and rocks and creaks and moans in the eternal breeze.
>
> Through all ages—when the pavement was grass, when
> it was swamp, through the age of tusk and mammoth,
> through the age of silent sunrise, the battered woman—for
> she wore a skirt—with her right hand exposed, her left
> clutching at her side, stood singing of love—love which
> has lasted a million years ... (122–23).

Again, universal love that transcends time and space. Again, an isolated being or moment that melts into the vast pattern of vision.

So in *Mrs. Dalloway,* through characterization and symbol, Virginia Woolf has presented the varied levels of fact and vision that pervade the world. Sir William and Hugh on the one hand and Septimus on the other define the extremes. Clarissa serves to attempt some reconciliation, however imperfect, in herself and in her parties. Thus within this novel, both ends and means have been defined. In those to come Virginia Woolf will be able to deal with the more delicate nuances of her central theme.

5

To the Lighthouse

In all of her novels from *The Voyage Out* to *Mrs. Dalloway* Virginia Woolf has wrestled with the problem of how to imagine and how to present a world that combines finite and infinite truth—that recognizes limitation and isolation, and at the same time realizes the presence of a transcendent unity encompassing all spatial and temporal existence. She has demonstrated the deficiencies in lives totally divorced from the external world or totally integrated with it. But there remains a need to balance the inspiration of characters like Mrs. Hilbery with the incorruptible honesty of St. John, Peter Walsh, and their kind. In *The Voyage Out* and *Night and Day* she hovered over the theme of marriage as a force that could combine the separated, at least on a small scale. In *Mrs. Dalloway* she began to enlarge the symbolic possibilities of her characters by making them represent various aspects of fact or vision. Now in *To the Lighthouse* she combines these themes and techniques to present the marriage of two vast personalities who stand for the factual and visionary approaches to the reality of life. She then goes on step further in her search for synthesis and sets this symbolic marriage before the eye of an artist, showing how an abstract scale art can accomplish the balancing of the two worlds.

From the outset, the themes and structure of *To the Lighthouse* were clear in Virginia Woolf's mind as the reader can see from various entries in her diary. It was to include, she said, "all the usual things I try to put in—life, death, etc."[1] "It might contain all characters boiled down; and childhood; and then this impersonal thing, which I'm dared to do by my friends, the flight of time and the consequent break of unity in my design . . . (I conceive the book in 3 parts. 1. at the drawing-room window; 2. seven years passed; 3. the voyage.)"[2] Perhaps because it is so controlled, so concentrated, so precise in its treatment of its theme, this novel has received more perceptive critical attention than any of Virginia Woolf's other works. Although a few theories about *To the Lighthouse* differ sharply from others, there is a general agreement among most of the critics about both theme and technique: the novel treats symbolically the marriage of opposites and discusses art as another means of combining opposing attitudes toward life.[3] Because little attention has been paid to Virginia Woolf's general concern with fact and vision, no one has yet attempted to view the novel in this light, so that several aspects of the work remain to be illuminated.

The theme of marriage is central to *To the Lighthouse* as most critics would agree. The meaning of this union, however, receives varying interpretations. Herbert Marder feels that Virginia Woolf "viewed marriage from two essentially different points of view, describing it, in an intensely critical spirit as a patriarchal institution, but also expressing a visionary ideal of marriage as the ultimate relation."[4] This explanation describes both the conflict and the ultimate harmony of Mr. and Mrs. Ramsay's relationship to each other. James Hafley, who associates Mrs. Ramsay with the sea, Mr. Ramsay with the land,[5] focuses his attention more on the opposition between the two, saying, "*To the Lighthouse* is really a story of a contest between two kinds of truth—Mr. Ramsay's and Mrs. Ramsay's. For him, truth is factual truth; for her, truth is the movement toward truth."[6] Melvin Friedman, too, sees in the marriage of the Ramsays an irreconcilable dualism between subject and object.[7] In his extremely perceptive study of Virginia Woolf's novels, John Graham probably comes closest to recognizing the full significance of the Ramsays' marriage: "Crudely put," he says, "Mrs. Ramsay equals eternity, Mr. Ramsay equals time; they are married. . . . Together they fulfill each other, and are the creators of life."[8] Time and eternity are only part of the greater worlds of fact and vision, but Mr. Graham has recognized that the marriage represents an ideal harmony between seemingly divergent truths.

Part One of *To the Lighthouse,* "The Window," shows us the essential personalities of Mr. and Mrs. Ramsay and the intricacies of their relationship with one another, exploring in the process both the narrow and the expansive meanings of marriage. Because this is the only section in which Mrs. Ramsay appears physically, the greater attention is given to her function in the Lighthouse world; but the portrait of her husband is presented with such precision that we are left in no doubt about his role in her life and in the novel as a whole. The first thing we discover about Mr. Ramsay is that he is "lean as a knife, narrow as the blade of one. . . ."[9] Immediately Peter Walsh's knife comes to mind, and we anticipate that Mr. Ramsay will be another disciple of abstract truth. Our expectations prove justified as we learn that "What he said was true. It was always true. He was incapable of untruth; never tampered with a fact; never altered a disagreeable word to suit the pleasure or convenience of any mortal being, least of all his own children, who, sprung from his loins, should be aware from childhood that life is difficult; facts uncompromising . . ." (10–11). And what is this truth that he insists upon imposing on his offspring and wrestles with himself? It is fact, isolated, objective, cut off from beauty or any other distracting element that might cloud its outline. Lily Briscoe expresses it concretely: "Whenever she 'thought of his work' she always saw clearly before her a large kitchen table. It was Andrew's doing. She asked him what his father's books were about. 'Subject and object and the nature of reality,' Andrew had said. And when she said Heavens, she had no notion what that meant. 'Think of a kitchen table then,' he told her, 'when you're not there' " (38). That Mr. Ramsay is larger than life in this dedication to unvarnished truth is seen instinctively by Lily, too: "Naturally, if one's days were passed in this seeing of angular essences, this reducing of lovely evenings, with all their flamingo clouds and blue and silver to a white deal four-legged table (it was a mark of the finest minds so to do), naturally one could not be judged like an ordinary person" (38). Although Mr. Ramsay's devotion to truth is admirable and his refusal to bend under ordinary human pressure an attitude to inspire fear or awe in less colossal mortals, his apprehension of total truth, even in his own eyes, is incomplete. To reduce this truth to its most abstract essence, he sees it stretching before him like a piano keyboard or the alphabet, made up of gradual and progressive steps. If reaching "Z," then, means attaining perfect truth, he has failed; for try as he will, he can proceed no further than "Q." Pacing about the garden within sight of his wife, he brings all his factual powers to bear on the problem: "Qualities that would have saved a ship's company exposed on a broiling sea with six biscuits and a flask of water—endurance and justice, foresight, devotion, skill, came to his help. R is then—what is R?" (54). Something is missing in Mr. Ramsay's conception of life, but the truth he does perceive he grasps bravely and uncompromisingly, keeping watch over it with "a vigilance which spared no phantom and luxuriated in no vision . . ." (69). Virginia Woolf sums up this virtue symbolically when she writes:

> It was his fate, his peculiarity, whether he wished it or not, to come out thus on a spit of land which the sea is slowly eating away, and there to stand, like a desolate sea-bird, alone. It was his power, his gift, suddenly to shed all superfluities, to shrink and diminish so that he looked barer and felt sparer, even physically, yet lost none of his intensity of mind, and so to stand on his little ledge facing the dark of human ignorance, how we know nothing and the sea eats away the ground we stand on—that was his fate, his gift (68–69).

Like the body of the lighthouse, then, Mr. Ramsay stands, facing the limitations, the fact of isolation in life. Without being able to accept a truth that is based upon unity and boundlessness, without, in other words, sensing the vision, he provides the firm foundation that lies at the core of that vision, the fact that must be perceived as solid before it can take on transcendence.

If the merits of factual truth are great, the vision in Virginia
Woolf's novels is always greater. As a result, the visionary characters in each of her works seem to hover over their worlds,
providing infinite order and unity; and most critics would
agree that Mrs. Ramsay is one of those creative characters. (One
notable exception is Glenn Pederson who sees her as "the negative force which usurps the lighthouse and thus prevents the
integration of the family while she lives."[10]) Thus when Mrs.
Ramsay finds a moment in which to uncover her essential self,
instead of contracting to a bare, spare point like her husband,
she feels herself a "wedge-shaped core of darkness, something
invisible to others' (95). "Her horizon seemed to her limitless.
. . . This core of darkness could go anywhere, for no one saw it"
(96). At these moments when her soul shakes off its physical
limitations to venture into the world, it often seems naturally
drawn into the visionary atmosphere of the Roman church:
"she felt herself pushing aside the thick leather curtain of a
church in Rome" (96) or felt she heard "men and boys crying
out the Latin words of a service in some Roman Catholic
cathedral" (166). Although this fact gives some support to
F. L. Overcarsh's Christian interpretation of *To the Lighthouse*,[11] it is clear that Mrs. Ramsay's all-pervasive self is only
symbolized by religious unity, not defined by it. For if her
visionary approach to life is at home in a church, it is equally a
part of the natural world. "It was odd, she thought, how if one
was alone, one leant to inanimate things; trees, streams, flowers; felt they expressed one; felt they became one; felt they
knew one, in a sense were one . . ." (97). Like Katharine, Ralph,
Peter, and Rachel, Mrs. Ramsay connects the infinity of life
with trees; for when she hears the words "And all the lives we
ever lived and all the lives to be are full of trees and changing
leaves" (166), "She did not know what they meant, but, like
music, the words seemed to be spoken by her own voice, outside her self, saying quite easily and naturally what had been
in her mind the whole evening while she said different things"
(166). Because her vision is fluid, pervasive, it is not surprising
that it is associated with one aspect of the sea, and if her husband stands as the body of the lighthouse, holding off the

destruction of the waves, Mrs. Ramsay becomes the light from its great lamp, the beam that includes waves, land, and men in its unifying stroke. When her soul goes out to embrace the whole of life "there rose to her lips always some exclamation of triumph over life when things came together in this peace, this rest, this eternity; and pausing there she looked out to meet that stroke of the Lighthouse, the long steady stroke, the last of the three, which was her stroke . . ." (96).

For all her sense of the infinite expanse of life, for all her realization that men are not bounded by the limits of factual truth to which her husband is so loyal, Mrs. Ramsay is not unaware of a menacing undercurrent that continually threatens the vision. She does not deny the desolation that Mr. Ramsay defines as existence but only determines not to let this side of life swallow up the more important unity that can find order in seeming chaos, hope in despair. This pull between unity and formlessness is best represented by the sea itself.

> . . . the monotonous fall of the waves on the beach, which for the most part beat a measured and soothing tattoo to her thoughts and seemed consolingly to repeat over and over again as she sat with the children the words of some old cradle song, murmured by nature, "I am guarding you—I am your support," but at other times suddenly and unexpectedly, especially when her mind raised itself slightly from the task actually in hand, had no such kindly meaning, but like a ghostly roll of drums remorselessly beat the measure of life, made one think of the destruction of the island and its engulfment in the sea, and warned her whose day had slipped past in one quick doing after another that it was all ephemeral as a rainbow . . . (27–28).

Like the clocks in *Mrs. Dalloway,* the sea in *To the Lighthouse* can either unite the separated or proclaim the limits of life. To maintain its visionary sense the sea must be perceived through the eyes of effort, through the determination of the vision-makers to keep the vision alive. If Mrs. Hilbery could wander unhindered through a dream world from which the ugliness of life was excluded, Mrs. Ramsay cannot. Subjected to the test of time, the vision has been threatened by the facts of sorrow, poverty, and loneliness. *To the Lighthouse*, then, reflects a new maturity accompanied by a certain loss of naïveté in the view of vision. For even in a world removed from time-driven London society, the vision must deal with the most frightening of facts. In an honest reconciliation of the dual worlds, full power must be recognized in each.

Thus, Mrs. Ramsay, even in her absorption into the beam from the Lighthouse, cannot set aside her own responsibilities in maintaining the vision that that light represents.

> Often she found herself sitting and looking, sitting and looking, with her work in her hands until she became the thing she looked at—that light, for example. And it would lift up on it some little phrase or other which had been lying in her mind like that—"Children don't forget, children don't forget"—which she would repeat and begin adding to it, It will end, it will end, she said. It will come, it will come, when suddenly she added, We are in the hands of the Lord.
>
> But instantly she was annoyed with herself for saying that (97).

The infiniteness of religion she can accept; its leaving all things to God she cannot. "How could any Lord have made this world? she asked. With her mind she had always seized the fact that there is no reason, order, justice: but suffering, death, the poor. There was no treachery too base for the world to commit; she knew that. No happiness lasted; she knew that" (98). To preserve the unity that her soul discerns she cannot overlook the other truth, the truth that her mind perceives. Yet it is because of her instinctive awareness of the possibility of unity and happiness that she cannot, like her husband, accept this intellectual truth as everything. He is content with proclaiming the world's bleakness; she with her vision must try to turn desolation to communion. Thus "with all his gloom and desperation he was happier, more hopeful on the whole than she was. Less exposed to human worries—perhaps that was it" (91). The vast difference between Mr. and Mrs. Ramsay is brilliantly condensed into their opening argument about the Lighthouse. They both recognize its frightening isolation, a symbol of every man's essential loneliness, but while Mr. Ramsay accepts this fact as inevitable, says that a trip to the Lighthouse is impossible, Mrs. Ramsay insists on the possibility of relieving the loneliness, prepares magazines and stockings for the isolated, and flies in the face of facts to preserve the truth of vision.

The marriage of Mr. and Mrs. Ramsay is not merely the living together of two separate individuals as we shall see. It is a real union characterized by mutual understanding and support. This closeness, however, does not preclude an occasional clashing of their opposite natures. When, for example, Mrs. Ramsay suggests that the weather may change after her husband has carefully explained that bad weather will make a Lighthouse excursion impossible, "The extraordinary irrationality of her remark, the folly of women's minds enraged him. He had ridden through the valley of death, been shattered and shivered; and now, she flew in the face of facts, made his children hope what was utterly out of the question, in effect, told lies. He stamped his foot on the stone step. 'Damn you,' he said" (50). If Mr. Ramsay cannot accept any attitude that opposes his hard-won facts, his wife is equally shocked by her husband's narrowness: "To pursue truth with such astonishing lack of consideration for other people's feelings, to rend the thin veils of civilization so wantonly, so brutally, was to her so horrible an outrage of human decency that, without replying, dazed and blinded, she bent her head as if to let the pelt of jagged hail, the drench of dirty water, bespatter her unrebuked" (51). Devastating as Mr. Ramsay's inflexibility may be, however, it provides the support upon which his wife may rest her vision, gives her a reference point round which to weave a pattern out of surrounding confusion: "she often felt she was nothing but a sponge sopped full of human emotions. Then he said, Damn you. He said, It must rain. He said, It won't rain; and instantly a Heaven of security opened before her" (51). Even though she is unable to accept his general view of life, Mrs. Ramsay needs her husband's factual strength as a foundation for her vision. So during her dinner party, "she let it uphold her and sustain her, this admirable fabric of the masculine intelligence, which ran up and down, crossed this way and that, like iron girders spanning the swaying fabric, upholding the world . . ." (159). When Lily conceives of a painting that eventually will include the truths of both Mr. and Mrs. Ramsay, "She saw the colour burning on a framework of steel; the light of a butterfly's wing lying upon the arches of a cathedral" (75). Both lives are a necessary part of the total truth.

Although some of the sustaining force of their marriage manifests itself in altercation, in general the Ramsays exist on a plane of unspoken understanding: "they looked at each other down the long table sending . . . questions and answers across, each knowing exactly what the other felt" (144). This intimacy is seldom consciously of the possessive kind, for when one needs privacy, the other grants it (49, 100). Yet whenever help is needed it is freely offered. If Mr. Ramsay gives his wife a factual nail upon which to hang the boundlessness of her vision, she in turn provides him with a fertile atmosphere of creativity in which he can refresh the soul he desiccates with chalk-dry truth. Sometimes just the sight of her "fortified him and satisfied him and consecrated his effort to arrive at a perfectly clear understanding of the problem which now engaged the energies of his splendid mind" (53). At others his need is so great that she must call up her entire visionary being in order to flood his parched mind with a vision he cannot descry, can only profit from, unknowing.

> Mrs. Ramsay, who had been sitting loosely, folding her son in her arm, braced herself, and, half turning, seemed to raise herself with an effort, and at once to pour erect into the air a rain of energy, a column of spray, looking at the same time animated and alive as if all her energies were being fused into force, burning and illuminating (quietly though she sat, taking up her stocking again), and into this delicious fecundity, this fountain and spray of life, the fatal sterility of the male plunged itself, like a beak of brass, barren and bare (58).

Even Mr. Ramsay senses that the gift of vision in the face of fact always weakens the giver. Yet vision denies limitation, so whenever he asks, she gives. "She was aloof from him now in her beauty, in her sadness. He would let her be, and he passed her without a word, though it hurt him that she should look so distant, and he could not reach her. . . . And again he would have passed her without a word had she not, at that very moment, given him of her own free will what she knew he would never ask, and called to him and taken the green shawl off the picture frame, and gone to him" (100). The only thing Mrs. Ramsay cannot do, even to please her husband, is to betray her vision by accepting any limitations to it. Thus she cannot tell him in words that she loves him; for words, as we have seen in *Mrs. Dalloway*, imply restriction, and love is boundless. Instead she acknowledges the truth of his facts, without denying the validity of her own perception of truth. " 'Yes, you were right. It's going to be wet tomorrow. You won't be able to go.' And she looked at him smiling. For she had triumphed again. She had not said it: yet he knew" (186).[12] So to the end in their own relationship Mrs. Ramsay protects her vision, bathing her husband in it in return for his support. Fact is strong, but, during her lifetime at least, vision prevails.

Mrs. Ramsay's creative vision, which shelters and unites, is not, of course, shared only with her husband. "Indeed, she had the whole of the other sex under her protection . . ." (13) as well as her children and any others who cross her path. During the time in which *To the Lighthouse* unfolds, we watch her weaving her vision, sometimes successfully, sometimes unsuccessfully, around a representative assortment of people staying in the Ramsays' summer home. The first problem she tackles is Charles Tansley, "the little atheist" (12), a disciple of her husband's. "He was such a miserable specimen, the children said, all humps and hollows. He couldn't play cricket; he poked; he shuffled" (15). His fidelity to factual exactitude is, if possible, even more fanatical than that of Mr. Ramsay, a limitation reflected not only in his denial of religion, but also in his fastidious eschewal of any exaggeration, however rhetorical. Mrs. Ramsay "could not help laughing herself sometimes.

She said, the other day, something about 'waves mountains high.' Yes, said Charles Tansley, it was a little rough. 'Aren't you drenched to the skin?' she had said. 'Damp, not wet through,' said Mr. Tansley, pinching his sleeve, feeling his socks'' (15). If Mr. Ramsay at times succumbs to a self-centered fear that his life is wasted and turns to his wife for praise, Charles Tansley is so knotted into himself that, as the Ramsay children put it, "he would go to picture galleries . . . and he would ask one, did one like his tie?" (16). To someone so caged in by fact, vision can be given only in a totally nonfactual form; and in the case of Mrs. Ramsay, this visionary medium is her beauty. In an essay called "Reading," Virginia Woolf writes, "perhaps one of the invariable properties of beauty is that it leaves in the mind a desire to impart. Some offering we must make; some act we must dedicate."[13] Mrs. Ramsay's beauty gradually loosens the bonds that encircle the limited Charles. Under the influence of the emotion she calls up in him, "he was coming to see himself, and everything he had ever known gone crooked a little" (24). Then, as realization of her power floods over him, he is moved, as Virginia Woolf predicts, to make his small offering:

> . . . all at once he realised that it was this: it was this:—she was the most beautiful person he had ever seen.
>
> With stars in her eyes and veils in her hair, with cyclamen and wild violets—what nonsense was he thinking? She was fifty at least; she had eight children. Stepping through fields of flowers and taking to her breast buds that had broken and lambs that had fallen; with the stars in her eyes and the wind in her hair—He took her bag (25).

Because Mr. Tansley is so bound to the limited world, it is not surprising that after Mrs. Ramsay's influence is gone he ends up "lean and red and raucous, preaching love from a platform . . ." (292–93). Yet for the moment, Mrs. Ramsay has succeeded in making him believe in cooperation rather than egotistical domination.

With Augustus Carmichael, however, her kind of power is ineffectual. Because she depends so completely on love and beauty to create harmony in her world, Mrs. Ramsay does not recognize another form of vision in the mind of this elderly man, who writes poetry that "said something about death; it said very little about love" (290). From *The Voyage Out* to *Jacob's Room* to *Mrs. Dalloway,* death has been presented as the final unifier, the mist that erases individual identities and represents infinity. Yet it is always a frightening force to be embraced only as a last resort. So Mr. Carmichael's poetry of death and detachment does not become popular until wartime, until after Mrs. Ramsay herself has become infinite by dying. And while she is alive Mrs. Ramsay can offer no communication through love to a man who is immersed completely in a formless world of his own. All she can do is offer him a retreat from an unhappy home life, where he can nurture his private dreams until their time comes due. So he sits every morning, out on the lawn "with his yellow cat's eyes ajar, so that like a cat's they seemed to reflect the branches moving or the clouds passing, but to give no inkling of any inner thoughts or emotions whatsoever . . ." (19).[14] Being content to let his soul exist apart from others, he rejects any form of living unity tendered by Mrs. Ramsay and reflects back at her a cold picture of herself, making her feel that her vision is incomplete, "that she was suspected; and that all this desire of hers to give, to help, was vanity. For her own self-satisfaction was it that she wished so instinctively to help, to give, that people might say of her, 'O Mrs. Ramsay! dear Mrs. Ramsay . . . Mrs. Ramsay, of course!' and need her and send for her and admire her?" (65). To create unity that weakens with time is one thing. To see her offer of communion rejected is another. Only after her death, when Lily brings together the whole Lighthouse world on canvas, will Mrs. Ramsay and Mr. Carmichael be joined in the vision.

But if Mr. Carmichael is immune to love as a source of vision, others remain who are not; and Mrs. Ramsay's power to create unity brings together Minta Doyle and Paul Rayley who tacitly accept her vision of marriage: "for what could be more serious than the love of man for woman, what more commanding, more impressive . . ." (151). In their case, like that of Charles Tansley, the vision fades when Mrs. Ramsay is no longer alive to foster it, and the pair cease to devote the necessary effort to preserve it; but through her they experience, for a time at least, the miniature unity of love.

Because Mrs. Ramsay has incorporated the vision into her own life through marriage, she often relies on this method too implicitly, prescribing it even where it is inappropriate. For example, as she sits in her window, knitting comfort for the loneliness of the Lighthouse keepers, she sees William Bankes pass by with Lily Briscoe and suddenly thinks it an admirable idea that the two should marry. It is true that both these individuals are open to vision and that Mrs. Ramsay inspires this vision in each of them, but in neither case is marriage the means by which they will achieve their sense of infinite unity.

Because of his own flexibility, William Bankes can experience the revelation of Mrs. Ramsay's beauty with far greater visionary effect than Charles Tansley, or even Paul and Minta. He feels that "The Graces assembling seemed to have joined hands in meadows of asphodel to compose that face" (47) so that "the sight of her reading a fairy tale to her boy had upon him precisely the same effect as the solution of a scientific problem, so that he rested in contemplation of it, and felt, as he felt when he had proved something absolute about the digestive system of plants, that barbarity was tamed, the reign of chaos subdued" (74). As this impression indicates, William Bankes's love of scientific precision does not restrict him to one sense of truth as it does Mr. Ramsay. He "was rather unusual . . . he never let himself get into a groove" (133). Since marriage would destroy this flexibility for him, he prefers to remain free so that he can maintain an unfailing friendship for Mr. Ramsay and at the same time appreciate Lily's painting and love Mrs. Ramsay with a love far more visionary than the limited affection of one man for one woman. Lily, with her infallible artist's eye, recognizes this vision springing up in Mr. Bankes. "It was love, she thought, pretending to move her canvas, distilled and filtered; love that never attempted to clutch its object; but, like the love which mathematicians bear their symbols, or poets their phrases, was meant to be spread over the world and become part of the human gain. So it was indeed" (73–74).

Lily Briscoe, too, as artist, cannot involve herself permanently in the intimacy of marriage; for she must be able to maintain her objectivity in order to weigh all of life equally and so capture in her art the balanced reconciliation of fact and vision. The first thing William notices in Lily is that "Her shoes were excellent. . . . They allowed the toes their natural expansion" (31). As we are well aware by now, Virginia Woolf feels that a person's boots express his character, and the one thing Lily cannot relinquish is room for natural expansion. Whenever she senses that Mrs. Ramsay is pushing her to marry, ". . . gathering a desperate courage she would urge her own exemption from the universal law; plead for it; she liked to be alone; she liked to be herself . . ." (77). Thus when she goes walking with William Bankes, the two observers of life leave the intimacy of the garden and are drawn naturally to the universality of distant views that "seem to outlast by a million years (Lily thought) the gazer and to be communing already with a sky which beholds an earth entirely at rest" (34). Because she insists on remaining somewhat aloof from the lives of others, Lily develops a nearly infallible sense for the moods and personalities of those around her. Time and again her analysis of another's thoughts proves justified until she seems to be able to see people "as in an X-ray photograph" (137). It is she who perceives precisely both the merits and the limitations implicit in Mr. Ramsay's approach to life; and it is she, too, who realizes that Mrs. Ramsay holds the key that can turn all flux into infinite pattern. At moments, caught up in the vision herself, Lily can apprehend that both Mr. and Mrs. Ramsay are a part of the transcendent unity:

Directly one looked up and saw them, what she called "being in love" flooded them. They became part of that unreal but penetrating and exciting universe which is the world seen through the eyes of love. The sky stuck to them; the birds sang through them. And, what was even more exciting, she felt, too, as she saw Mr. Ramsay bearing

down and retreating, and Mrs. Ramsay sitting with James in
the window and the cloud moving and the tree bending,
how life, from being made up of little separate incidents
which one lived one by one, became curled and whole like
a wave which bore one up with it and threw one down
with it, there, with a dash on the beach (72–73).

Thus Lily recognizes that the marriage of the truth-driven
Mr. Ramsay to the unity-seeking Mrs. Ramsay is more than
just a social fact but is actually symbolic of the visionary totality of life.

And suddenly the meaning which, for no reason at all, as
perhaps they are stepping out of the Tube or ringing a
doorbell, descends on people, making them symbolical,
making them representative, came upon them, and made
them in the dusk standing, looking, the symbols of marriage,
husband and wife. Then, after an instant, the symbolical
outline which transcended the real figures sank down again,
and they became, as they met them, Mr. and Mrs. Ramsay
watching the children throwing catches (110–11).

If Mrs. Ramsay in her marriage, and her inspiring those about
her, creates the vision in life, makes time stand still and imposes order on confusion, Lily, by her objective reserve and
keen perception, attempts to create the same vision in her art:
a combination of Mrs. Ramsay's pervasiveness and Mr. Ramsay's precision in "the light of a butterfly's wing lying upon the
arches of a cathedral" (75)—her painting. As she approaches
her canvas, Lily recognizes that the problem is "how to connect this mass on the right hand with that on the left" (82–83);
but though the problem may be easily definable, the solution
is not; and "It was in that moment's flight between the picture
and her canvas that the demons set on her who often brought
her to the verge of tears and made this passage from conception
to work as dreadful as any down a dark passage for a child"
(32). To create unity is an overwhelmingly difficult task, and
Lily knows that she cannot achieve it by accepting the com-

promise vision of marriage that Mrs. Ramsay, sensing Lily's kinship with vision, offers her.

Lily's attempts to unite the whole of the Lighthouse world on canvas involve a struggle second only to Mrs. Ramsay's efforts to unite this world in life; and just as Lily's talents often fail her, so Mrs. Ramsay's experiments, as we have seen, are not always successful—Lily and William are not meant to marry; Mr. Carmichael rejects all offers of communion. Yet Mrs. Ramsay, no more than Lily, will admit defeat; for to let the formlessness of life engulf all hope of pattern, unity, or order is to betray the vision. So she carries the vision bravely into life, offers to go to town for Mr. Carmichael, suggests the unity of marriage wherever it seems appropriate. Nor does she limit her fight against the disruptive forces in life entirely to her own family and friends. To do battle against isolation and sorrow she campaigns for clean dairies, visits the widow, and brings aid to the poor. But her visionary triumphs take place in her own home where her gift pervades every room and where, like Mrs. Dalloway, she has the greatest control over her life.[15] Here "Men, and women too, letting go the multiplicity of things, had allowed themselves with her the relief of simplicity" (65), and here, too, the culminating unification takes place in a dinner party, a miniature counterpart of the Dalloway gathering.

On the evening of the day in which Part One of *To the Lighthouse* takes place, Mrs. Ramsay presides over a special dinner at which every detail has been carefully planned to promote harmony and union: the individual fruits in the centerpiece have been arranged into an artistic, unified whole; the Boeuf en Daube, gem of the feast, has been simmering oil, olives, bay leaves, wine, and tender brown and yellow meats together for two days until the different ingredients have become one splendid savory stew. But when Mrs. Ramsay faces her guests at the table, "They all sat separate. And the whole of the effort of merging and flowing and creating rested on her" (126). The task is not easy; all her strength is needed to work the miracle; but when it comes, it comes in a flood of joy that seemed now for no special reason to stay there like a smoke, like a fume rising upwards, holding them safe together. Nothing need be said; nothing could be said. There it was, all round them. It partook, she felt, carefully helping Mr. Bankes to a specially tender piece, of eternity; as she had already felt about something different once before that afternoon; there is a coherence in things, a stability; something, she meant, is immune from change, and shines out . . . in the face of the flowing, the fleeting, the spectral, like a ruby; so that again tonight she had the feeling she had had once today, already, of peace, of rest. Of such moments, she thought, the thing is made that endures (158).

Because Mrs. Ramsay is aware that the waves of dissolution are always beating at the vision, she knows that such moments cannot last, but when they pass, they remain as symbols of the eternal possibility of coherence, of vision, and provide a motivation for renewed effort. So, although "directly she went a sort of disintegration set in . . ." (168), she knows that, for a moment, unity was reality. Still suspended in that sense of communion, she goes to work her magic in the nursery, remembering that "Children don't forget" (97). "She felt, with her hand on the nursery door, that community of feeling with other people which emotion gives as if the walls of partition had become so thin that practically . . . it was all one stream" (170). In the nursery lie James and Cam, the two Ramsay children who will live to continue that reconciliation of fact and vision begun by their parents. Already displaying those qualities that reflect their inheritance and forecast their future, these two are quarreling when Mrs. Ramsay enters. The bone of contention is an animal skull, symbol of death: ". . . Cam couldn't go to sleep with it in the room, and James screamed" (171) if anybody touched it. Like his father, James insists upon the bare facts of life, while Cam, inheriting her mother's sensitivity, is disturbed by them. Mrs. Ramsay, always the peacemaker, solves the difficulty as is her wont by swathing the fact in vision, never denying it is there, only asserting that there is something more. So by wrapping the skull in the green shawl that symbolizes her vision,[16] she teaches both her children to combine the two kinds of truth; and just as the shawl envelops the bone, so Mrs. Ramsay, who is not to see her children again in the course of the novel, will be "wound about in their hearts, however long they lived" (170).

"Time Passes," the second section of this novel, interrupts the story of the Ramsays, save for a few concentrated and highly significant parenthetical remarks, and watches the Lighthouse world—the house, the shore—as ten years, scarcely touched by civilization, wash over it. We know from Virginia Woolf's own statement, quoted earlier, that this break in the unity of design was intentional, that it was meant to be a test of the validity of that design. Because this section is built upon suggestion rather than statement, pattern rather than proposal, it has caused and probably will continue to cause some disagreement among critics. Thus when Virginia Woolf opens the last section of the book with "What does it mean then, what can it all mean?" (217), the question is not far from the mind of anyone who has just emerged from "Time Passes." From its title alone we can see that the emphasis of this section will be upon the question of movement in time. Jean Guiguet feels that "after the personal reign of Duration, ["Time Passes"] asserts the impersonal triumph of time."[17] Joan Bennett, too, recognizes that "it is not merely a particular ten years that is represented, but time in relation to eternity, the short span of mortal lives contrasted with the recurring seasons and the enduring world."[18] She feels, however, that this interweaving of natural seasons and human events creates "the illusion of nature's sympathy . . . the irony of nature's indifference,"[19] thus emphasizing the contrast between the fact of dissolution and the human hope for unity. In general, the feeling is that this section demonstrates the apparent triumph of fact over vision,[20] yet there are many elements in "Time Passes" that suggest that this interpretation is incorrect. In the first place, the rhythm of this section, the repetition of images and phrases, creates a reiterative pattern in itself that imposes order on the passage of the years and gives an impression of permanence. Second, the alternation of hope and despair, light and darkness, which flickers across these pages, unites "Time Passes" to Mrs. Ramsay's vision of the winking Lighthouse, and again makes stasis out of change. In the third place, the most momentous signs of decay, the deaths of Mrs. Ramsay, Prue, and Andrew, are carefully understated, so that the presence of these figures is not erased, only muffled. Just as Mrs. Ramsay's shawl made something visionary of the skull, letting it melt into mountains and valleys, flowers and birds, so do Mrs. Woolf's parentheses imbed the actuality of death in a pattern of waves, petals, and butterflies. We have seen in "The Window" that vision must be achieved by effort. In "Time Passes" we discover that many years after this effort has ceased through death, the most momentous sign that its power has faded at all is that two folds of Mrs. Ramsay's shawl have loosened from around the skull.

Perhaps the best way to examine the possibility that "Time Passes" presents the triumph of vision rather than its disintegration is to follow the wavelike rise and fall of the alternating passages of joy and sorrow that compose it. In this way we can discover whether the beam from the Lighthouse, which is Mrs. Ramsay's stroke, burns out, or continues to illuminate the world around it. The section opens in the dark:

> So with the lamps all put out, the moon sunk, and a thin rain drumming on the roof a downpouring of immense darkness began. Nothing, it seemed, could survive the flood, the profusion of darkness which, creeping in at keyholes and crevices, stole round window blinds, came into bedrooms, swallowed up here a jug and basin, there a bowl of red and yellow dahlias, there the sharp edges and firm bulk of a chest of drawers. Not only was furniture confounded; there was scarcely anything left of body or mind by which one could say, "This is he" or "This is she" (189–90).

Night then succeeds to night until it seems impossible that truth or light will ever emerge again. The visionary who might seek answers to the questions of life upon the beach will find nothing to bring the night to order or make "the world reflect the compass of the soul" (193). Then, as if to destroy the last vestige of hope, at the moment of deepest night Mrs. Ramsay dies. What then? Does even greater, unimaginable darkness succeed her end and reflect a defeat inherent in her passage? No, quite the opposite; the subsection following immediately upon her parenthetical departure opens not with night succeeding to night, but "day after day, light turned, like a flower reflected in water . . ." (194). So, even in the face of death,

> Loveliness and stillness clasped hands in the bedroom, and among the shrouded jugs and sheeted chairs even the prying of the wind, and the soft nose of the clammy sea airs, rubbing, snuffling, iterating, and reiterating their questions —"Will you fade? Will you perish?"—scarcely disturbed the peace, the indifference, the air of pure integrity, as if the question they asked scarcely needed that they should answer: we remain (195).

Now, in comes Mrs. McNab, like the beggar woman in *Mrs. Dalloway,* weaving further continuity with her song, which, "coming from the toothless, bonneted, care-taking woman, was robbed of meaning, was like the voice of witlessness, humour, persistency itself, trodden down but springing up again . . ." (196–97). In this period of light "The mystic, the visionary, walking the beach on a fine night . . . had suddenly an answer vouchsafed them . . . so that they were warm in the frost and had comfort in the desert" (197–98). As the illumination continues, the vision grows until "there came to the wakeful, the hopeful, walking the beach, stirring the pool, imaginations of the strangest kind—of flesh turned to atoms which drove before the wind, of stars flashing in their hearts, of cliff, sea, cloud, and sky brought purposely together to assemble outwardly the scattered parts of the vision within" (198). But, as Mrs. Ramsay herself knew, such moments never last, and in the midst of light Prue dies and the shawl begins to unwind. Then a new darkness descends with the war and the death of Andrew, and once again the dreamer, walking on the beach, sees his vision dissolve. Storms, too, return with the chaos that ran wild at the opening of this section, "until it seemed as if the universe were battling and tumbling, in brute confusion and wanton lust aimlessly by itself" (203). But this darkness is shorter than the one before, and Mrs. McNab is soon back again with such vivid imaginings of Mrs. Ramsay that we begin to wonder whether death is not a mere dip in the road of life. "She could see her now, stooping over her flowers; and faint and flickering, like a yellow beam or the circle at the end of a telescope, a lady in a grey cloak, stooping over her flowers, went wandering over the bedroom wall, up the dressing-table, across the washstand, as Mrs. McNab hobbled and ambled, dusting, straightening" (205). Mrs. Ramsay, in her death, has become the long stroke of light from the Lighthouse, wandering about the house and land like a protective spirit. We have caught a glimpse again of the vision. But, as always, the revelation fades: "The long night seemed to have set in . . ." (206); once again the messengers of chaos "seemed to have triumphed" (206). But because this darkness has become part of the pattern of hope and despair, we have learned to expect the returning light. So if disorder seems to rule, artichokes spring up among roses, we simply wait for the vision to return. And the Lighthouse beam, entering the darkened rooms for a moment every few minutes, reinforces our hope; for have we not just learned for certain that Mrs. Ramsay is in that light? As we expect, as we hope, now comes that moment again, "that hesitation when dawn trembles and night pauses, when if a feather alight in the scale it will be weighed down" (208). Again we have touched the brink of disaster; once more we ascend into order and light. So the cycle begins again. The Ramsays write that they are returning and the house emerges from the dark so much the same as before that when "Lily Briscoe had her bag carried up to the house late one evening in September" (213) and once again Mr. Carmichael reads his book by candlelight (214), we look at the title of the section, "Time Passes," and realize that the pattern, the vision, has triumphed. "Then indeed peace had come. Messages of peace breathed from the sea to the shore. Never to break its sleep any more, to lull it rather more deeply to rest, and whatever the dreamers dream holily, dreamt wisely, to confirm . . ." (213).

"What does it mean then, what can it all mean?" (217). Now that the cycle has begun again, are we closer to the vision or farther from it? As the novel opened Mr. and Mrs. Ramsay were in significant disagreement about whether or not one could go to the Lighthouse. Mr. Ramsay declared the excursion impossible, and, for the moment, his view triumphed. Now at the beginning of the last section, the formerly forbidden trip is about to take place. Mr. Ramsay, Cam, and James prepare to set sail, unsure, without Mrs. Ramsay to instruct them, what to take with them, how to proceed: "What does one send to the Lighthouse?—opened doors in one's mind that went banging and swinging to and fro and made one keep asking, in a stupefied gape, What does one send? What does one do?" (218). When she lived and influenced directly the lives of those around her, Mrs. Ramsay forced herself to acknowledge her husband's facts while keeping a close grasp on the vision. Now it is Mr. Ramsay's turn, when all the power belongs to him, to make his own token offering to his wife—what he must send to the Lighthouse is himself and so accept symbolically her belief that men, in spite of facts, may communicate, join, help each other to weave a pattern of unity. Cam and James, too, must make the trip and learn to see the Lighthouse through eyes that contain the shadows of two truths, that unite the double vision of their parents.

Thus great symbolic weight hangs on both the voyage and the Lighthouse itself, so that every critic who examines *To the Lighthouse* must attempt to unveil these symbols. As might be expected, interpretations have been many and varied. One critic sees the Lighthouse as "unattained perfection";[21] another understands it to represent "the rhythm of joy and sorrow in human life."[22] Still others interpret it as a symbol of Mrs. Ramsay herself.[23] Because of its complexity, several critics have given the Lighthouse a composite meaning. William York Tindall, for example, feels that "the Lighthouse is a suitable goal; for in it each quester can see himself and what he wants."[24] Margaret Church says "The Lighthouse with its revolving beam is superficially like a clock; on another level, its light represents security for those tossed by the restless flux of the waves. The Lighthouse is static in the midst of flux; it symbolizes the movement toward a synthesis of time and eternity."[25] Because Virginia Woolf compares Mr. Ramsay to a channel marker, or sets him lonely on a spit of land, the waves lapping at his feet; and because she specifically connects the signal light with Mrs. Ramsay, the most perceptive interpretations belong to Kaehale and German, and C. B. Cox. The former pair see that the Lighthouse contains the "harmonious union of their [Mr. and Mrs. Ramsay's] complementary qualities,"[26] while Mr. Cox states even more precisely, "The lighthouse symbolizes the essential isolation and independence of the individual, but the beams of the lighthouse crossing the dark waters at night represent the love of Mrs. Ramsay which unites all her friends and gives meaning to their lives."[27] Thus, in terms of fact and vision, the physical Lighthouse is factual truth, Mr. Ramsay's truth, representing both the loneliness of man and his courage in standing firm amidst the formlessness of life. The light from the Lighthouse, Mrs. Ramsay's vision, is not bounded by physical limitations, but pervades the darkness and gives direction to the traveler. Neither is complete without the other: vision needs fact as a reference point in order to function in the factual world; fact needs vision in order to escape its own limitations. In interpreting the final voyage, David Daiches says that "to reach the lighthouse is, in a sense, to make contact with a truth outside oneself, to surrender the uniqueness of one's ego to an impersonal reality";[28] but in the context of the story, it seems more consistent to see the successful trip in a double light. For Mr. Ramsay, the voyage to the Lighthouse is an admission that the vision exists, that death has not erased the essence of his wife, that although men are isolated from one another factually, some greater force unites them. When Cam and James set out for the Lighthouse, they know it only by its beams, understand only that side of it that represents their mother's form of truth. In experiencing the solid physical Lighthouse without denying the mystical one that shone in their early childhood, they fulfill their inheritance and see that the Lighthouse is not true in one way only, but in both. The greatest life is a combination of fact and vision.

That the journey to the Lighthouse is not merely a day's outing is made clear from the start as is the fact that this final section must concentrate on Mr. Ramsay's role in the voyage in order to create a balanced vision that includes both Mr. and Mrs. Ramsay. Lily Briscoe, who has returned to complete the vision in her painting, sees that the short sail is a major event in Mr. Ramsay's life, when she says, "There was no helping Mr. Ramsay on the journey he was going" (230). In making the trip, he cannot set aside his lifelong devotion to objective fact, but must carry it with him. The kitchen table, "bare, hard, not ornamental" (232), still rules his world. He "kept always his eyes fixed upon it, never allowed himself to be distracted or deluded, until his face became worn too and ascetic and partook of this unornamented beauty" (232). But Mr. Ramsay has never lacked courage. "He liked that men should labour and sweat on the windy beach at night; pitting muscle and brain against the waves and wind . . ." (245). So bravely he begins the voyage he had formerly denied, reminding himself even as he journeys toward communion that "We perished, each alone"; "and like everything else this strange morning the words became symbols . . ." (219). As he herds together his reluctant children, forcing them to undertake a voyage they no longer want, Lily sees the coercion as a tragedy and remembers the continual sacrifices Mrs. Ramsay made for her husband. In a sense it is tragic that children should be compelled to accept the limits of fact; yet as we have seen in the case of Mrs. Ramsay and as we shall see again before the story is through, both the skull and the shawl are real, both the Lighthouse and its light. In order to be able to appreciate life in its entirety, then, Mrs. Ramsay's children must accept the validity of their father's truth and blend it with that revealed to them by their mother.

Both Cam and James, as they set sail, sense the inflexibility and often unwitting cruelty of their father and realize that he makes little effort to understand or appreciate them for their individual qualities. When Cam, for example, cannot find their house from the sea, she sees that "he could not understand the state of mind of any one, not absolutely imbecile, who did not know the points of the compass" (249). So the two children "vowed, in silence, as they walked, to stand by each other and carry out the great compact—to resist tyranny to the death" (243).

The first to recognize that Mr. Ramsay's rigidity is honesty rather than tyranny is, of course, Cam; for she has inherited that sense of vision from her mother that seeks harmony rather than discord. Time and again as the voyage progresses we see these reflections of Mrs. Ramsay shining in Cam's mind, as, for example, when she finds in the sea a pattern "where in the green light a change came over one's entire mind and one's body shone half transparent enveloped in a green cloak" (272), and so takes on Mrs. Ramsay's green shawl of vision. As this newly expanded visionary self sends fingers out into the world, she, like her mother, alights on "Greece, Rome, Constantinople" (281). With her mother's instinct she sees that Mr. Ramsay, for all his occasional selfishness, is primarily a courageous defender of the truth, who, while insisting on life's loneliness and ugliness, offers stability and protection for those who need it. As the Lighthouse looms large just ahead, Cam sits by her father and thinks, "Now I can go on thinking whatever I like, and I shan't fall over a precipice or be drowned, for there he is, keeping his eye on me . . ." (304). Like Mrs. Ramsay, Cam recognizes her need for the austerity of factual truth upon which to hang her visions of infinity.

For James, the voyage to the Lighthouse is a voyage of self-discovery in which he learns to reconcile the fact and vision in himself. As a small child, he was totally absorbed into his mother's world, learning from her the value of vision, taking sides with her against his father. But even then his legacy from Mr. Ramsay was clear to others if not to himself: "he appeared the image of stark and uncompromising severity, with his high forehead and his fierce blue eyes, impeccably candid and pure, frowning slightly at the sight of human frailty . . ." (10). During the course of the trip he begins, first of all to see the virtue of his father's way of life, then to recognize his father in himself. When, in defining the tyranny he opposes, he weaves a metaphor of a great wheel crushing a helpless foot to describe his father, James suddenly sees that if the foot is innocent, so is the wheel. If his father seems cruel, it is only that he is uncompromising. "Yes, thought James, while the boat slapped and dawdled there in the hot sun; there was a waste of snow and rock very lonely and austere; and there he had come to feel, quite often lately, when his father said something or did something which surprised the others, there were two pairs of footprints only; his own and his father's" (274–75). As he begins to sense a kindred love of truth in himself, James unconsciously takes on his father's mannerisms as well. " 'We are driving before a gale—we must sink,' he began saying to himself, half aloud, exactly as his father said it" (302). Then his father praises the precision of his sailing, and with this final moment of communion with his father, James is ready to recognize the truth of his reaction to the suddenly factual Lighthouse:

> The Lighthouse was then a silvery, misty-looking tower with a yellow eye, that opened suddenly, and softly in the evening. Now——
>
> James looked at the Lighthouse. He could see the whitewashed rocks; the tower, stark and straight; he could see that it was barred with black and white; he could see windows in it; he could even see washing spread on the rocks to dry. So that was the Lighthouse, was it?
>
> No, the other was also the Lighthouse. For nothing was simply one thing. The other Lighthouse was true too (276–77).

So James's voyage has made him see that life includes both his mother's vision and his father's objective fact just as he contains the stuff of both his parents.

If Cam, James, and Mr. Ramsay achieve a symbolic reconciliation of fact and vision in life by their Lighthouse excursion, on shore Lily Briscoe is attempting to create the same harmony in her painting. As we saw in "The Window," the artist can become a successful vision-maker only by living a life that recognizes all truth, without favoring one attitude to the exclusion of another. Such a life demands objectivity and personal freedom, but insists, too, upon sufficient involvement with others to allow for sympathy and understanding. When we first come upon Lily in "The Lighthouse" section, she is "Sitting alone . . . among the clean cups at the long table," where she feels "cut off from other people, and able only to go on watching, asking, wondering" (218). On the surface she is prepared to approach her canvas with a reverent and objective mind, but until she recognizes the full significance of Mr. Ramsay in the Lighthouse world, she will be unable to begin her painting. Although she knows that the encounter with him must come, she recognizes that it will be painful and tries to postpone it as long as possible. When he looks at her in passing, then, "she pretended to drink out of her empty coffee cup so as to escape him—to escape his demand on her, to put aside a moment longer that imperious need" (219). With his wife gone and the voyage not yet begun, Mr. Ramsay must seek the solace of vision in others, at the same time imposing upon them the weight of his burden of fact. Having, like James, allowed the power of Mrs. Ramsay's vision to cast a shadow on the necessity of Mr. Ramsay's precepts, Lily must make her sacrifice to him before she can attempt to make time and truth stand still upon her canvas. Hoping to avoid the unavoidable, she sets up her easel, cleans her brushes, pretends to be busy, but "You shan't touch your canvas, he seemed to say, bearing down on her, till you've given me what I want of you" (224). He stands waiting, and she is paralyzed, unable to give him what he asks. Then, in an inspired moment, almost unconsciously, she looks down at his boots, "sculptured; colossal; like everything that Mr. Ramsay wore, from his frayed tie to his half-buttoned waistcoat, his own indisputably. She could see them walking to his room of their own accord, expressive in his absence of pathos, surliness, ill-temper, charm. 'What beautiful boots!' she exclaimed" (228–29). In praising his boots while recognizing that they bear the imprint of his soul, she is in fact praising him, acknowledging his power and importance to her

own vision. Thus once she has spoken, the barrier to her painting is removed and she can begin.

To create vision is never easy as we have seen, and Lily,
confronting her blank canvas thinks:

> what could be more formidable than that space? Here she
> was again, she thought, stepping back to look at it, drawn
> out of gossip, out of living, out of community with people
> into the presence of this formidable ancient enemy of
> hers—this other thing, this truth, this reality, which
> suddenly laid hands on her, emerged stark at the back of
> appearances and commanded her attention (236).

Then "before she exchanged the fluidity of life for the concentration of painting she had a few moments of nakedness
when she seemed like an unborn soul, a soul reft of body . . ."
(237). In this moment of vision she is flooded with a fountain
of memories that begin to bring together the presence of the
concrete Mr. Ramsay and that of his visionary wife. At first
Lily is unaware that Mrs. Ramsay's death has changed nothing.
"It must have altered the design a good deal," thinks Lily,
"when she was sitting on the step with James" (239). But if
she cannot yet sense her presence, Lily can remember Mrs.
Ramsay's gift: "what a power was in the human soul! she
thought. That woman sitting there writing under the rock
resolved everything into simplicity . . ." (239). "Oh, Mrs. Ramsay! she called out silently, to that essence which sat by the
boat, that abstract one made of her . . ." (266); and, answering
the call, Mrs. Ramsay appears, relieving Lily "for a moment
of the weight that the world had put on her, staying lightly by
her side and then . . . raising to her forehead a wreath of white
flowers . . ." (269). This vision, seen so clearly and experienced
with such emotion, fades, as all such moments must. Reality
breaks in, requires and gets "an effort of attention, so that the
vision must be perpetually remade" (270). Lily, like Mrs.
Ramsay, realizes that when one asks, "What is the meaning of
life?" (240), the great revelation never comes. "Instead there

were little daily miracles, illuminations, matches struck unexpectedly in the dark . . ." (240). Then, as each is extinguished, new moments must be fought for, until a pattern begins to emerge, such as we saw in "Time Passes." So Lily and Mrs. Ramsay both attack the flux of life with the tools of vision.

> . . . Mrs. Ramsay making of the moment something permanent (as in another sphere Lily herself tried to make of the moment something permanent)—this was of the nature of a revelation. In the midst of chaos there was shape; this eternal passing and flowing (she looked at the clouds going and the leaves shaking) was struck into stability. Life stand still here, Mrs. Ramsay said (241).

And so too says Lily, taking her brush in hand.[29]

As she works toward the completion of her painting, Lily feels that it includes "so many lives. The Ramsays'; the children's; and all sorts of waifs and strays of things besides . . . . some common feeling held the whole" (286). She senses too that in her work she is creating this unity through a special kind of love, the visionary force that pervades so many of Virginia Woolf's novels: "Love had a thousand shapes. There might be lovers whose gift it was to choose out the elements of things and place them together and so, giving them a wholeness not theirs in life, make of some scene, or meeting of people (all now gone and separate), one of those globed compacted things over which thought lingers, and love plays" (286). The scope of this vision makes one feel "One wanted fifty pairs of eyes to see with . . ." (294), for it extends far beyond the limits of a single mind to embrace infinity.

The moment when Lily will complete this vision is at hand. Out in the bay Mr. Ramsay, Cam, and James have almost reached their goal. To help her unite past and present, to create the momentarily infinite world, Lily calls again to Mrs. Ramsay, and "Mrs. Ramsay—it was part of her perfect goodness—sat there quite simply, in the chair, flicked her needles to and fro, knitted her reddish-brown stocking, cast her shadow on the step. There she sat" (300). Quickly, thinks Lily, "Where was that boat now? And Mr. Ramsay? She wanted him" (300).

For both husband and wife must be present for her to capture the fleeting vision that, like Mrs. Ramsay, "should be . . . feathery and evanescent, one colour melting into another like the colours on a butterfly's wing; but beneath the fabric must be clamped together with bolts of iron" (255), the iron of Mr. Ramsay's fact. The painting must make one "feel simply that's a chair, that's a table, and yet at the same time, It's a miracle, it's an ecstasy" (300). The moment has come to connect the opposite poles of truth; Mr. Ramsay has landed at the Lighthouse, and Lily "With a sudden intensity, as if she saw it clear for a second . . . drew a line there, in the centre. It was done; it was finished. Yes, she thought, laying down her brush in extreme fatigue, I have had my vision" (310). So, as Sharon Kaehale and Howard German so perceptively put it, Lily "combines the perspectives of both Mr. and Mrs. Ramsay and makes reality simultaneously factual and miraculous."[30]

Thus, by the end of the novel, Virginia Woolf has sent Mrs. Ramsay's vision through the refining fire of fact, bringing it forth unscathed to be finally united both in life and in art with the bare factual truth, making that truth transcendent. This testing and proving of vision, while it has demanded the inclusion of factual existence, has taken place primarily on a symbolic plane in which the full force of change has been kept at a remove and let in only through token members of society or images of chaos. Because of the success of this "visionary" method of reconciling fact and vision, symbolized itself by the remoteness of Lily from the distractions of husband, children, or financial affairs, Virginia Woolf will devote her next major novel, *The Waves,* to an even more detailed presentation of the factual/visionary world and present that world within an artistic form that in itself is purely visionary.

6

The Waves

Of the eight major novels that Virginia Woolf wrote, *The Waves* is by far the most intricate, both structurally and thematically. One year before she began to work on it, she conceived of an "abstract mystical eyeless book,"[1] a book that would stand "away from facts; yet concentrated; prose yet poetry; a novel and a play."[2] Then, as the idea grew denser, more concrete, she described her nascent book this way: "The idea has come to me that what I want now to do is to saturate every atom. I mean to eliminate all waste, deadness, superfluity: to give the moment whole; whatever it includes. Say that the moment is a combination of thought; sensation; the voice of the sea. Waste, deadness, come from the inclusion of things that don't belong to the moment; this appalling narrative business of the realist."[3] *The Waves,* then, was to be a book that would include all of life without being weighted down by fact, in other words, a book that would serve, as Lily Briscoe's painting served, to concentrate all forms of reality into as economic a space as possible; to unite the factual and visionary worlds, but all within the symbolic structure of vision. This novel, when it emerged, fulfilled all the early foreshadowings of its magnitude. In a little over two hundred pages, Virginia Woolf has succeeded in presenting not only the individual lives of six very different human beings, all faced with the problem of reconciling fact and vision; she has also, in these few characters, managed to examine nearly every possible method of attacking this problem in life. Because it is true that there is little dross in this work, no single study of anything other than book length could reveal all the nuances, unveil all the meanings, of each scene, each speech. It is even doubtful whether such a study could include everything, so that all any shorter examination can attempt is to send one thin beam of light through the book, illuminating a single aspect of the whole.

Perhaps because the task of interpreting *The Waves* is so immense, few critics have done more than to suggest one or two themes that might prove fruitful to those who should dare more thorough exploration. David Daiches, for example, says "again time, death, and personality, and their interrelations, provide the main theme; here, the emphasis is on time."[4] Other critics, too, have settled on one or more of these three themes in trying to sum up the central concern of the novel: James Hafley finds in the style of *The Waves* a mirroring of the theme, "life's flux is precisely its unity";[5] Winifred Holtby feels that the book "concerns the preparation of the individual for life and death and the effect of death upon the survivors";[6] A .D. Moody sees it as achieving "a wonderful poise between the pervasive reality of death and the continuing reality of human energy,"[7] Jean O. Love, a "movement from diffusion to partial differentiation to diffusion."[8]

Because an understanding of the six main characters is so obviously crucial to an intelligent interpretation of the novel as a whole, most critics have suggested at least one theory to elucidate their unusual lives. Bernard Blackstone explains their isolation from the rest of the world by saying that "reality and society do not go together . . . . the solitary mind alone can glimpse ultimate truth,"[9] a theory that seems valid when looking at the novel solely from a stylistic point of view but collapses under exposure to the themes of the book. At least four critics, Harvena Richter,[10] Dorothy Brewster,[11] Aileen Pippett,[12] and Jean Guiguet,[13] view the six as different aspects of a single individual; while others such as John Graham, Michael Payne, and Joan Bennett see unifying forces at work in the lives of the six without concluding that they are really one. Graham sees these forces as simply "human communion."[14] Payne as the power of art,[15] and Bennett as "an integrity of purpose which gives them the power to discover the principle of their own nature."[16]

And if the six main characters have obvious symbolic import, so, of necessity, has the title of the novel, which washes regularly into the italicized interludes and at times into the body of the book as well. Several critics have paused to suggest some translation of "The Waves." M. C. Bradbrook interprets the sea as "a symbol of the eternal and indifferent natural forces";[17] Peter and Margaret Havard-Williams as "the perfect image of the ceaseless flow of dreams and images"[18] that keeps Rhoda from the factual world; and James Hafley provides what is probably the most illuminating interpretation, saying, "the individual life is a wave, and life itself the sea; to look at oneself as only one wave is to perish when that single wave breaks, but to see oneself as an indivisible part of the sea, composed of innumerable drops of water—as part of wave after wave—is to gain immortality."[19]

Almost any one of these approaches to *The Waves* could lead to a better understanding of the work; but I have chosen yet another, feeling that this novel provides the most complete presentation thus far of Virginia Woolf's many-faceted theme of the duality of fact and vision in the life of every man, and in life in general.

Because *The Waves* is so tightly woven, the scenes and the characters so elaborately interrelated, any study that attempts a vertical rather than a horizontal approach is certain to create unnatural fractures in the fabric of the work. Therefore, to explore the development of the central problems and to appreciate fully the final summation, one must work section by section rather than theme by theme. Virginia Woolf herself, to help illuminate the main text, set apart certain passages in the novel by opening each new section with a densely symbolic description of a beach scene as it changes in appearance from dawn to night. These italicized interludes mirror on a small scale the entire movement of the novel and, in themselves, serve several purposes. First of all, each time of the day they describe corresponds to a certain period in the lives of the six main characters. Second, by embracing so large a scope of life

within a single day, these passages, like "Time Passes" in *To
the Lighthouse*, suggest that change is illusory when set in
the infinite context of the vision, and that life, like the cycle
from dawn to dusk to dawn again, is an endless pattern of
rising and falling. Third, they provide a set of images, drawn
from factual reality, which are separated from the subjective
thought-speeches of the six characters. When fragments of
these scenes appear in their minds, the reader is then able to
see how each of them reacts to the real world. Thus, for example, when these images spring up word for word in Bernard's
phrase-making, his role as reliable spokesman is demonstrated
by the fact that he can see clearly and report poetically the
objective world around him.

The prelude to the first section begins:

> *The sun had not yet risen. The sea was indistinguishable
> from the sky, except that the sea was slightly creased as if a
> cloth had wrinkles in it. Gradually as the sky whitened a
> dark line lay on the horizon dividing the sea from the sky
> and the grey cloth became barred with thick strokes moving,
> one after another, beneath the surface, following each
> other, pursuing each other, perpetually.*
>
> *As they neared the shore each bar rose, heaped itself,
> broke and swept a thin veil of white water across the sand.
> The wave paused, and then drew out again, sighing like a
> sleeper whose breath comes and goes unconsciously.*[20]

At the dawn of the day the waves, which serve as one of the
symbols for the six characters, seem almost to merge with the
sky. So, too, at the dawn of life the child feels so close to the
world around him that he cannot distinguish between himself
and others. Yet the wrinkles of individuality are there, and
soon each child takes on a separate form that shapes itself,
disperses, then reshapes, suggesting a perpetuity in life, an
association with an eternal pattern that is represented by the
image of waves breaking and reforming, breaking and
reforming.

When we look back to Rachel Vinrace in *The Voyage Out*,
we remember her inchoate spiritual childhood and her need

to confront the factual world in order to develop a sense of self. In these interludes of *The Waves,* the light of day symbolizes this objective reality that brings out the contours of land and sea. Before the formative process begins, the sun has not yet risen, but as it climbs over the horizon, *"the air seemed to become fibrous and to tear away from the green surface . . ."* (179), just as sensation, caused by contact with factual reality, makes the child differentiate between himself and the outside world.

To increase the density of these interludes and thus provide yet another mirror to the text, Virginia Woolf introduces two other symbols to reflect her characers' progress through life: a flock of birds in a garden; and a house. As the sun illuminates the sea,

> . . . *light struck upon the trees in the garden, making one leaf transparent and then another. One bird chirped high up; there was a pause; another chirped lower down. The sun sharpened the walls of the house, and rested like the tip of a fan upon a white blind and made a blue fingerprint of shadow under the leaf by the bedroom window. The blind stirred slightly, but all within was dim and unsubstantial. The birds sang their blank melody outside* (179–80).

At this early hour the birds are just beginning to find their voices and as yet have no form to their song. The house, too, its walls bathed in reality, has assumed only a shell of substance while its inner rooms are still darkened. So Rhoda, Louis, Jinny, Neville, Susan, and Bernard, who are slowly waking in one of these shadowy rooms, have not yet stepped out into the full light of fact. Like the birds, they have only begun to test their own voices.

> "I see a ring," said Bernard, "hanging above me. It quivers and hangs in a loop of light."
> "I see a slab of pale yellow," said Susan, "spreading away until it meets a purple stripe."
> "I hear a sound," said Rhoda, "cheep, chirp; cheep, chirp; going up and down."

"I see a globe," said Neville, "hanging down in a drop against the enormous flanks of some hill."

"I see a crimson tassel," said Jinny, "twisted with gold threads."

"I hear something stamping," said Louis. "A great beast's foot is chained. It stamps, and stamps, and stamps" (180).

As yet, the six children are separated from one another only by the thinnest lines. Each receives his first taste of the reality of the factual world in small doses and expresses what he perceives in simple, compact, parallel phrases. Exposure to sensation has just begun, and for each the new experience is brief and elementary. Yet even in these abbreviated reactions lie hidden the clues to the path each character will follow into life. Already Bernard, the nascent phrase-maker, builds embryonic metaphors and small alliterations around his observations with his "loop of light." Susan, in her careful factual observation of essential attributes of objects, foretells her own future as a woman who lives simply and close to the basic elements of life. Rhoda, with Louis, perceives a sound rather than a visual image, indicating that both these children will have difficulty in apprehending life's tangible aspects. Neville, who perceives the microscopic world in a raindrop against the great expanse of a hill, will later be torn between the miniature life of a carefully enclosed room and the expansive life involved in following truth across mountains and deserts. And Jinny, who will grow up to glitter in silks and jewelry, to live in a world dominated by sex and socializing, is immediately and symbolically attracted to the crimson and gold of a curtain tassel. In his first encounter with fact, each child settles on one facet of the world around him, but because Virginia Woolf made of this novel a vision that could absorb all reality in symbol by "saturating every atom," even these solid objects blossom into symbol and, like Neville's raindrop, hold a world within a little space.

In the fragments of perception that follow the opening lines, these hints about each character grow broader. Bernard's phrase-making expands ("Now the cock crows like a spurt of hard, red water in the white tide" [181], he says). Neville's love of precision is reflected even in his experience of sensation ("Stones are cold to my feet . . . I feel each one, round or pointed, separately" [181], he says). The fearful Rhoda identifies herself with the one bird that sings by the window alone while the rest flock after seed, realizing that she will never be able to participate naturally in the ordinary actions of life.

When faced with the classroom and the task of working out Latin translations, the children grow more and more distinct from one another in their reactions. Louis, while acknowledging secretly his own superior comprehension of the lesson, waits to imitate Bernard's way of speaking in order to hide his Australian accent. So all through life he will force himself to conform to the actions of the masses and never fit the ordinary pattern instinctively. Susan avoids the abstraction of words, seeing them as natural objects, "stones one picks up by the seashore" (188). Bernard revels in words and begins to use his observations of the factual world to give added meaning to less tangible ideas: "They flick their tails right and left as I speak them," says Bernard of the Latin words. "They wag their tails; they flick their tails; they move through the air in flocks, now this way, now that way, moving all together, now dividing, now coming together" (188). He has seen the birds and seen them accurately, but transforms them into metaphor for words in order better to understand the power of language. Jinny, like Susan, avoids the abstraction of words and thinks, "Those are yellow words, those are fiery words. . . . I should like a fiery dress, a yellow dress, a fulvous dress to wear in the evening" (188). If Bernard mixes words and birds to enhance the existence of both, Neville, another man of words, sees only the precise, factual side of language as of life. "Each tense," says Neville, "means differently. There is an order in this world; there are distinctions, there are differences in this world . . ." (188).

In every daily action in which the children participate each reveals his own idiosyncracies. Do they play in the garden? Each devises a different amusement. Do they eat bread and milk together? Rhoda dreams over it; Bernard makes his bread into pellet "people;" Louis looks into the distance, ignoring his meal; Neville eats neatly and decisively; Jinny makes her fingers do pirouettes on the table cloth. Before this childhood day is over, the six characters, for all their unfamiliarity with themselves, each other, and life in general, have begun to reveal their own methods of balancing fact and vision.

Rhoda, as her reaction to the solitary bird has already revealed, is somehow unable to follow the others and step out of the unconscious world of vision in which all forms and faces are intermingled; thus she cannot assume a solid, factual identity. When she is alone, she exists in a kingdom of dreams, floating petals in a basin and calling them her ships. These blossom boats must all be white, for colors belong to the solid world that Susan and Jinny inhabit; and they must remain at sea, for the mainland is too concrete for Rhoda to comprehend. If they call in at any port, it is in some foreign island, totally unlike the actual world in which Rhoda lives, and most of them end up at the bottom of her little sea. In the classroom, while the others sit working out their arithmetic problems, Rhoda becomes overwhelmed by the abstract figures and slips further and further from specific time and specific space to float about in the amorphous sea of unconscious, universal formlessness.

> ". . . I cannot write," [she cries to herself.] "I see only figures. The others are handing in their answers, one by one. Now it is my turn. But I have no answer. . . . Look, the loop of the figure is beginning to fill with time; it holds the world in it. I begin to draw a figure and the world is looped in it, and I myself am outside the loop; which I now join—so—and seal up, and make entire. The world is entire, and I am outside of it, crying, 'Oh, save me, from being blown for ever outside the loop of time!' " (189).

Because he, too, is something of an outsider, Louis recognizes Rhoda's agony, and says, ". . . as she stares at the chalk figures, her mind lodges in those white circles; it steps through those white loops into emptiness, alone. They have no meaning for her. She has no answer for them. She has no body as the others

CHAPTER 6

have" (189). She has no body. Like a shell-less snail, Rhoda is missing a concrete self. So fact to her is something always alien, to be grasped as her petal-boat sailors grasp at straws when their ships go under. At night, when the light of fact gives way to the unifying darkness of vision, Rhoda must press her toes against the bed rail in order not to lose all contact with physical reality. Like Septimus, she is too much a part of vision, has become too much absorbed into insubstantiality, to be able to weld this truth to the solid factual world.

Louis, like Rhoda, is a visionary. When he is alone he says,

> I hold a stalk in my hand. I am the stalk. My roots go down to the depths of the world, through earth dry with brick, and damp earth, through veins of lead and silver. I am all fibre. All tremors shake me, and the weight of the earth is pressed to my ribs. Up here my eyes are green leaves, unseeing. I am a boy in grey flannels with a belt fastened by a brass snake up here. Down there my eyes are the lidless eyes of a stone figure in a desert by the Nile. I see women passing with red pitchers to the river; I see camels swaying and men in turbans. I hear tramplings, tremblings, stirrings round me (182).

While Rhoda is so absorbed in vision that nothing concrete has meaning for her, Louis comes closer to giving some form to his perception of infinite universality. Instead of merging with infinity, he absorbs all times and places into himself, sees that he includes the past as well as the present. In her fantasy, *Orlando,* Virginia Woolf presented this same hyperbolic embodiment of the fact that all time is one, by making the hero/ heroine of that book a figure who lives for hundreds of years without growing old. Louis, in the present, senses that he lives in a universe of infinite time and space. Yet perception of the vision of unity is not enough. Somehow this sense of pattern must be integrated with life in the factual world, and Louis, like Rhoda, fails to achieve this balance. As his behavior in Latin class has already shown, Louis betrays his great knowledge by setting it aside in order to imitate others. When Jinny comes upon him as he dreams of his pervasive being and forces him to confront contracted reality by kissing him, his vision is shattered. He cannot create a factual identity that does not conflict with his visionary self, and his life's effort will be devoted both to molding himself to match the world and attempting (surreptitiously) to reshape that world to fit himself, a hopelessly circular way of life.

Jinny, in her dreams of golden dresses and crimson tassels, in her kissing Louis and rejoicing in the world of the senses, is already revealed as the embryonic social and sexual creature. "I dance," she says. "I ripple. I am thrown over you like a net of light. I lie quivering flung over you" (183). Jinny has all the physical magnetism of Clarissa Dalloway or Mrs. Ramsay, with none of the greater visionary sense behind it. Time for her is limited to the passing moment, space to the social scene surrounding her body in ballroom or bedroom. Since she sees no universal unity, she contents herself and the men she loves with temporary sexual merging, never tying herself to one man or letting time turn her blossom to fruit through marriage and childbearing. Thus, in her own factual realm, she mimics visionary oneness and so solves in her own simple way the complexities of life.

Susan's answer to the question of how to create meaning and unity within a world of bounded fact is just as simple as Jinny's, but unconsciously comes closer to uniting pure fact with the wholeness of vision sensed by Louis and experienced by Rhoda; for Susan, instead of immersing herself in the sterile superficialities of society, becomes one with the natural world of earth, trees, and raw, straightforward emotions—love, hate, jealousy. Even in her childhood this affinity with the unpolished side of life is fully developed. For example, when she sees Jinny kiss Louis, Susan screws her anguish into her handkerchief and, hiding her tears and her jealousy, runs to the beechwood, away from the abstractions of the classroom, to examine her emotion under the trees and make it part of the concrete world of nature that she loves. When Bernard comes to comfort her, she tells him ingenuously of her own limitations and emotions, saying, "I love . . . and I hate. I desire one thing only. My eyes are hard. Jinny's eyes break into a thousand lights. Rhoda's are like those pale flowers to which moths come in the evening. Yours grow full and brim and never break. But I am already set on my pursuit. I see insects in the grass" (185). Susan's clear eyes see each fact precisely; her emotions are never mixed. She does not aspire to visionary heights but instead is tied to the world "with single words" (185) describing single facts. Like Jinny, Susan is conscious of no mystical unity; but, as her adherence to the natural world grows stronger and stronger, it soon unites her to the perpetual cycle of seasons, until, by merging with a cycle composed of time but transcending it through repetition, she stands unwittingly outside the door to vision.

If Susan consecrates her body and her emotions to the natural world of fact, loving it and living at its roots, Neville, from his earliest childhood, subjects all events, emotions, men, and objects to continuous mental analysis, thus devoting himself to abstract rather than concrete fact. His careful dissection of Latin grammar foretells his future as a scholar and his coming membership in Virginia Woolf's family of fact-driven men: St. John Hirst, Mr. Hilbery, Peter Walsh, Mr. Ramsay. When Bernard hurries off to comfort the crying Susan, the limiting precision of Neville's mind is unveiled by his thoughts: "Where is Bernard? . . . He has my knife. . . . He is like a dangling wire, a broken bell-pull, always twangling. He is like the seaweed hung outside the window, damp now, now dry. He leaves me in the lurch; he follows Susan; and if Susan cries he will take my knife and tell her stories. . . . I hate dangling things; I hate dampish things. I hate wandering and mixing things together" (187). The complexities and confusions of life annoy Neville. He searches out a private place in which to examine his observations, cuts through them with an intellectual knife, and lays bare their core of abstract truth. Even overpowering emotion receives this dispassionate analysis. For example, one night as a child, while climbing the stairs, Neville overhears the servants talking about a man found with his throat cut. Carefully, he examines his reaction to this first encounter with death.

The apple-tree leaves became fixed in the sky; the moon glared; I was unable to lift my foot up the stair. . . . I shall call this stricture, this rigidity, "death among the apple trees" for ever. There were the floating, pale-grey clouds; and the immitigable tree; the implacable tree with its greaved silver bark. The ripple of my life was unavailing. I was unable to pass by. There was an obstacle. "I cannot surmount this unintelligible obstacle," I said. And the others passed on. But we are doomed, all of us by the apple trees, by the immitigable tree which we cannot pass (191).

On the factual plane, death is the end. Only in the context of the vision does it assume the infinite unifying proportions that the disciples of intellectualized fact never see.

Bernard is the most complex, as well as the most reliable observer, of all the six. His eye is keen. If the objective prelude describes the leaf-shadows on the house as blue fingerprints (180), he sees "blue, finger-shaped shadows of leaves beneath the windows" (181); so that the reader trusts Bernard's descriptions of himself and the others. In *To the Lighthouse* the artist Lily Briscoe kept herself aloof from others in order to retain her objectivity, but when Bernard senses in one of his companions a loneliness, a sorrow, or a joy that must be shared, he hurries to involve himself and weaves a bandage of words for wounds or a shelter of story for the lonely. So when Susan cries in jealousy, Bernard creates a fantasy about the town of Elvedon with its lady in the window writing and its threatening gardeners sweeping the lawns so that he and she must run and escape the sorrow. Under the influence of the love that Susan's candor inspires, he makes his first small poem: "The pigeon beats the air; the pigeon beats the air with wooden wings" (186). Though Susan cannot understand his phrase-making, she has drawn comfort from his story. So the artist must bring his vision into life and use it widely to give it validity.

Everything Bernard sees is material for his endless chronicle of life. Crawling in among the roots and stems where the birds hop about in the interludes, Bernard builds pearls of story for Jinny around each grain of fact he finds, a foreshadowing of his later symbol-making; worms become cobras; sparrows are eagles. "Everything is strange. Things are huge and very small" (190). Because life itself provides no real endings, Bernard's narrations lead him on and on. "My hair is untidy," he says, "because when Mrs. Constable told me to brush it there was a fly in a web, and I asked, 'Shall I free the fly? Shall I let the fly be eaten?' So I am late always" (184). He cannot retreat from complexity to look for an abstract system as does Neville, or, with Louis, attempt to impose his own sense of order on the world. But if Bernard cannot fabricate boundaries where they do not exist, he can interpret and express his own experience and that of others, giving form to life by setting it in the context of art. Thus each stage of life is carefully observed by Bernard, then woven in the form of images into a momentary and fragmentary summation. In the first stage, in which six unformed children are exposed to the shock of factual reality and so begin to take on to some degree the outlines of selfhood, Bernard describes a representative example of this new encounter with sensation in a single scene in which a great sponge, heavy with water, is squeezed over him during his bath. "Water pours down the runnel of my spine," he says. "Bright arrows of sensation shoot on either side. I am covered with warm flesh" (192). Fact, then, puts flesh on the bones of vision, and at the end of the day, Bernard recounts in an image of the bath the way in which he and his friends have been flooded with these exterior, objective events: "Rich and heavy sensations form on the roof of my mind; down showers the day —the woods; and Elvedon; Susan and the pigeon. Pouring down the walls of my mind, running together, the day falls copious, resplendent" (192).

In the brighter light of the second interlude, with the sun risen higher into the sky, *The rocks which had been misty and soft hardened and were marked with red clefts* while the *Blue waves, green waves swept a quick fan over the beach, circling the spike of sea-holly and leaving shallow pools of light here and there on the sand. A faint black rim was left behind them"* (194). Life is beginning to assume greater solidity. The outer world has taken on a reality of its own upon which the newly formed waves leave their mark. So most of the six characters, who have begun to discover their individual identities, have reached that point of selfhood at which they can begin to have some effect on others. The garden and the birds, here in this early scene, are scattered into fragments, each substantial but alone. *"Sharp stripes of shadow lay on the grass, and the dew dancing on the tips of the flowers and leaves made the garden like a mosaic of single sparks not yet formed into one whole. The birds, whose breasts were specked canary and rose, now sang a strain or two together, wildly, like skaters rollicking arm-in-arm, and were suddenly silent, breaking asunder"* (194).

The six characters, too, are concentrating on self-definition and are not yet ready to form a harmonious pattern with others. This period of separation, as we have seen before, is necessary if the individual is to learn to build visionary unity in a disordered factual world. Unless one is aware of division, how can one hope to create a union? So the scene of beach and garden, having emerged from the unity of unconsciousness, has splintered into distinct segments. Inside the house, whose rooms represent the furnishings of the individual mind, everything is still *"softly amorphous, as if the china of the plate flowed and the steel of the knife were liquid"* (194). The first step into reality is an awareness of the otherness of the world that surrounds one. Then comes an understanding of the self.

Rhoda, the visionary, longs to make some offering that would convey her dreams to others, and thinks, "I will pick flowers; I will bind flowers in one garland and clasp them and present them—Oh! to whom?" (213). Because she is unable to find her way from the formless sea of life's infancy to the substantial shore of fact, she has no base to stand on from which to make her symbolic gesture. She cannot gather her flowers of vision into the factual world until she herself can arrive there. "I have no face," she thinks. "Other people have faces; Susan and Jinny have faces; they are here. Their world is the real world. The things they lift are heavy. . . . They know what to say if spoken to. They laugh really; they get angry really; while I have to look first and do what other people do when they have done it" (203–4). Because she understands her factual self only by imitation and comparison, Rhoda attaches herself to names and faces and hoards them "like amulets against disaster" (204). As the months go by, she gains no greater substantiality but seems instead to drift further and further into unrealized vision, saying: "Month by month things are losing their hardness; even my body now lets the light through; my spine is soft like wax near the flame of the candle. I dream; I dream" (205). Thus before she has even achieved a hold on reality it begins to slip through her fingers. She is losing the battle of life even before she enters the unsheltered world.

The night, though she longs for its anonymity, is one of her greatest threats, for as she lies in bed alone with no names or faces to clutch for protection against dissolution, she falls into nothingness and has to bang her hand against something hard to recall her factual self. So if night threatens to undo her, death is far more dangerous. In her childhood games she let her imaginary sailors drown in a basin sea. Now, faced with a puddle in the middle of a courtyard, she is paralyzed. "I could not cross it," she says. "Identity failed me. We are nothing, I said, and fell. I was blown like a feather. I was wafted down tunnels" (219). Yet somehow she prevails and extricates herself from chaos with the help of a cold brick wall against which to lay her hands and catch fact through momentary sensation. Because the shock of factual reality is so alien, so painful to her, Rhoda's life is the most difficult of the six. She knows that objective life is real, that she cannot make it otherwise, but each new encounter with the world is like the spring of a tiger, and as she fights her way through each day, she longs for the formlessness of night.

Louis, too, thinks of night as the time when he can give free rein to the vision:

. . . when darkness comes I put off this unenviable body—
my large nose, my thin lips, my colonial accent—and inhabit

space. I am then Virgil's companion, and Plato's. I am
then the last scion of one of the great houses of France. But
I am also one who will force himself to desert these windy
and moonlit territories, these midnight wanderings, and
confront grained oak doors. I will achieve in my life—
Heaven grant that it be not long—some gigantic amalgama-
tion between the two discrepancies so hideously apparent
to me (210–11).

Like Rhoda, Louis sees the great gap between fact and vision,
but, unlike her, he has the power to forge for himself an
effective outward identity and attack the problem within the
life of the world. Although he would like to let himself melt
into his personal vision, he realizes that by ignoring the factual
side of life he defrauds human history "of a moment's vision,"
and says, "Its eye, that would see through me, shuts . . ." (220).
To find some means, familiar to the rest of the word, by which
to convey his sense of infinite progression, Louis turns to established forms of order. He admires the formal procession by
which he and his friends enter church, and once inside de-
clares, "Blessings be on all traditions, on all safeguards and
circumscriptions!" (214); for within the context of traditional
Christianity he finds the authority, the sense of continuity,
and the belief in communion that form his conception of the
vision. As he listens to the headmaster read he sees himself
emerge from the pattern of history and thinks, "I recover
my continuity, as he reads. I become a figure in the procession,
a spoke in the huge wheel that turning, at last erects me, here
and now. I have been in the dark; I have been hidden. . . .
There is no crudity here, no sudden kisses" (198). In his determination to force the vision of unity and order into life, Louis
makes two mistakes that are already beginning to show themselves here. In the first place, his idea of reconciliation neces-
sitates restriction, cannot include the cruder forms of life, and
so loses the very universality it professes. Second, because the
fight to bridge the gap between fact and vision is so much
involved in his own personal struggle with life, Louis loses his
sense of perspective. Every sentence in his pondered plan to
recover unity and continuity begins with "I." In true vision

the self is merged with others, but when Louis transfers the timeless, spaceless unity to life, he stands out as dictator. In Louis's inflexibility are the signs of conversion that the predatory Sir William Bradshaw displayed on a factual plane in *Mrs. Dalloway*. Somewhere between the vision and life, Louis's sense of unity grows hard, loses its fluidity, and becomes encased in unyielding fact like a fly in amber.

For Jinny there is never any conflict between factual and visionary existence. Even before she bursts upon society she admits her limitation to the immediate factual world: ". . . I cannot follow any word through its changes. I cannot follow any thought from present to past. . . .I do not dream" (203), she says. So in this second section, Jinny is revealed as a daylight person: "I hate darkness and sleep and night," she says, "and lie longing for the day to come" (212). The great expanse of vision, blossoming in the night, means nothing to her. Continuity does not exist, for there is only the body and the momentary, passing present. So Jinny's world, as the opposite to that of the visionary Rhoda, is a world of the body, always in the light. Her only dreams are of "a thin dress shot with red threads that would gleam in the firelight" (197) and would billow as she walked and "make a flower shape" (197) as she sank down onto a gilt chair. Because her selfhood is so simply factual, Jinny is fully formed by the time she passes out of the second section and can already leave her faint mark upon a gentleman against whom she brushes in a train. Her body lives a life of its own and that life is all she has.

As the six characters take on firmer definition in this second stage of life, they become more aware of differences amongst them, and each learns to set himself against the others in order to understand himself the better through contrast. So Susan, seeing herself beside Jinny in a mirror, says, "I do not want, as Jinny wants, to be admired. I do not want people, when I come in, to look up with admiration. I want to give, to be given, and solitude in which to unfold my possessions" (211). Where Jinny flourishes at school, testing her powers of attraction on teachers and other students before she puts them into practice in the world of men, Susan hates the limited days of order and discipline and looks forward to the natural flow of the seasons in the country. As she tears off each day from the calendar and crushes it with passion in her hand, just as she had crushed her handkerchief in jealousy when a little child, Susan says, "They have been crippled days, like moths with shrivelled wings unable to fly. There are only eight days left. In eight days' time I shall get out of the train and stand on the platform at six-twenty-five. Then my freedom will unfurl, and all these restrictions that wrinkle and shrivel— hours and order and discipline, and being here and there exactly at the right moment—will crack asunder" (211). Thus while Rhoda clutches the regimental life, mimicking the others as they follow orders and maintain discipline (for her selfhood, seen in the mirror, is a blank); and while Jinny thrives in the social atmosphere of the school, knowing instinctively when she may break a rule with impunity (so that her mirrored self is whole in this limited world); Susan rejects man-made restrictions. She does not need them, like Rhoda, to find herself, or adopt them as her own, as does Jinny; for her selfhood is as large and simple as the natural world. When she looks into the mirror she sees not an emptiness, not a rippling self-contained body, but a wide landscape with farm wagons and banging doors, and meadows full of hay.

So even at this early stage, all three girls are beginning to see how they will fit into the world. The totally visionary Rhoda will succeed in the factual world only by painfully submitting herself to sudden sensual shocks that will keep her from dissolution. Jinny, who represents social existence, will live a life bounded by her body and by the rapidly moving moment, ignoring visionary claims to unity. Susan will become one with the farmland and the cycle of seasons, merging with natural fact to fulfill one aspect of vision. For Rhoda, time is undefined; for Jinny it is the passing present. Susan combines these views to illustrate in her own life a time that is defined by nature but that assumes an infinite pattern in its endless repetition.

Neville, in this second section, begins a conscious formulation of the life-style of precision and privacy that he had chosen instinctively while a small boy. Upon entering his new school, he immediately rejects the vagueness of Christianity and turns to the rigors of classical scholarship, saying, "Those are laboratories perhaps; and that a library, where I shall explore the exactitude of the Latin language, and step firmly upon the well-laid sentences, and pronounce the explicit, the sonorous hexameters of Virgil; of Lucretius . . ." (196). Accepting the sacrifices inherent in such a choice, Neville says proudly, "That is my triumph; I do not compromise" (223). Yet those who reject all but the scholar's intellectualized factual world are forced into compromise. They search for pure truth in abstraction, excluding the less definable matters of emotion, vision, and the multiplicity of life. These imprecise sides of life, however, will not be denied; they manage to step into even the most private rooms and ordered minds. So if Neville finds the fullness of nature "too vegetable, too vapid" and rejects the shadowy "sublimities and vastitudes and water and leaves" (210), when he runs to his secluded, firelit room, he welcomes a compromise in "the limbs of one person" (210) whose single body represents, on a limited scale he can understand, the body of nature. So physical reality, which Neville omits in his studies, enters his life in the form of one body, Percival, who then sparks in him a glimmer of vision through love and so provides both the natural and transcendent aspects of the world that Neville's scholarly exactitude does not include. Percival is all body. He cannot read, but excels in the physical realm. He accepts Neville's devotion naturally, as he accepts all of life; for he, like Susan, seems one with the concrete, eternal, natural world. So as an emblem of all that is unlike Neville, he shatters the scholar's precise intellectual theories, suggesting that total truth can never be achieved solely in the mind. The reconciliation of fact and vision that approaches infinity demands the union of body, soul, and mind to be complete.

Bernard, even at this early stage in his life, comes closest to perceiving the unity and pattern of life. When the rest of his friends are busy searching for a single, distinct, definable identity, he says, "I do not believe in separation. We are not single.

Also I wish to add to my collection of valuable observations upon the true nature of human life" (221). Believing in infinite community, Bernard attempts to bring together as much of human life as possible, attacking the problem with the tools of the literary artist, and saying, "The bubbles are rising like the silver bubbles from the floor of a saucepan; image on top of image. I cannot sit down to my book, like Louis, with ferocious tenacity. I must open the little trap-door and let out these linked phrases in which I run together whatever happens so that instead of incoherence there is perceived a wandering thread, lightly joining one thing to another" (208). So he weaves his friends together with words, and they appreciate his creating sequence out of formlessness. But because a story with an ending implies limitation, Bernard's chronicles always trail away indefinitely. He desires to include everything and so can never round off his sentences with a flourish. Instead he begins to collect compact and careful images, rejecting the tremendous, sonorous, and seductive sentences of authority as being "too hearty to be true" (196).

So too he must reject the detached exactitude that he admires in Louis and Neville, for rigidity is anathema to anyone who attempts to build stories around life and so catch the vision. Because his phrases depend on factual reality for a base, Bernard can create only in the presence of others; for his words do not describe an ideal dream world but instead preserve the essence of reality. "The fact is," he says, "that I have little aptitude for reflection. I require the concrete in everything. It is so only that I lay hands upon the world. A good phrase, however, seems to me to have an independent existence" (222). Once he has extracted the substance of a fact and set it in a phrase, that phrase assumes a reality more powerful than the object it describes. In the same way Lily's painting in *To the Lighthouse,* by combining Mr. and Mrs. Ramsay, became something universal—greater than both of them. So already, Bernard is assuming the visionary role of artist.

By the third interlude, illumination of the individual has fully begun. *"Light almost pierced the thin swift waves as they raced fan-shaped over the beach. . . . Their quivering mackerel sparkling was darkened; they massed themselves; their green hollows deepened and darkened and might be traversed by shoals of wandering fish"* (225). Now that the self has begun to solidify, the individual must step into the turmoil of unsheltered life and face the task of reconciling his inward being with his outward existence. Because this unprotected life is new to him, he clings to others in each unfamiliar setting, imitating the actions of those who feel at home there, testing discretely his newly formed self against others, but never relinquishing that self entirely. This adventure into life with all its joy and terrors is mirrored here by the action of the birds. *"In the garden the birds that had sung erratically and spasmodically in the dawn on that tree, on that bush, now sang together in chorus, shrill and sharp; now together, as if conscious of companionship, now alone as if to the pale blue sky. They swerved, all in one flight, when the black cat moved among the bushes, when the cook threw cinders on the ash heap and startled them. Fear was in their song, and apprehension of pain, and joy to be snatched quickly now at this instant"* (225). If at moments of fear or sense of community they sing and fly together, they also maintain their individual concerns and gaze intently at snail or flower, apple leaves or pendant rain drops on the hedge, towering elms or sun. In the same way, in the section that follows this interlude, the six characters leave the regulated life of school and venture into the outer world, each one trying to fit into the pattern in which he finds himself but retaining his secret self as well. By this time the inner being of each character has taken on an integrated form, a development which is reflected in the growing illumination of the house. *"Now, too, the rising sun came in at the window, touching the red-edged curtain and began to bring out circles and lines. Now in the growing light its whiteness settled in the plate; the blade condensed its gleam. Chairs and cupboards loomed behind so that though each was separate they seemed inextricably involved"* (226). Now that the self has found form, it is ready to launch out against the world, attack the enemy, life, and bring it under the scepter of the self. *"The wind rose. The waves drummed on the shore, like turbaned*

warriors, like turbaned men with poisoned assegais who, whirl-
ing their arms on high, advance upon the feeding flocks, the
white sheep" (227).

Rhoda and Jinny are both launched into society; but the
success of each in this glittering world has already been antici-
pated in their earlier experiences at school. When Rhoda
steps fearfully into the ballroom, the sudden encounter with
reality puts her to flight: "The door opens, the tiger leaps. The
door opens; terror rushes in; terror upon terror, pursuing me.
Let me visit furtively the treasures I have laid apart. Pools lie
on the other side of the world reflecting marble columns.
The swallow dips her wings in dark pools" (247). Even at this
stage in her life she cannot reconcile the fact that she is a
single person in a single place with the pervasive sense that she
is merely the foam on the wave (249), an unformed part of an
infinite whole. "I hate all details of the individual life," she
says, "but I am fixed here to listen. An immense pressure is on
me. I cannot move without dislodging the weight of centuries.
A million arrows pierce me" (248). Like Septimus in *Mrs. Dalloway,* Rhoda is martyred by social reality because of her immersion in vision; so she cries out, "Hide me, . . . protect me,
for I am the youngest, the most naked of you all" (248).

Jinny, as Rhoda's opposite, glories in the physical world of
society, saying, "I feel myself shining in the dark. Silk is on my
knee. My silk legs rub smoothly together. The stones of a
necklace lie cold on my throat. My feet feel the pinch of shoes"
(245). At the center of all eyes she ripples first toward one man,
then toward another, welcoming the patterned limits of the
dance, communicating with each new man not with words,
but with her body. "This is my calling," she says. "This is my
world" (245).

If Rhoda feels herself the youngest, the most naked, of all
her friends when exposed to the social world, Louis experiences the same sense of defenselessness as he goes into business.
He, like Rhoda, never feels at ease with others, never trusts
his instinct to dictate his behavior. And as she suffers torments
at a party, he sits at his little restaurant, mimicking the other
workers at their meal. "Here is the central rhythm,' he feels:

"here the common mainspring. I watch it expand, contract; and then expand again. Yet I am not included" (240). If Rhoda feels her vision being torn to shreds by the confusion of reality around her and runs to her dim world of dreams, Louis experiences the same pain, but does not run. Instead, he resolves to reduce this confusion to order, to forge an iron ring around it and make it suit his idea of unity. Bernard recognizes that Louis looks upon people as inconsequential fragments to be set into a mold, saying, "I . . . often feel his eye on us, his laughing eye, his wild eye, adding us up like insignificant items in some grand total which he is for ever pursuing, in his office. And one day taking a fine pen and dipping it in red ink, the addition will be complete; our total will be known; but it will not be enough" (238). Because he cannot accommodate himself naturally to ordinary life, Louis will never achieve his grand reconciliation.

While Rhoda, Jinny, and Louis leave school for bounded lives in society or business, Susan flies to her farmland like an uncaged bird and spreads herself into the natural flowing life of planting and harvest, morning and evening, seasonal change. "At this hour, this still early hour," she says, "I think I am the field, I am the barn, I am the trees. . . . I cannot be divided, or kept apart. . . . I think sometimes . . . I am not a woman, but the light that falls on this gate, on this ground. I am the seasons, I think sometimes, January, May, November; the mud, the mist, the dawn" (242–43). Where Jinny at the dance flutters from man to man, Susan waits for her own form of fulfillment in one man and the simplest and most basic relationship the world offers: "To his one word I shall answer my one word. What has formed in me I shall give him. I shall have children; I shall have maids in aprons; men with pitchforks; a kitchen where they bring the ailing lambs to warm in baskets, where the hams hang and the onions glisten" (243). Susan's life lies ahead of her as one of giving and taking, baking and feeding, a rhythmic life rocked by the rise and fall of the seasons. She is not, like Jinny, a glittering point among people, or like Rhoda a bit of foam on the wave of life; she is not social fact and action, or formless vision, but an integrated part of the natural whole—a symbol, actually, of the natural world upon which poets build their phrases and visionaries their vision.

Neville, deep in the university at this stage of life, wavers continually between the truth embodied in nature and love, and the drier truth of abstraction. He sits by the river, letting the beauty of the scene wash over him unanalyzed, and cries, "A leaf falls, from joy. Oh, I am in love with life!" (231). Then, as he watches the trees and boat form a rhythmic pattern, he feels the poetic urge welling up inside him and says,

> Now begins to rise in me the familiar rhythm; words that have lain dormant now lift, now toss their crests, and fall and rise, and fall and rise again. I am a poet, yes. Surely I am a great poet. Boats and youth passing and distant trees . . . I see it all. I feel it all. I am inspired. My eyes fill with tears. Yet even as I feel this, I lash my frenzy higher and higher. It foams. It becomes artificial, insincere. Words and words and words, how they gallop—how they lash their long manes and tails, but for some fault in me I cannot give myself to their backs; I cannot fly with them, scattering women and string bags (231–32).

The devotion to precision and order that is so great a part of Neville forces him to distrust inspiration, makes him approach words not as the tools of vision but as the precise instruments of fact. He realizes the limitations of this approach to poetry, admits that "one cannot go on for ever cutting these ancient inscriptions clearer with a knife" (235); but he cannot renounce his desire for order and so withdraws from the inspiring but confused rhythm of life, "draws his curtain; and bolts his door" (237). If uncontrolled life sends Neville back to the protection of his books, it follows him in through the keyhole and disturbs him at his work. Although he recognizes that it "would be a glorious life, to addict oneself to perfection; to follow the curve of the sentence wherever it might lead, into deserts, under drifts of sand, regardless of lures, of seductions . . ." (235), he admits to himself, "I would rather be loved, I would rather be famous than follow perfection through the sand" ('235–36). Tossed back and forth between love and learning, poetry and precision, Neville turns to Bernard for a story that can unify the conflicting sides of his identity, and Bernard offers:

> Let me then create you. (You have done as much for me.)
> You lie on this hot bank, in this lovely, this fading, this still
> bright October day, watching boat after boat float through
> the combed-out twigs of the willow tree. And you wish
> to be a poet; and you wish to be a lover. But the splendid
> clarity of your intelligence, and the remorseless honesty of
> your intellect . . . bring you to a halt. You indulge in no
> mystification. You do not fog yourself with rosy clouds,
> or yellow (233).

So where Louis attempts to reconcile these opposing views by choosing one and forcing it upon the other, the more honest Neville watches the balance rise and fall without putting a dogmatic thumb on either side.

If Bernard produces an accurate miniature of the opposing forces of Neville's life, Neville tears off the multiple layers of Bernard's soul and says, "'You are not Byron; you are your self'" (236). But Bernard realizes that this single concentrated self, although true in part, is not complete, saying,

> The complexity of things becomes more close. . . . Every
> hour something new is unburied in the great bran pie.
> What am I? I ask. This? No, I am that. Especially now, when
> I have left a room, and people talking, and the stone flags
> ring out with my solitary footsteps, and I behold the moon
> rising, sublimely, indifferently, over the ancient chapel—
> then it becomes clear that I am not one and simple,
> but complex and many (227).

Within himself Bernard is both disparate and integrated, a feeler and a reasoner. Like Jacob in *Jacob's Room* he walks across the courtyard of the university and absorbs infinite numbers of identities; yet, when asked, he can slice through complexity to reveal essence and simplicity. Because he is as honest with himself as Neville is, Bernard recognizes that these flashes of inspired summary soon disperse. Some fragment of new reality always intrudes and makes the seeming whole imperfect. At times too when alone, he watches all his images slip from him, for without someone to share them with he loses his creative urge. But it always returns. The artist who is fully aware of the depth and complexity of life recognizes with Lily Briscoe that the vision must be continually remade.

As the next interlude begins, the waves have assumed a powerful regularity and the entire natural scene is charged with suppressed activity, full of assurance and strength. The waves

> ... *drew in and out with the energy, the muscularity of an engine which sweeps its force out and in again. ... The hills curved and controlled, seemed bound back by thongs, as a limb is laced by muscles; and the woods which bristled proudly on their flanks were like the curt, clipped mane on the neck of a horse. ... The birds sang in hot sunshine, each alone. ... Each sang stridently, with passion, with vehemence, as if to let the song burst out of it, no matter if it shattered the song of another bird with harsh discord. ... They sang as if the edge of being were sharpened and must cut, must split the softness of the blue-green light, the dampness of the wet earth* ... (250).

With confidence born of experience the six characters in the section that follows are able to sit together and define themselves. This awareness of individuality, when exposed to the concentrated form of outward reality, Percival, leads to a moment of true communion, reflected in the song of the birds that suddenly *"ran together in swift scales like the interlacings of a mountain stream whose waters, meeting, foam and then mix, and hasten quicker and quicker down the same channel brushing the same broad leaves. But there is a rock; they sever"* (251). And so, too, the moment of visionary unity that the six experience must soon dissolve. Within the house a momentary miracle takes place, too, in the clear light of reality: *"Whatever the light touched became dowered with a fanatical existence. ... Everything was without shadow. ... And as the light increased, flocks of shadow were driven before it and conglom-*

erated and hung in many-pleated folds in the background"
(251). So Percival at the London dinner party disperses the
darkness of solitude and allows the six to stand distinct yet
united.

Percival, the one character to whom all the other six relate
but who never speaks himself, has proved to be an enigmatic
symbol in the eyes of the critics. Because he is central to the
lives of the narrators, his significance must be explained, but
no two people who approach the novel seem to agree on what
he represents. Harvena Richter sees him as "soul, spirit, or life-
force";[21] Aileen Pippett as "the Ordinary Man made perfect,
the all-containing, incomprehensible Norm";[22] Maxime Chastaing as God;[23] James Hafley as unadulterated action;[24] Ralph
Freedman as order.[25] Floris Delattre and Lotus A. Snow come
close to agreeing with one another when the former says that
Percival symbolizes to the six that which they loved in their
happy childhood[26] and the latter that he is "a symbol to each
of the six of the individual quality which would afford him
wholeness."[27] But since no consensus has been reached, perhaps a new suggestion may help. First of all, it is clear from
his many descriptions that Percival is a beautiful, animal
youth. Like a bear he buffets his followers "good-humouredly
with a blow of his paw" (231). "His magnificence is that of
some mediaeval commander" (200). He blunders through the
artificial ring of steel with which Louis attempts to impose
order on the world (202); he inspires poetry (202); he is linked
by love and by nature to Susan (263, 272); and he is continually
compared to the sun (200, 207, and elsewhere). These facts,
gleaned from the impressions of the six, suggest that Percival
symbolizes natural, factual reality. Sunlight in the interludes
gives form to flowers, waves, and furniture; Percival gives form
to the six. He can also, like the tree in *The Voyage Out,* lead
to unifying vision through the intensity of his reality. The
form of factual truth—shop girls and cabs, leaves and birds—
is never ordered by abstract law, so Percival contradicts Louis's
authority by his presence. Instead, the multiplicity of life is
ordered by the natural cycle of seasons that absorbs all disparity
into the vastness of its pattern. So Percival, representing this

natural law, is in love with Susan and is linked with her by the others.

Thus as the morning draws to a close, the six characters come together to say good-bye to Percival: the sun is reaching its height; reality has done its utmost in the formation of their lives; the time has come to sum up the factual self and begin to move toward the unifying darkness of night that symbolizes a conscious merging into vision. From this point on, the wave of life, which has been gathering into a mass, will begin to roll in toward the beach where it will be dissolved, only to begin to cycle again.

When Rhoda enters the restaurant where the six are to meet, Louis, her spiritual brother, recognizes the conflict inside her, saying, "We wake her. We torture her. She dreads us, she despises us, yet comes cringing to our sides because for all our cruelty there is always some name, some face which sheds a radiance, which lights up her pavements and makes it possible for her to replenish her dreams" (258). Because she has no core of concrete selfhood to hold her together, Rhoda must fall like moonlight "here on a tin can, here on a spike of the mailed sea holly, or a bone or a half-eaten boat" (265), must cling to the tangible in order to exist at all. Time for her does not progress minute to minute: she does not grow older, nor does the "shock of sensation" (265) grow less severe. So she must brave the tiger's spring again and again, saying, "I am drawn here across London to a particular spot, to a particular place, not to see you or you or you, but to light my fire at the general blaze of you who live wholly, indivisibly and without caring in the moment" (266). Once having endured reality for a moment, she can safely float into her vision again; but she realizes that "these pilgrimages, these moments of departure, start always in your presence, from this table, these lights, from Percival and Susan, here and now" (272). The vision, even in its most ineffectual form, needs the solidity of natural fact upon which to ground itself.

When Louis approaches, he puts on his factual mask to fit himself to the social pattern that Jinny, Neville, and Bernard seem to demand. But since he recognizes that both Susan and

Percival accept and absorb all natural facts, including ugliness or an Australian accent, he admires them and sees that they are never limited to the world that states " 'I am this, I am that'' (270) but instead coincide naturally with his visionary sense of being rooted in all of time.

Because the factual self Louis wears is only a mask, covering a sense of universal selfhood, and because Rhoda hasn't even a factual disguise to muffle herself in, these two, watching the celebration of the reality of Percival, can predict his death, can imagine the shucking off of the external, factual bounds as a step toward final unity.

> "The flames of the festival rise high," said Rhoda. "The great procession passes, flinging green boughs and flowering branches. Their horns spill blue smoke; their skins are dappled red and yellow in the torchlight. They throw violets. They deck the beloved with garlands and with laurel leaves. . . . The procession passes. And while it passes, Louis, we are aware of downfalling, we forbode decay. The shadow slants. We who are conspirators, withdraw together to lean over some cold urn, note how the purple flame flows downwards."
>
> "Death is woven in with the violets," said Louis. "Death and again death" (272–73).

If Percival, upon entering, draws everything together in the clear light of concrete truth, Jinny, who represents social fact, accomplishes the same thing on a purely sexual level. "She seems to centre everything; round her tables, lines of doors, windows, ceilings, ray themselves, like rays round the star in the middle of a smashed window-pane. She brings things to a point, to order" (258), says Susan, who senses the irreconcilable contrast between her diffusion and Jinny's concentration. Jinny herself is completely aware of the effect she has on others, but readily admist that the pattern she inspires is only an ordering of bodies, not of souls. It is Neville who points out most clearly the flaw in Jinny's physical method of creating unity as he says to her, " 'When you stand in the door . . . you inflict stillness, demanding admiration, and that is a great impediment to the freedom of intercourse' " (264). Jinny's center is Jinny, while Percival's is a reality that gives equal light wherever it shines. Yet Jinny, in her straightforward way, is well aware of the significance of the gathering, saying, "Emerged from the tentative ways, the obscurities and dazzle of youth, we look straight in front of us, ready for what may come. . . . All is real; all is firm without shadow or illusion. . . . Our differences are clear-cut as the shadows of rocks in full sunlight" (273). This meeting marks the moment of greatest factual reality, the reality chosen by Jinny as a way of life.

Susan as she enters shows little diffidence or consciousness of self. Her movements and reactions are instinctive and natural. "She seems to find her way by instinct in and out among these little tables, touching no one, disregarding waiters . . ." (258). When she reaches her friends, her face assumes a certainty of love that includes them all. She has chosen the life she is best suited for and recognizes its scope and limitations, declaring, "The only sayings I understand are cries of love, hate, rage and pain. . . . I shall never have anything but natural happiness. It will almost content me. I shall go to bed tired. I shall lie like a field bearing crops in rotation; in the summer heat will dance over me; in the winter I shall be cracked with the cold. But heat and cold will follow each other naturally without my willing or unwilling" (266). She sees that this natural life will involve the hypocrisy and possessiveness that seem to be inherent in the raising and protecting of children, that in order to keep this life whole she must sacrifice her love for Bernard who slips beyond natural fact in the phrase-making she cannot understand. But she adheres to her choice, sensing the freedom and order in its natural progression.

For Neville, nothing at the restaurant is real until Percival arrives. As he sits waiting he says, "This table, these chairs, this metal vase with its three red flowers are about to undergo an extraordinary transformation. . . . Things quiver as if not yet in being" (257). Percival will "pump into this room this prickly light, this intensity of being . . ." (257) that he longs for. Without this light, Neville's scholarship, his poetry, his private curtained room, are meaningless and without order. Thus when Percival arrives, "the reign of chaos is over" (260). He imposes order that lies at the heart of all Neville's desires.

When Bernard appears at the beginning of this fourth stage in the rise and fall of *The Waves,* he prepares the way for the moment of communion to come at the restaurant. As he sits in the train that steams toward London and the meeting of the six, he recognizes the power of a common goal to unite the unconnected, looking at his fellow passengers and saying, "Over us all broods a splendid unanimity. We are enlarged and solemnised and brushed into uniformity as with the grey wing of some enormous goose . . . because we have only one desire—to arrive at the station" (252). If common interest can join the unacquainted commuters on Bernard's train, the power of Percival to unite the six friends at luncheon should be tremendous. Yet even when brought together into a connected whole, the six will maintain their individual selfhoods, acquired through constant exposure to the factual world. This, too, Bernard recognizes, having himself "walked bang into a pillar-box" (273), become engaged, only the day before and so having been "charged in every nerve with a sense of identity" (253). Since Bernard is at his most real in his relationship with others, his engagement, being for him the most concentrated form of connection, has brought him to the peak of defined selfhood. Having reached this summit of distinct identity, he and the others can afford to relax their grasp upon themselves and allow for the intersection of their closely guarded beings. As Bernard puts it, "I . . . now wish to unclasp my hands and let fall my possessions . . ." (253). "I wish to go under; to visit the profound depths; once in a while to exercise my prerogative not always to act, but to explore; to hear vague, ancestral sounds of boughs creaking, of mammoths, to indulge impossible desires, to embrace the whole world with the arms of understanding, impossible to those who act" (254). Action is integral to fact as we see in Percival's athletics, Jinny's dancing, Susan's patterned life, and Louis's efforts to bring the world to order. Vision involves a relaxing of this concentrated action, a contemplation and gradual outbowing of energy to pervade the entire world rather than to attack it at a single point. So Bernard recognizes that once having formed a "diamond" self of action and definition, he is ready to approach the vision. With his newly acquired insight, he sees a fluid pattern of repetition lying before him in the thought of generations upon generations springing from himself. "We come up differently, for ever and ever" (254), he says, having now achieved selfhood and so having conquered the mountain of limited fact. Standing upon the hard-won summit, he can see that his private peak is part of the endless and visionary pattern of hill after hill. Yet, as always, the expansive vision contracts: "One cannot extinguish that persistent smell. It steals through some crack in the structure—one's identity" (254). Each experience of vision, however, leaves behind it "one moment of enormous peace" (255) that inspires the man who has known it to rebuild what he has lost. So Bernard approaches the meeting place, saying, "I conceive myself called upon to provide, some winter's night, a meaning for all my observations— a line that runs from one to another, a summing up that completes" (255). Having sensed the possibility of embracing the whole world with arms of understanding, he determines to collect each insight in the hope that some day he may add up all his observations and so create the infinite vision. With his keen eye for essences he realizes that somehow Louis and Rhoda in their private lives inhabit this visionary realm, yet he sees, too, that his effective creation of vision for others within a context of fact will "contribute more to the passing moment" (268) than the secret relations of any of his friends. So he enters the restaurant and catches each of the other five in a careful phrase to be stored away until the day of summation: "I see Louis, stone-carved, sculpturesque; Neville, scissor-cutting exact; Susan with eyes like lumps of crystal; Jinny dancing like a flame, febrile, hot, over dry earth; and Rhoda the nymph of the fountain always wet" (256). His perception gives his concise phrases a depth of significance that comes close to making each a miniature vision of the totality of the person described. For the word "stone-carved" connects Louis with the ancient Sphinx and so his vision of continuity, yet also reflects the limitations, the inflexibility of his plans to bring this vision into the factual world. Neville's incisive mind cuts through to abstract essence, yet trims away the vision. Susan's eyes are lumps of crystal because they reflect the unpolished but precious raw material of the natural world that, refined by the poet, makes the stuff of vision. Jinny's flame is full of the reality of light but parches the land, thus drying out any traces of the visionary sea and denying the continuity implied in the fecundity of irrigated soil. Rhoda has never left the sea of vision, presented in the first chapter, and so is always wet. Because of his ability to bring his friends together at their moment of greatest factual selfhood, knitting a story in which they achieve unity without losing their identities, Bernard as vision-maker can almost complete the pattern made by the six. But his time for summation and gathering together has not yet come, for distinctness and definition remain paramount at this stage of life. So the group, while appreciating Bernard's gift, still needs the factual reality of Percival to achieve its greatest unity. Neville articulates this attitude when he sees Bernard enter and says, "He bears down with such benignity, with such love of mankind (crossed with humor at the futility of 'loving mankind'), that, if it were not for Percival, who turns all this to vapour, one would feel, as the others already feel: Now is our festival; now we are together. But without Percival there is no solidity" (259).

Now Percival enters, and Bernard, always the one to catch the moment in words, says:

> He is a hero. Oh, yes, that is not to be denied, and when he takes his seat by Susan, whom he loves, the occasion is crowned.... We who have been separated by our youth ... who have sung like eager birds each his own song and tapped with the remorseless and savage egotism of the young our own snailshell till it cracked ... or perched solitary outside some bedroom window ... now come nearer ... sitting together now we love each other and believe in our own endurance (260).

In the bright light of Percival, the moments that were most

important in the formation of the six individuals leap to their minds: Bernard's sensation of the watery sponge; Susan's watching two servants embracing; Neville and his "death among the apple trees"; Jinny's kissing Louis, and so on through school and university, business and society, to the present moment when the sum of each person is combined into a single total. "We have come together," says Bernard, "to make one thing, not enduring—for what endures?—but seen by many eyes simultaneously. There is a red carnation in that vase. A single flower as we sat here waiting, but now a seven-sided flower, many-petalled, red, puce, purple-shaded, stiff with silver-tinted leaves—a whole flower to which every eye brings its own contribution" (263). He has seen how each of the seven represents some aspect of fact and vision and realizes that the final summation, which encompasses all life, all time, all space, must include them all.

In this single visionary moment, each character sees a fragment of the entire vision: Bernard, the future; Susan, the sequence of days and months; Rhoda, her visionary world; Neville, the quiet of ordinary things; Louis, a solid ring of unity. Even Jinny sees the greatness of the event, saying, "Let us hold it for one moment . . . love, hatred, by whatever name we call it, this globe whose walls are made of Percival, of youth and beauty, and something so deep sunk within us that we shall perhaps never make this moment out of one man again" (276). She is right. As Rhoda and Louis have predicted, Percival when he leaves has gone for good. The reality of fact clearly seen, sharply experienced, is over. From this stage on the identity begins to lose its form in habit, and not until the outlines of the six have been worn away by time to let the great expanse of infinite merging take place will another moment such as this be possible.

Now it is noon: ". . . *the sun burnt uncompromising, undeniable. It struck upon the hard sand, and the rocks became furnaces of red heat; it searched each pool and caught the minnow hiding in the cranny, and showed the rusty cartwheel, the white bones, or the boot without laces stuck, black as iron, in the sand. It gave to everything its exact measure of colour . . ."* (278). This is the last moment of total illumination in which factual reality may be perceived most clearly, the self defined most precisely before the sun begins to sink, and the outlines of the self and the world grow indistinct. At this moment the little scene of house and garden expands, and the sun reveals the solid forms of southern villages, mosques, and foreign women, showing that this rise and fall of day and life is the same everywhere. But within the garden itself, the birds have already ceased their strident song of selfhood and have renounced detachment for domesticity. Each *"sang passionate songs addressed to one ear only and then stopped. Bubbling and chuckling they carried little bits of straw and twig to the dark knots in the higher branches of the trees"* (279). With the sun overhead, the inner rooms are darkened and the windows reflect only the outside world of leaves and branches, as the lives of settled adults often reflect the world around them. Yet the waves still fall and withdraw *"like the thud of a great beast stamping"* (280), suggesting that effort must never cease. This, then, is the time when Percival, who represents unadulterated factual reality, must die in order not to lose any of his distinctness. The section that follows this noontime interlude presents the fact of his death and describes the effect this event has on those characters whose lives remain flexible and who come closest to understanding the full significance of the vision of unity that Percival created by his presence at their first gathering.

Percival is dead. Bernard Blackstone sees his death as "the pathos of promise unfulfilled,"[28] but this dissolution of formative reality is only a necessary step in the journey from unconscious vision to fact to conscious vision that *The Waves* describes. For three of the six, this event will make no changes, since, one way or another, fact sums up their lives. Jinny will continue to pirouette through society. Susan "will stand for a second with the telegram before her, holding a plate; and then, with a kick of her heel, slam to the oven door" (287), for death is simply a natural event in her cyclical world of spring and winter, birth and death. Louis will "smooth out the death of Percival to his satisfaction" (287) by setting the loss into his personal system of order. But for Neville and Rhoda, Percival's passing takes something essential from their lives; and to Bernard, to whom all beginnings and endings are of great interest, this moment provides an opportunity to discover the meaning of death.

For Neville, Percival's death is the tree that he cannot pass (280), the destruction of light in the world. This disappearance of Percival means the loss of reality and love; and from now on Neville's life, like Jinny's, will become a series of superficial physical unions to maintain factual selfhood and a passing sense of order in life that has been proved ephemeral by death.

For Rhoda, this event is the puddle of dissolution she cannot cross. When factual reality departs, she totters on the brink of eternal formlessness. Yet she has always known that Percival would die, for fact is never permanent in her world. But now it is gone forever, become as misty as her vision. Although Percival, by dying, has snatched Rhoda's fragile foundation from under her, he has also given her a moment in which the two worlds that tear her apart are finally combined. Reality becomes one with dissolution. Now she begins to see the possibility of making her longed-for offering, saying, "On the bare ground I will pick violets and bind them together and offer them to Percival, something given him by me. Look now at what Percival has given me. Look at the street now that Percival is dead. The houses are lightly founded to be puffed over by a breath of air" (286). In order to understand the significance of this passing of concrete reality, Rhoda turns for a moment to music that shows her the importance of Percival's death. As the quartet begins to play she asks,

> ... what is the thing that lies beneath the semblance of the thing? Now that lightning has gashed the tree and the flowering branch has fallen and Percival, by his death, has made me this gift, let me see the thing. There is a square; there is an oblong. The players take the square and place it upon the oblong. They place it very accurately; they make a perfect dwelling-place. Very little is left outside.

The structure is now visible; what is inchoate is here
stated; we are not so various or so mean; we have made
oblongs and stood them upon squares. This is our triumph;
this is our consolation (288).

From Rachel Vinrace's piano-playing to Lily Briscoe's painting to Bernard's phrases we have seen the power of art to combine fact and vision. Here music, the most visionary of the
arts, unites these two worlds for Rhoda by presenting fact in
its most abstract, intangible form as geometric shapes. In this
way Rhoda can understand that her world of vision and the
world of fact that Percival embodied when alive are not con-
tradictory but can be intermeshed through careful effort.
When death reduces Percival's fact to symbol, Rhoda can
reconcile it to her own unformed way of life and so become
free for a moment, with the dead Percival's help, to plunge
completely into vision. "Now I will at last free the checked,
the jerked back desire to be spent, to be consumed," she says.
"We will gallop together over desert hills where the swallow
dips her wings in dark pools and the pillars stand entire. Into
the wave that dashes upon the shore, into the wave that flings
its white foam to the uttermost corners of the earth I throw
my violets, my offering to Percival" (289).

If music can reveal to Rhoda the full force of vision in
Percival's death, Bernard as artist can experience the same
revelation. "My son is born," he says; "Percival is dead. I am
upheld by pillars, shored up on either side by stark emotions;
but which is sorrow, which is joy?" (281). In a sense, birth
and death are one, being part of the eternal pattern, one
emerging from the formlessness of vision, the other returning
to it. Bernard recognizes that this is his great chance "to find
out what is of great importance" (281–82), discover the impact upon life of the death of factual reality, the death of a
single human being. So he confronts the event squarely, understands its every implication, and says, " . . .'But this is better
than one had dared to hope,' I say, addressing what is abstract,
facing me eyeless at the end of the avenue, in the sky, 'Is
this the utmost you can do?' 'Then we have triumphed' "

(282). Death ends nothing, only creates another of those brief moments of vision one experiences within the factual world. Soon "signals begin, beckonings" (282), calling one back to the endless pattern of living. "One cannot live outside the machine for more perhaps than half an hour," (282) says Bernard. "The sequence returns; one thing leads to another—the usual order" (283). Bernard realizes that even after death Percival exists somewhere, is part of the unbounded universe that includes action and contemplation, fact and vision. One way to capture this unity of life for a moment is in art, as Rhoda's experience at the concert has indicated; so Bernard, to keep his momentary understanding of the import of Percival's death alive a little longer, turns to painting in a gallery to help him find the "something unvisual beneath" (283) that will contain Percival, alive and dead, and inspire Bernard to return to his own form of vision-making in words. In the gallery he experiences the vision for a space, but realizes that the time has not yet come for him to create it himself, saying, "Yet something is added to my interpretation. Something lies deeply buried. For a moment I thought to grasp it. But bury it, bury it; let it breed, hidden in the depths of my mind some day to fructify. After a long lifetime, loosely, in a moment of revelation, I may lay my hands on it, but now the idea breaks in my hand. Ideas break a thousand times for once that they globe themselves entire" (284–85). So, the vision over, Bernard returns again to the world of fact and goes off to visit Jinny.

By the opening of the sixth section, the sun is no longer high in the sky. *"Its light slanted, falling obliquely"* (290). There is a suggestion, too, not only of diurnal but of seasonal decline in the rustling of the brittle leaves. So the peak of life has passed, and the birds sit still, now and again pausing ". . . *in their song as if glutted with sound, as if the fullness of midday had gorged them"* (290). Inside the house the finish of the furniture seems to crack under the long daggers of afternoon light and darkness heaps up *"in mounds of unmoulded shape"* (290). The waves, meanwhile, have washed up on the shore in the fullness of high tide and then drawn back, leaving a fish stranded in a pool. Within the text of this section those characters who have resolved their lives in habitual existence, whose days fill and empty to the same degree month after month, year after year, describe the existence they have built for themselves, while Rhoda and Bernard, the two whose experience of vision keeps them from becoming sated by a changeless life, do not speak.

Now that the tide of life is ebbing, those who have limited themselves to factual truth in one form or another watch their lives roll slowly downhill without seeing any hope for greater meaning or greater fulfillment before them.

Louis is one of those who have chosen fact as a way of life. To adapt himself to the concrete world he has devised an inflexible rule for himself and others and has nailed a factual shell of identity onto his visionary form with such persistency that his childhood sense of pervasiveness is all but smothered, leaving only a core of loneliness inside the factual armor he has forged for himself.

> "I have signed my name," said Louis, "already twenty times. I, and again I, and again I. Clear, firm, unequivocal, there it stands, my name. Clearcut and unequivocal am I too. Yet a vast inheritance of experience is packed in me. I have lived thousands of years. . . . all the furled and close-packed leaves of my many-folded life are now summed in my name; incised cleanly and barely on the sheet. Now a full-grown man; now upright standing in sun or rain, I must drop heavy as a hatchet and cut the oak with my sheer weight, for if I deviate, glancing this way, or that way, I shall fall like snow and be wasted" (291).

So Louis has reduced the infinite range of his vision to the scoring of the globe with shipping lines; uniting the world with fact, not vision. Blinded by his insistence on one thing only, he feels that "The weight of the world is on our shoulders. This is life" (293). But he keeps his attic room and retreats there to Rhoda, for a hidden part of him still yearns toward visionary unity and the dissolution of petrified selfhood.

Jinny, who chose the life of the body and the fleeting moments in society, sees that her journey through life grows more precarious as the years go by, saying, "I have lived my life I must tell you all these years and I am now past thirty, perilously, like a mountain goat leaping from crag to crag; I do not settle long anywhere; I do not attach myself to one person in particular . . ." (296). Her physical attraction remains, but she knows that once it is gone she will have nothing to fall back upon. She ". . . cannot take these facts into some cave and, shading [her] eyes, grade their yellows, blues, umbers into one substance" (297) for infinity and vision are beyond her grasp. But because she has chosen the path of fact, she determines to follow it without hesitation, saying, "Let us decorate our Christmas tree with facts and again with facts. People are so soon gone; let us catch them" (296). She knows that in some way her life is necessary to the creation of a whole and resolves to live it to the utmost.

Susan, sitting now always by her cradle, sees that her life is bounded by the pattern she had predicted for herself. The seasons now pass so naturally that they go unnoticed and her days are devoted to keeping the human rhythm alive, protecting her children, waiting until they can carry her spirit into the world. No longer is she free to walk alone through the fields, feeling herself one with the forests and grasses; for by choosing the natural life she herself had to become an active part of the pattern of endless fruition. Her verbal prediction is now solidified into fact and at times she wishes for respite, declaring, "So life pours through my limbs. So I am driven forward, till I could cry, as I move from dawn to dusk opening and shutting, 'No more. I am glutted with natural happiness.' Yet more will come, more children; more cradles, more baskets in the kitchen and hams ripening; and onions glistening; and more beds of lettuce and potatoes" (295).

Neville, too, has slipped into factual pattern, embracing a series of new loves to counterbalance his endless search for abstract order and so failing to achieve either fruitful pattern in poetry and love, or the pure perfection he once dreamed of. "We must oppose the waste and deformity of the world," he says:

its crowds eddying round and round disgorged and trampling. One must slip paper-knives, even, exactly through the pages of novels, and tie up packets of letters neatly with green silk, and brush up the cinders with a hearth broom. Everything must be done to rebuke the horror of deformity. Let us read writers of Roman severity and virtue; let us seek perfection through the sand. Yes, but I love to slip the virtue and severity of the noble Romans under the grey light of your eyes. . . . Hence I am not a disinterested seeker, like Louis, after perfection through the sand (300–301).

So neither of Neville's two dreams, to create order and to be a poet/lover, is fulfilled, for each interrupts and shatters the other. He cannot reconcile the fact and the vision and so accepts a compromise for each.

In the seventh interlude the sun has sunk so low that shadow intermittently succeeds to light. The tide, too, has fallen. In the garden all the birds but one *"raced in the furrows of the wind and turned and sliced through them as if they were one body cut into a thousand shreds"* (302). This wind unites the leaves, too, and only when it flags do they regain their individual identities. At the window of the room, curtains blow in and out, letting in the light in *"flaps and breaths. . . . All for a moment wavered and bent in uncertainty and ambiguity, as if a great moth sailing through the room had shadowed the immense solidity of chairs and tables with floating wings"* (303). In the section that follows, the six characters pause for a moment, seeing their lives begin to dissolve one into the other, and quickly sum up what they have gained, what they have lost, accepting their lot while realizing that their individual suns are sinking.

Now comes the period of life in which habit has worn away the edges of definite self for those living in the factual realm so that all six characters can now summarize their lives before they melt into one another and the world. Louis and Rhoda have always been ready for this moment, for they never stopped beating their "wings against the storm in the belief that be-

yond this welter the sun shines. . . . They say truth is to be
found there entire, and virtue, that shuffles along here, down
blind alleys, is to be had there perfect" (313). So Rhoda, setting
the pain of her life behind her for a moment, makes a pil-
grimage to the southern coast of Spain where, from a mountain
top, she can look out over the sea to Africa which, in its vastness, represents her vision. Standing on the brink, she looks
toward her own dissolution, saying,

> We launch out now over the precipice. Beneath us lie the
> lights of the herring fleet. The cliffs vanish. Rippling
> small, rippling grey, innumerable waves spread beneath
> us. I touch nothing. I see nothing. We may sink and settle
> on the waves. The sea will drum in my ears. The white
> petals will be darkened with sea water. They will float for a
> moment and then sink. Rolling me over the waves will
> shoulder me under. Everything falls in a tremendous
> shower, dissolving me (319).

After this second symbolic return to the sea, Rhoda's actual
dissipation in suicide is only a fulfillment of her life.

Louis, too, at the moment of summation, has little important selfhood. He has not participated in the natural rhythm of
life, has "known little natural happiness" (316). For he has
never forgotten his early resolution to unite the true, visionary
"Nile" world with that of the hard "oak door." Thus he has
spent his life trying to weave the two truths together, that of
"our long history" and that "of our tumultuous and varied
day" (316). But when he attempts to "make reason of it all—
one poem on a page, and then die" (316), that poem emerges as
another's work, the anonymous "O western wind, when wilt
thou blow" (317) that, sung by a nameless voice, tells of loneliness and unhappiness.[29] So his system has failed him; for
vision cannot be encircled by the ring of steel he tried to
forge around it, and he stands, like Rhoda, on the brink of
anonymity.

Jinny, who has always lived without vision, sees that the fullness of her physical life has ended. The body whose law she
has obeyed grows old and will soon fail to call men to her.

But she faces the future bravely, seeing that death is the end of the body, but determining to "march forward" (312) till that end.

Neville's lovers have come and gone. He says, "I have picked my own fruit. I look dispassionately" (312). Always honest with himself, he can stand back and see where time has carried him and his friends, see at last that ugliness and beauty are all part of the rhythm of life, that repetition gives order to the unordered. "He says, she says, somebody else says things have been said so often that one word is now enough to lift a whole weight" (312), says Neville. The poetry he longed to write is now woven into life itself. The present contains the past. So as he turns from Virgil to the poetry of life that surrounds him, he realizes that one needs the eyes of many in order to understand all of it: "There are no commas or semicolons" (314) in life. All things, after the years have mellowed his understanding, flow together, and the moment of vision is at hand. Yet for Neville, as for any who approach the vision by any road, the habits of life interrupt; and, for now, he returns to the partial vision created by a new love.

Bernard, fleeing from his habitual English existence to Rome in order to find enough detachment to sort out his past, sees that he stands and has always stood in between the devotees of precise and limited fact and the followers of vision, saying, "The truth is that I am not one of those who find their satisfaction in one person, or in infinity. The private room bores me, also the sky. My being only glitters when all its facets are exposed to many people" (304). So he sees that no one truth can explain everything and that to try to pin down the vision is to destroy it. He recognizes, too, that his life and the lives of his friends have progressed from stage to stage, falling drop by drop in endless flowing rhythm. His notebooks are full of innumerable phrases, gleaned from each stage, waiting for the story that will unite them. And so, too, Bernard waits for the winter's night when he will be asked to combine all these fragments of fact and vision into a whole. Until then, he determines to greet each new stage as it comes, maintaining his fluidity until solidity is required. So he, with all his friends, stands on the brink of unity.

At the eighth interlude darkness is rapidly engulfing the world of waves and rooms. *"The hard stone of the day was cracked. . . . the waves, as they neared the shore, were robbed of light, and fell in one long concussion, like a wall falling, a wall of grey stone, unpierced by any chink of light"* (320). Color is gone; the trees, the hills, the sea are a single grey of liquid shadow. Inside the house the few last rays of evening make of the knife, the fork, something portenteous. *"Rimmed in a gold circle the looking-glass held the scene immobile as if everlasting in its eye"* (321). Again, *". . . rocks lost their hardness"* (321), and the water is dark. At midmorning the six characters gathered to define themselves and celebrate factual reality. Now has come another moment for coming together, this time to form an immortal scene of total unity in which, for an instant, the six become one in vision. Having braved factual existence, they, like Rachel Vinrace before them, have earned a moment of vision, complete, and comprehended; an interlocking of their differing efforts to create a successful reconciliation.

A final meeting is planned, and once again the six enter a single door, this time that of an inn at Hampton Court. By now Rhoda has learned to face the shock of encounter unflinchingly, but the shock remains. She walks bravely up to her friends, sensing that this gathering will approximate her vision. ". . . There are moments," she says, "when the walls of the mind grow thin; when nothing is unabsorbed, and I could fancy that we might blow so vast a bubble that the sun might set and rise in it and we might take the blue of midday and the black of midnight and be cast off and escape from here and now" (331). Louis, too, sees in the evening a "moment of reconciliation, when we meet together united," and asks "How can I reduce these dazzling, these dancing apparitions to one line capable of linking all in one?" (328). At this gathering, neither of the two visionaries predicts death or disaster; for death by now means vision to them and casts no shadow on their sense of unity. "All seems alive," says Louis. "I cannot hear death anywhere tonight. Stupidity, on that man's face, age, on that woman's, would be strong enough, one would think, to resist the incantation, and bring in death. But where is death tonight? All the crudity, odds and ends, this and that, have been crushed like glass splinters into the blue, the red-fringed tide, which, drawing into the shore, fertile with innumerable fish, breaks at our feet" (336).

Even Jinny, facing her time-ravaged body bravely in the mirror, sees that unity is the goal of their lives and tells of her own attempts to create this communion: "The torments, the divisions of your lives have been solved for me night after night, sometimes only by the touch of a finger under the tablecloth as we sat dining—so fluid has my body become, forming even at the touch of a finger into one full drop, which fills itself, which quivers, which flashes, which falls in ecstasy" (329). And where Jinny suggests the physical path to merging, Susan, since Percival is gone, presents the pattern of natural fact that lies below the surface confusion of all fact. ". . . I have seen life in blocks," she says, "substantial, huge; its battlements and towers, factories and gasometers; a dwelling place made from time immemorial after an hereditary pattern" (325), showing how time can unify, make permanent, as well as shatter the vision of life. Neville, another fact-driven individual, seeing his abstract self as "a net whose fibres pass imperceptibly beneath the world" (324), senses the permanence that this pattern of time has cast over all of them, saying, "Change is no longer possible. We are committed" (324).

But Bernard refuses to see the vision as fixity. ". . . It is only my body," he cries, "—this elderly man here whom you call Bernard—that is fixed irrevocably—so I desire to believe" (326). He sees that the red lines that fact seems to have drawn round himself and the rest are false, that habit has begun to erase the desire for impenetrable selfhood that used to make them think always of "I or of you" (326). "We are ready to consider any suggestion that the world may offer quite impartially" (332), he says. Then all at once he realizes that the

unity he looks for is neither fixity nor fluidity but effort, endless rebuilding of vision and battle against the flux of fact.

Arm in arm, as though to march against isolation and disorder, the six at once combine to create this sense of visionary
unity:

"The iron gates have rolled back," said Jinny. "Time's
fangs have ceased their devouring. We have triumphed
over the abysses of space, with rouge, with powder, with
flimsy pocket-handkerchiefs."

"I grasp, I hold fast," said Susan. "I hold firmly to this
hand, any one's, with love, with hatred; it does not matter
which."

"The still mood, the disembodied mood is on us," said
Rhoda, "and we enjoy this momentary alleviation (it is
not often that one has no anxiety) when the walls of the
mind become transparent. Wren's palace, like the quartet
played to the dry and stranded people in the stalls, makes
an oblong. A square is stood upon the oblong and we
say, 'This is our dwelling-place. The structure is now
visible. Very little is left outside.' "

"The flower," said Bernard, "the red carnation that
stood in the vase on the table of the restaurant when we
dined together with Percival is become a six-sided flower;
made of six lives."

"A mysterious illumination," said Louis, "visible
against those yew trees" (334–35).

Then, as with every vision, this moment passes. "Let us stop
for a moment," says Bernard; "let us behold what we have
made. Let it blaze against the yew trees. One life. There. It is
over. Gone out" (335). So the six, after combining their varying efforts to triumph over the destruction of death and so
creating an instant of vision, must begin again to rebuild
what has just been lost.

The ninth interlude completes the cycle from dark to sun-
lit individuality to dark unity again—the pattern of visionary
growth that this novel describes. *"Now the sun had sunk. Sky*

and sea were indistinguishable" (340). But however much this darkness may be like that of the opening interlude, it is not the night of unconscious vision that united the six characters in their childhood. It is a darkness that embraces the ravages of time, recognizing them as a necessary part of the pattern of life, the pattern formed of vision, broken vision, and the effort to rebuild this shattered unity. Thus this all-inclusive darkness cannot exist in the innocence of childhood but washes in only in the winter of life when it can absorb all the symbols of decay—the empty nest, the rotten apple—which are scattered through this final interlude. Within the room, *"All colours . . . had overflown their banks. The precise brush stroke was swollen and lopsided; cupboards and chairs melted their brown masses into one huge obscurity"* (340); while outside, *"As if there were waves of darkness in the air, darkness moved on, covering houses, hills, trees, as waves of water wash round the sides of some sunken ship. Darkness washed down streets eddying round single figures, engulfing them. . . ."* (340–41). That this infinite unity is not merely the darkness of a death that ends life is shown in two ways in the section that follows. First of all, the novel ends as dawn once again lifts the weight of night from life, ends with renewed effort, not with defeat. And second, the force that combines the six characters whose story has comprised *The Waves* is not death but art, represented by Bernard who has absorbed into his own life through momentary revelations of unity the lives of the other five, both living and dead.

The artist, because he recognizes that his vision cannot be limited to one truth only, attempts to collect into his work as many sides of life as he has had the experience or insight to have observed. Lily Briscoe, in *To the Lighthouse,* called together the vision of Mrs. Ramsay and the fact of Mr. Ramsay to unite them in her painting, her moment of total vision. So Bernard, now that his phrases are to be welded into a story, gathers all his memories and fragments of vision to his side. And just as Lily could not have completed her picture until the possibility of oneness that shone in Mrs. Ramsay's life was tested by time and death, so Bernard could not begin his summation until this winter's evening when the dreams and struggles of himself and each of his friends have been exposed to all the stages of life. As a child he knew too little of the external world to paint a finished portrait of totality; at the noon hour of his life, he and all his friends were too divided by this factual individuality to let their selfhoods fade and blend together. Now, after the six have linked arms and marched against the common enemy, decay and separation, they are ready to assume one many-faceted form; and Bernard, as artist, must create this final vision for them.

So he begins: "Now to sum up. . . . Now to explain to you the meaning of my life. . . . But in order to make you understand, to give you my life, I must tell you a story—and there are so many, and so many—stories of childhood, stories of school, love, marriage, death, and so on; and none of them are true" (341). No single side of life is true without all others joining with it; and Bernard recognizes that his phrases, no matter how keen and clear, can never catch the whole:

> "How tired I am of stories, how tired I am of phrases that come down beautifully with all their feet on the ground! Also, how I distrust neat designs of life that are drawn upon half sheets of notepaper. I begin to long for some little language such as lovers use, broken words, inarticulate words, like the shuffling of feet on the pavement. I begin to seek some design more in accordance with those moments of humiliation and triumph that come now and then undeniably" (341–42).

He needs a language as pervasive as the passing vision, a language that does not exist. But since the time has come for statement, he must make do with the tools he has, pretending "that life is a solid substance, shaped like a globe, which we turn about in our fingers" (350) and that his fragile phrases can support this imaginary sphere.

Because this summary story is interwoven with the past of all the six friends, Bernard must follow the thread from its source. "In the beginning," he says, "there was the nursery . . ." (342), and the first sensations of an outer world—a brass handle gleaming in the sun, a raised sponge and the surprise of water on the skin, defining physical form. This was the time when each of the six began to discover an identity distinct from the others. "It was Susan who cried," says Bernard, "that day when I was in the tool-house with Neville; and I felt my indifference melt. Neville did not melt. 'Therefore,' I said, 'I am myself, not Neville,' a wonderful discovery" (343). With the sensation of selfhood came realization of "the presence of those enemies who change, but are always there; the forces we fight against. To let oneself be carried on passively is unthinkable" (343). Even as a child Bernard chose words as his weapon, making, for example, a wood-pigeon poem to sooth Susan's tears and capture the sudden transparency of vision that his love for her gave him. As he paints with phrases his picture of childhood, Bernard shows that even then his friends were choosing separate and limited paths into life, saying, "But we were all different. The wax—the virginal wax that coats the spine melted in different patches for each of us. . . . Louis was disgusted by the nature of human flesh; Rhoda by our cruelty; Susan could not share; Neville wanted order; Jinny love; and so on. We suffered terribly as we became separate bodies" (343–44).

After the nursery came the stage of school, further separation, and Percival, who stood for "what is startling, what is unexpected, what we cannot account for, what turns symmetry to nonsense" (345), who contained in himself all the sudden surprise of a sponge full of water, of natural, myriad reality. At school Louis emerged as cutting, apt, severe. "He was without those simple attachments by which one is connected with another. He remained aloof; enigmatic; a scholar capable of that inspired accuracy which has something formidable about it" (346). Then Neville grew more distinct and ". . . with a mind like the tongue of an ant-eater, rapid, dexterous, gluttonous, he searched out every curl and twist of those Roman sentences, and sought out one person, always one person to sit beside" (346). Bernard's waxy coat, too, began to melt off in patches, revealing the man beneath who saw clearly and tried to experience everything. Using a metaphor plucked

from the interlude mirroring this second stage of life, Bernard
describes the three girls in adolescence as bits of mosaic, un-
harmonized bird songs; Jinny exhibiting the first social talent;
Rhoda staying wild and aloof; and Susan growing quickly into
womanhood and developing "some quality in accordance with
the high but unemphatic beauty of pure style which those who
create poetry so particularly admire" (348), for she held the
rhythm of nature within her.

Then came the period of life in which each of the six finished forming a self to measure against the world. While the
others took on solidity in business, society, or country living,
Bernard, at the university, "buried match after match in the
turf decidedly to mark this or that stage in the process of
understanding. . . ." (349). He donned any number of factual
identities, changing from Hamlet, to Shelley, to Napoleon,
to Byron, and attempting to absorb all realms of experience in
preparation for the day in which he should be called upon
to summarize everything. In the process of crystallization, he
uncovered "that which is beyond and outside our own predica-
ment . . . that which is symbolic, and thus perhaps permanent . . ." (349); and, being a man to catch the abstract in the
solid, he attached this newly won symbolic reality to the willow tree, saying, "The tree alone resisted our eternal flux"
(349). Like Rachel's miraculous tree in *The Voyage Out,* this
willow with "Its shower of falling branches, its creased and
crooked bark had the effect of what remains outside our illu-
sions yet cannot stay them, is changed by them for the moment,
yet shows through stable, still, and with a sternness that our
lives lack" (350–51). This tree unites in itself the limited and
the limitless worlds: it is the pure fact that serves as the foundation for vision. It is separate from vision yet changed by it.
Like the Lighthouse it stands firm amid the flux of chaos
and supports the visionary beams. So this tree becomes the
ideal against which Bernard must measure his phrases and
the others their lives. At this stage each stood his completed
self beside the symbol of totality. Rhoda, because she had not
succeeded in forming a factual self, watched the tree shrivel
before her eyes; Jinny made the leaves dance "but not with

illusion; for she saw nothing that was not there" (351), under-stood only the fact of the tree and not its vision. Louis's un-compromising demand for "some diamond of indissoluble ve-racity" (352), which emerged fully formed at this stage of sharpest selfhood, and Neville's extreme precision both left out important sides of life.

So Bernard continued to polish his phrases and look for that fragile "crystal, the globe of life as one calls it" (354), which would include within its thin walls the combined truths of Jinny, Neville, Louis, Rhoda, Susan, and every other truth as well. Since each phrase he made caught only a fragment, each truth only a part of the whole, Bernard had to enlarge his own life in order to make his phrases create the total vision. Thus while choosing outwardly a pattern of domesticity and social existence in which "Tuesday follows Monday; then comes Wednesday" (355), he kept always in mind the con-tradictory side of life represented by Louis and Rhoda, who, in their own individual lives, insisted upon total vision. So when the others had carved out a self for themselves and a solid habitual life, Bernard, even in his days of wife and children, retained that multiplicity of being that the artist must never lose if he is to be able to make his work a vision composed in a context of fact.

Then, at the moment of most tangible reality, when the six had discovered their factual selves and knew where their lives would lead, Percival died. Exposed to this stunning event, Bernard uncovered "the sense that a burden has been re-moved; pretence and make-believe and unreality are gone, and lightness has come with a kind of transparency, making oneself invisible and things seen through as one walks . . ." (359). This death of factual reality marked the turning point in the lives of the six, for from that moment on the edges of limited selfhood began to wear away and a new possibility of conscious visionary unity began to emerge. With Percival dead, the six were able to join in their common refusal to sit passive, in their determination to fight against the destruc-tion of meaning in death and preserve a transcendent Percival in vision. Each of the six made his own distinct contribution to this many-sided unity of effort: Louis his desire for perfection, Rhoda her rejection of limited fact, Neville his careful relationship with one person, Susan her natural rhythmic life, Jinny her animality. To Bernard was left the task of weaving together these disparate attempts to conquer the disruptive power of death; for as artist he had to find the phrase to realize the whole.

But as he grew older and the presence of the enemy no longer came as a shock, the need for opposition lost its sting and he was continually tempted to accept passively the fact of limitation and the inescapable doom of death. New phrases did not come easily: the familiar tended to repeat themselves. So at the moment when effort was most needed, it came most slowly; but, at last it came, and Bernard leaped to his task. Describing his renewal of effort he says,

> I jumped up, I said, "Fight." "Fight," I repeated. It is the effort and the struggle, it is the perpetual warfare, it is the shattering and piecing together—this is the daily battle, defeat or victory, the absorbing pursuit. The trees, scattered, put on order; the thick green of the leaves thinned itself to a dancing light. I netted them under with a sudden phrase. I retrieved them from formlessness with words (363–64).

So as the sun of life began to set and each of the six looked back on what he had done and what he had failed to do, Bernard realized that his life was not definable, like those of the others, saying, ". . . what I call 'my life,' it is not one life that I look back upon; I am not one person; I am many people; I do not altogether know who I am—Jinny, Susan, Neville, Rhoda, or Louis: or how to distinguish my life from theirs" (368). Because he had always been called upon to make stories to include everything, his life had never developed the shell-like surface that would divide him from others.

So, with the weight of life behind them, the six met at Hampton Court. Bernard describes what they all experienced when he says, "We saw for a moment laid out among us the body of the complete human being whom we have failed to be, but at the same time, cannot forget. All that we might have been we saw; all that we had missed, and we grudged for a moment the other's claim, as children when the cake is cut, the one cake, the only cake, watch their slice diminishing" (369). Then slowly as they ceased to envy and compare, lost their distinct identities, they were caught up in the formlessness of time and space that tears life to shreds. Faced with this threat, the six rose up together and forged an ephemeral but single wholeness, combining all their lives, and "burnt there triumphant" (369). Of course this moment faded and the wave they had made burst asunder as each surrendered again to the insistency of distinct and varied sensation. Only Louis and Rhoda kept the vision entire, but even they could sustain it only in their private dreams. So the gathering divided.

"Was this then," asks Bernard concerning this momentary oneness, "this streaming away mixed with Susan, Jinny, Neville, Rhoda, Louis, a sort of death? A new assembly of elements? Some hint of what was to come?" (370). Is death, then, perhaps, a fulfillment of the hope for wholeness? As though to answer him, Rhoda, who was always drawn toward infinite, formless vision and who had already returned to the waves symbolically, commits suicide and so flows back into the unity she never really left. Since Bernard had absorbed Rhoda into his multiple self, her death fulfills that part of him that longs for dissolution just as Septimus preserves Mrs. Dalloway by dying for her. But before he can create the vision of which Rhoda is a part, Bernard must, for a moment, accept the meaning of her death, discard his many selves, his many limited phrases and so apprehend that coherence "that sense of generations, of women carrying red pitchers to the Nile . . ." (373), which the pure visionary experiences. The moment comes. He calls, and his self does not answer. He experiences death in the midst of life and the weight of emptiness and despondency. Then slowly, miraculously, light returns "in thin stripes" (375) to his shadow world. The earth puts on mass and color, though he himself is still "Thin, as a ghost, leaving no trace . . . perceiving merely . . . alone in a new world, never trodden; brushing new flowers, unable to speak save in a child's words of one syllable . . ." (376). Carrying the essences of all his friends within him, he has died, and now emerges a child again as he was when *The Waves* began: ". . . that thin, hard shell which carries the soul, which, in youth, shuts one in . . ." (377) is gone; all obstacles that separated him from others are dissolved and the vision is complete. He has seen for a moment the purpose of death, the need for dissolution to achieve communion. So, now, as the moment grows, he feels on his forehead the blow that killed Percival, on his neck the kiss Jinny gave Louis, in his eyes Susan's tears, in his mind the dream Rhoda leaped toward in her death. The winter night has come and Bernard can set before his unknown listener the whole of all his lives, both the fact and the vision, purified and combined. "Immeasurably receptive," he says, "holding everything, trembling with fullness, yet clear, contained—so my being seems. . . . It lies deep, tideless, immune, now that he is dead, the man I called 'Bernard,' the man who kept a book in his pocket in which he made notes . . ." (378–79). In this visionary fullness he overflows into the interludes that divided the oneness of *The Waves*: his phrases, pouring out, all spring from these isolated passages and make the vision of the book complete.

But even this tremendous revelation must end, or the pattern of build and rebuild will be broken, the continuity denied. So the infinite Bernard contracts, becomes an "elderly man, rather heavy, grey above the ears, who . . . leans one elbow on the table . . ." (379). "Lord," thinks Bernard, "how unutterably disgusting life is! What dirty tricks it plays us, one moment free; the next, this. . . . I who had thought myself immune, who had said, 'Now I am rid of all that,' find that the wave has tumbled me over, head over heels, scattering my possessions, leaving me to collect, to assemble, to heap together, summon my forces, rise and confront the enemy" (380). In spite of this shock of reality, however, the vision has been achieved; Bernard has tasted the infinite self and, for a moment longer, sits relishing the experience and leaving his shards of phrases in his notebook on the floor. Then the battle begins again and he must gather up his coat and muffler and be off. Yet once outside, he senses a change, saying,

> There is a sense of the break of day. I will not call it dawn. What is dawn in the city to an elderly man standing in the street looking up rather dizzily at the sky? Dawn is some sort of whitening of the sky; some sort of renewal. . . . Another general awakening. The stars draw back and are extinguished. The bars deepen themselves between the waves. . . . Yes, this is the eternal renewal, the incessant rise and fall and fall and rise again (382–83).

So, having passed from unconscious dawn to finite noon and into the vastness of death and vision, Bernard has emerged once more into the daylight of words of one syllable and begins his fight and phrase-making again, saying,

> And in me too the wave rises. It swells; it arches its back. I am aware once more of a new desire, something rising beneath me like a proud horse whose rider first spurs and then pulls him back. What enemy do we now perceive advancing against us, you whom I ride now, as we stand pawing this stretch of pavement? It is death. Death is the enemy. It is death against whom I ride with my spear couched and my hair flying back like a young man's, like Percival's, when he galloped in India. I strike spurs into my horse. Against you I will fling myself, unvanquished and unyielding, O Death! (383).

Since death creates the infinity of vision by erasing each man's carefully developed temporal selfhood, it is always, paradoxically, half enemy and half savior to those living in a fact-dominated world. Yet even as enemy it serves as a spur to that effort that is needed to build and rebuild the ephemeral vision in life. As savior it can offer the final, eternal vision only after effort is no longer possible, after fact is gone.

So the wave rises and falls, the pattern of effort and vision, effort and vision continues. Bernard in his summary and in his life has displayed the artist's ability to create unity. And

Virginia Woolf, in *The Waves,* has done the same. All over-
tures toward life, pure fact, pure vision, and the representative
combinations of the two have been presented. Each individual's own progress from vision to fact to vision has been
traced. The need for effort that Mrs. Ramsay professed in
To the Lighthouse has here been shown to be part of the
endless pattern. And finally, the importance of the artist's
own efforts to conquer chaos and give form to the vision has
been demonstrated in the character of Bernard and in the
vision of the novel as a whole. Having examined fact and
vision so carefully within the context of vision, Virginia
Woolf devotes her next effort to testing the pattern within
a purely factual context, exposing the vision to all the disruptive elements of war, poverty, long illness, disappointment,
and failure. This she attempts in her next novel, *The Years.*

7

The Years

In *The Waves* Virginia Woolf made it clear theoretically that both fact and vision are essential to a comprehensive understanding of life. Within the course of this novel she also developed the supposition that this understanding can be achieved solely by constant effort and then only momentarily, so that the life of the perceptive individual becomes a pattern of effort, vision, loss of vision, and renewal of effort. Because of the symbolic complexion of *The Waves,* these theories could be articulated, but not demonstrated; for Virginia Woolf had resolved to trim away all of the factual narration characteristic of realistic fiction. As a result, her ideas retained a certain abstract quality inconsistent with the notion that fact is necessary to the pattern of revelation. In *The Years,* however, fact is presented outright: people do not merely talk figuratively about walking into pillar-boxes; they step out into the warm London night and run to the box in their slippers, and once there they come face to face with the most ugly sort of fact imaginable—a fact to shatter any fragile dream of vision. In this context of fact, then, the pattern and the vision are re-tested. Writing in her diary of her plans for the nascent *Years* —then to be called *The Pargiters*—Virginia Woolf declared: "What has happened of course is that after abstaining from the novel of fact all these years—since 1919—and *N&D* is dead—I find myself infinitely delighting in facts for a change, and in possession of quantities beyond counting: though I feel now and then the tug to vision, but resist it. This is the true line, I am sure, after *The Waves*."[1] Of course the vision soon crept back into the work, and a few months later Virginia Woolf wrote of her amended design, saying, "I want to give the whole of the present society—nothing less: facts as well as the vision. And to combine them both. I mean, *The Waves* going on simultaneously with *Night and Day*. Is this possible?"[2]

Several critics have answered this last question emphatically. A. D. Moody thinks *The Years* the "least inspired or inspiriting of Virginia Woolf's novels";[3] E. M. Forster says "in *The Years* as in *Night and Day* she deserts poetry, and again she fails";[4] while James Hafley, in total disagreement with his two fellows, finds the work "possibly the best, and certainly one of the most interesting, of Virginia Woolf's novels."[5] Those who agree at least in part with Hafley usually maintain as he does[6] that the novel is primarily a social study and is successful purely for that reason. Herbert Marder,[7] Dorothy Brewster,[8] and Carl Woodring[9] all see the central theme of *The Years* as the decline of the Victorian middle class and the emergence of a less constricted younger generation. Admittedly much of the novel is pervaded by this theme of social change, yet it fails to take into account a subtler underlying motif of permanence or continuity that is woven through the fabric of the work. To see *The Years* as another socially oriented *Night and Day* is to see only the fact and miss the vision. Since Virginia Woolf by her own admission intended to include the essence of *The Waves* as well as of her early realistic book, it seems a bit near-sighted to approach *The Years* solely as a social document. A few critics have given some attention to the less conspicuous aspects of the work. Margaret Church points out a "theme of return"[10] that gives the novel a circular structure. David Daiches notes that "the real subject of *The Years* is precisely what the title would indicate—the years, and the way their passage builds up, embryonically as it were, a transparent envelope which determines the nature and the limits of each individual consciousness";[11] and Jean Guiguet, who also recognizes this well-filled envelope of events, sees this multiplicity as "participating in the absolute and the eternal."[12] Herbert Marder, while emphasizing the social theme, does mention the vision,[13] interpreting it as a means to reform the world's confusion; and Bernard Blackstone, too, touches upon this theme when he finds *The Years* "a dark book showing male society crushing hope for vision."[14] But the theme of *The Waves* hovers over this novel with far greater persistency than many readers have recognized.

Certainly on first examination *The Years* seems to exhibit none of the intricate and regular order that held *The Waves* together. Instead of being divided into carefully measured sections, moving evenly through time, the novel is broken into irregular chunks, the chapters presenting first 1880, then 1891, 1907, 1908, 1910, 1911, 1913, 1914, 1917, 1918, 1936. Even the seasons described in the interludes preceding each section are conspicuous for their lack of order: autumn follows spring, summer autumn, spring summer, and so on—no two seasons follow each other in natural sequence. Nor is the diurnal pattern more systematic, for day often precedes day in these descriptive passages. Within the main body of the text, the ugliness from which the characters in *The Waves* were carefully shielded appears with alarming frequency, shattering the vision whenever it comes to light. Does Colonel Pargiter run for a glimpse of love to his mistress? She puts her dog affectionately on his knee and he finds the animal patchy with eczema.[15] Does Martin pause to give a penny to a flower seller? She looks up at him and reveals a noseless face (235). Nor is such physical deformity uncommon: Colonel Pargiter is missing several fingers and has a hand like a claw. "Bertie Levy's got six toes on one foot . . ." (14). Even Sara, the most visionary character in the book, was dropped as a baby and rendered crooked for life. Death, the vehicle for vision in many of Virginia Woolf's earlier novels, is presented here in its most hideous form. Mrs. Pargiter, who is hovering at the door of death when the novel opens, is described in the least poetic fashion possible: "Her face was pouched and heavy; the skin was stained with brown patches; the hair which had been red was now white, save that there were queer yellow patches in it, as if some locks had been dipped in the yolk of an egg" (21). Even food, served in a shoddy rooming house, reflects the ugliness in much of factual reality: a joint of mutton is a "rather stringy disagreeable object which was still bleeding into the well. The willow-pattern plate was daubed with gory streaks" (320–21). And party games consist of drawing "monsters" with the head of the queen and body made up of parts of birds, tigers, and elephants. War no longer enters obliquely through visionary shell-shock victims as in *Mrs. Dalloway* or parenthetical death and image-garlanded loss of ships as in *To the Lighthouse*. Its bombs fall outright, waking children, shattering the peace of social intercourse, and interrupting the vision with violence and destruction. This, then, is the setting within which the vision and the pattern of effort must survive. And survive they do.

If the interludes, in their outward disorder, reflect the superficial lack of pattern in the factual world, they also contain the subtle seeds of continuum, and the opening prelude provides the reader with most of the clues he will need to find the symbolic waves of exertion and vision that the mystical novel presented directly.

"Slowly wheeling, like the rays of a searchlight, the days, the weeks, the years passed one after another across the sky" (4). Thus the initial descriptive paragraph leads the reader into the story of the Pargiters. Time in this novel, in spite of occasional suggestions of disorder, will, like the rays of the searchlight, or the beams of the Lighthouse, embrace all aspects of life in its endless and constant progression. So whenever the clocks of London or Oxford chime out during the course of *The Years,* they seem to spread their message in an enveloping wave over every fragment of the day, uniting ugliness and beauty within a single continuous circle. Eleanor, for example, sits listening in her room at Abercorn Terrace. "As she spoke a faint sound boomed through the room. When the wind was in the right direction they could hear St. Paul's. The soft circles spread out in the air: one, two, three, four . . ." (41). No longer as in *Mrs. Dalloway* do leaden circles dissolve in the air. These hours are softer, more pervasive, and make the passage of time less irrevocable, more eternal. Even the fact-loving, scholarly Edward feels that the ringing of the bells rolls away the heavy solidity of life (49).

If the hours chiming out in this novel seem to suggest a permanence about time, the seasons presented in the interludes, for all their lack of sequence, provide another framework of eternity upon which the London world can rest. To begin with, these seasonal passages, describing the pattern of time in nature, reflect a natural cycle that the city seldom experiences in its confusion of traffic and social regimentation. Virginia Woolf makes this function of the country scenes quite clear when she writes in the introduction to "1910": "In the country it was an ordinary day enough; one of the long reel of days that turned as the years passed from green to orange; from grass to harvest. . . . In London, however, the stricture and pressure of the season were already felt . . ." (160). So these glimpses of the natural world serve as a reminder of the imperturbable cycle of days that rolls beneath the clutter and flutter of society. Then, too, each season is described in terms of a permanence that one is likely to overlook in the outward flux of society. "1918," for example, begins with this motionless November scene:

A veil of mist covered the November sky; a many-folded veil, so fine meshed that it made one density. It was not raining, but here and there the mist condensed on the surface into dampness; moistened the country roads and made pavements greasy. Here and there on a grass blade or on a hedge leaf a drop hung motionless. It was windless and calm. Sounds coming through the veil—the bleat of sheep, the croak of rooks—were deadened (302).

The stillness, the blurred and muffled uniformity that characterize this view of autumn carry over into the winter as well. January of "1913" covers all of England with a depth of snow that erases any distinctive aspects that might separate one scene from another.

The sky was nothing but a flurry of falling flakes. Lanes were levelled; hollows filled. . . . There was a faint murmur in the air, a slight crepitation, as if the air itself were turning to snow; otherwise all was silent. . . . Now and again a shaft of light spread slowly across the sky as a car drove through the muffled roads. But as the night wore on, snow covered the wheel ruts; softened to nothingness the marks of the traffic, and coated monuments, palaces and statues with a thick vestment of snow (214).

And when winter does not unite everything under a blanket of snow, it freezes life into fixity as in "1917" when ". . . the air seemed frozen, and, since there was no moon, congealed to the stillness of glass spread over England" (279). The summer interludes, too, bring unity to the world. Moonlight in "1907," falling "on water, made it white, inscrutable, whether deep or shallow" (129), and in "Present Day,"

> . . . the sky was blue still ,but tinged with gold, as if a thin veil of gauze hung over it, and here and there in the gold-blue amplitude an island of cloud lay suspended. . . . Sheep and cows, pearl white and parti-coloured, lay recumbent or munched their way through the half-transparent grass. An edge of light surrounded everything. A red-gold fume rose from the dust on the roads. Even the little red brick villas on the high roads had become porous, incandescent with light, and the flowers in cottage gardens, lilac and pink like cotton dresses, shone veined as if lit from within (306).

If the opening interlude in its roll of days and years across the sky begins a pattern of seasonal unity, it also contains the human pattern, the suggestion of uncertainty and frequent alternation between fact and vision that in itself is a necessary part of the continuum of life. "It was an uncertain spring," begins the prelude to "1880." "The weather, perpetually changing, sent clouds of blue and purple flying over the land. In the country, farmers, looking at the fields, were apprehensive; in London umbrellas were opened and then shut by people looking up at the sky" (3). The universality of this exposure to the rain of life is articulated in a fragmentary interlude within this opening chapter in which a sudden shower is described thus: "The fine rain, the gentle rain, poured equally over the mitred and the bareheaded with an impartiality which suggested that the god of rain, if there were a god, was thinking Let it not be restricted to the very wise, the very great, but let all breathing kind . . . share my bounty" (48). In *The Waves, To the Lighthouse,* and even *Mrs. Dalloway,* Virginia Woolf had made it clear that life is an endless struggle, that the vision is constantly being threatened by a rain of fact, and that the pattern of life is always one of fulfillment followed by disappointment and the need to rebuild the sense of unity. So this uncertain spring that begins the book prepares the reader for the many uncertainties that will interrupt the flow of life, for the innumerable intrusions of fact into vision. If Bernard in *The Waves* continually approached the moment when his phrases seemed to weave into a perfected story, only to watch sensation blunder in and shatter this increasing sense of harmony, the characters in *The Years* also experience the frustration of countless interruptions of their dreams. But in both cases, these momentary conflicts of fact and vision create a pattern of endeavor that leads to an ever-growing understanding of life's meaning. So if Rose makes "a great effort to tell her [Eleanor] the truth; to tell her about the man at the pillar-box" (42), only to be interrupted by the entrance of her nurse, she will grow to see that such obstructions in the road to truth serve to strengthen the soul and so to bring the seeker closer to his goal. If German bombs shatter Eleanor's train of thought, "as if some dull bore had interrupted an interesting conversation" (288), or if her message to others is cut off by the roar of a car engine (308), the hour will come when her vision will near completion and her thoughts permeate the minds of those who need to share her insights into the meaning of existence.

The endurance of the seasons and the unevenness of life are not the only fragments of the pattern that begin to reveal themselves in the opening prelude; for this passage rings with the sound of music, and snatches of melody run through this novel in a unifying thread of vision. Virginia Woolf indicated in *The Waves* both that repetition is the factual manifestation of the vision and that music with its harmonies and recurrent themes creates its own symbolic form of unity. So in this opening paragraph as pigeons "crooned over and over again the lullaby that was always interrupted" and "In the quieter streets musicians doled out their frail and for the most part melancholy pipe of sound, which was echoed, or parodied, here in the trees of Hyde Park, here in St. James's by the twitter of sparrows . . ." (3), the music begins. The pigeons' lullaby, "Take two coos, Taffy. Take two coos. Tak . . ." (75), appears again and again throughout the novel. Kitty hears it (75, 433), Eleanor hears it (75, 115, 176, 433), Edward and Martin hear it (433), Sara hears it (187), until it takes on a special meaning of vision interrupted and rebuilt. Street music, too, resounds as *The Years* unfolds: a barrel organ plays (91, 225), peddlars sing of "Old chairs and baskets to mend" (307) or "Any old iron to sell, any old iron" (91, 162), until "the rhythm persisted; but the words were almost rubbed out" (162). Then a trombone strikes up a tune (316), a woman practices her scales (316), and waltzes form a circle of sound "from Hammersmith to Shoreditch" "like a serpent that swallowed its own tail . . ." (129), making music into the symbol of eternity. As song and tune wind through the novel, they take on more and more of the ageless, wordless quality of the beggar woman's song in *Mrs. Dalloway* or Mrs. McNab's unrecognizable ditty in *To the Lighthouse,* increasing the sensation that repetition brings transformation and timelessness to life. So the incomprehensible song of the caretaker's children (429) with its almost frightening wordlessness and persistent rhythm that echoes the human rhythm inherent in the family reunion where it is sung, completes this musical motif and so unites the opening and closing scenes of the novel.

Repetition is not restricted to music in *The Years,* and the opening prelude provides several other clues to pattern that will evolve as the story progresses. "Interminable processions of shoppers in the West end, of business men in the East," for example, "paraded the pavements, like caravans perpetually marching . . ." (3); and "virgins and spinsters . . . carefully measured out one, two, three, four spoonfuls of tea" (4). So throughout the novel actions are repeated. If Milly in the opening scene frays the wick of the spirit lamp with a hairpin to make the water boil sooner (10), Eleanor does the same nearly twenty years and one hundred pages later (151). Political and social workers' meetings recur. Objects, too, reappear, often in different rooms. For example, the great crimson chair with gilt claws in Digby Pargiter's hall (128) turns up in a shabby apartment (165), a war-threatened drawing-room (287), and another dingy apartment (313) as the novel unfolds. Symbolic sounds, too, connect times and characters through repetition. Kitty hears someone hammering on a hen coop early in the book (68), then is reminded of this moment years later at the opera as she listens to Siegfried beat his sword on an anvil (183). At the other side of London that same evening, Sara listens to a drunk hammering on the door across the way (190) and sings, "Brandishing, flourishing my sword in my hand . . ." (186), thus joining Kitty to Sara and the rich world of operas to the poor world of drunkards.

In the midst of this constant rhythm of repetition—repeated symbols, actions, scenes, and sounds—the characters often lose their sense of definition and melt for a moment into a universal whole, thereby demonstrating the visionary power of pattern. "Where am I?" Delia asks herself at one point, feeling herself "to be in some borderland between life and death" (25). "Where am I?" says Eleanor. "She seemed to be alone in the midst of nothingness . . ." (43). "Where am I?" wonders Kitty. "She forgot where she was. The sky, blown into a blue open space, seemed to be looking down not here upon streets and houses, but upon open country, where the wind brushed the moors . . ." (74). Thus, by the opening of the actual story, the boundless waters of vision and unity have already begun to trickle over the jagged rocks of fact so that the reader is prepared to watch the rhythm of *The Waves* emerge and absorb the threat of disorder and limitation of *Night and Day*'s London world.

Because *The Years* is meant to include all of society, its characters are numerous and represent a wide assortment of social types. The Pargiters themselves, whose lives make up the bulk of the work, portray Virginia Woolf's usual activists and contemplatives, fact-seekers, and visionaries, all looking for meaning in the factual world. Colonel Pargiter, the father of the family, is a fact-bounded man like Captain Barfoot of *Jacob's Room*, combined with the less attractive characteristics of Mr. Ramsay. He rules his family with inflexible laws, can march through a London park, "looking straight ahead of him" (6) without pausing to notice the beauty that goes hand in hand with vision; and lives a life totally divorced from the non-factual world. His very deformity seems to stand as a symbol for his one-handed grasp on reality. "He had lost two fingers of the right hand in the Mutiny, and the muscles had shrunk so that the right hand resembled the claw of some aged bird" (13). It is with this hand that he attempts to caress his mistress, showing how his capacity for love, another road to vision, has shriveled away.

Edward, the eldest of the Colonel's three sons, is brother in spirit to all of Virginia Woolf's scholarly seekers of abstract factual truth. Like St. John Hirst and Neville before him, he spends hours in meticulous study of the classics.

> He caught phrase after phrase exactly, firmly, more exactly, he noted, making a brief note in the margin, than the night before. Little negligible words now revealed shades of meaning, which altered the meaning. He made another note; *that* was the meaning. His own dexterity in catching the phrase plumb in the middle gave him a thrill of excitement. There it was, clean and entire. But he must be precise; exact; even his little scribbled notes must be clear as print (50).

By the time he reaches old age, his precision has made him "too formed and idiosyncratic; too black and white and linear . . ." (408); yet his approach to life, although limited in itself, is part of the pattern that the novel unveils.

His brother Morris, too, follows a factual truth by going into Law, while Martin, the youngest, rejects the regulated London world and, like Peter Walsh in *Mrs. Dalloway*, seeks some purer truth in foreign lands. When also like Peter, he returns to England, not having caught enough of the vision to recognize it as a goal, he samples society again, but remains unsatisfied. His cousin Kitty recognizes his isolation when she says: "How many 'parties' would it need . . . to turn her satirical, uncompromising cousin into an obedient member of society?" (262). Of course he will never fit the social mold, and, walking by the empty house at Abercorn Terrace after the family has scattered out over London, he thinks of it as a place where "all those different people had lived, boxed up together, telling lies" (223). But if habitual social existence, bounded by facts and crippling restrictions, is the life of lies, what is the truth? Art, perhaps. And Martin, catching a glimpse of art's unifying power, looks at Saint Paul's and wishes he had been an architect: "He crossed over and stood with his back against a shop window looking up at the great dome. All the weights in his body seemed to shift. He had a curious sense of something moving in his body in harmony with the building; it righted itself: it came to a full stop. It was exciting—this change of proportion" (227). If Martin sees that art may lead to a clearer more universal truth, he senses that love can do the same—but not possessive love that restricts instead of freeing. So he never marries, for fear of growing inflexible. Instead he continues, like Peter Walsh, to sample both worlds without experiencing either completely or finding a goal toward which to aim his life.

The Pargiter daughters, too, choose different methods of seeking fulfillment in life. Milly, who even as a child imitates the manners of older people (11), steps naturally into married life with Hugh Gibbs, a man who "could only talk about girls. Girls and horses" (53). Never recognizing the existence of a world other than that of politics for him and housewifery for her, she becomes unwittingly and unconsciously confined to a life in which everything is half-conscious and habitual, like the mechanical life of Hugh Whitbread in *Mrs. Dalloway*. If Hugh was portrayed as a rather neutral inanimate object, Milly is described in explicitly negative terms; for as the ingredient of human effort becomes more and more important in Virginia Woolf's conception of the vision, people whose lives are marked by passivity seem less and less desirable. So when one of the more perceptive characters meets Milly at the final reunion, he notices "how the rings were sunk in her fingers, as if the flesh had grown over them" (373), and sees her conversation with her husband as "the half-inarticulate munchings of animals in a stall. Tut-tut-tut, and chew-chew-chew—as they trod out the soft steamy straw in the stable; as they wallowed in the primeval swamp, prolific, profuse, half-conscious . . ." (375). He recognizes, too, that Milly's love of her children is a restrictive love that sees the beloved as a piece of property, not a sharer in the vision. Only when she flashes out in a moment of bitterness toward a neighbor does she take on a spark of life; for real hatred, like real love, gives the person who feels the emotion a weapon against flux.

Milly's sister Delia, rejecting the easy habits of social repetition, dreams of a life of freedom and action at the side of Parnell, creating justice and helping the downtrodden. Because she chooses a life of effort, she earns a glimpse of vision and, at her mother's funeral, "she was possessed by a sense of something everlasting; of life mixing with death, of death becoming life. For as she looked she heard the sparrows chirp quicker and quicker; she heard wheels in the distance sound louder and louder; life came closer and closer . . ." (87). But then her growing awareness is interrupted by a platitude of passivity, and the vision is shattered. " 'We give thee hearty thanks,' said the voice, 'for that it has pleased thee to deliver this our sister out of the miseries of this sinful world——' What a lie! she cried to herself. What a damnable lie!" (87). Death is not an event to be accepted passively as a welcome end to the rhythm of life. Instead it is a part of that rhythm, being on the one hand an element of destruction to inspire opposition in the vision seeker, and on the other a moment of infinite unity, allowing for a renewal of the pattern. Bernard's and Rhoda's attitudes toward death in *The Waves* represent the dual nature of this phenomenon, and Delia perceives this duality at her moment of deepest understanding. Then, as the vision fades, she returns to her personal struggle for the cause of Irish independence. But her life of action does not last.

CHAPTER 7

After the death of Parnell, she marries and gradually becomes absorbed into a life not much more dynamic than that of Milly.

Rose Pargiter, on the other hand, never compromises her belief in the need for action, never allows the dream of visionary unity to enter her mind long enough to interrupt for more than a moment her various campaigns on behalf of truth, freedom, and justice. When she first enters the drawing-room at Abercorn Terrace at the opening of the novel, there is "a green smudge on her pinafore as if she had been climbing trees" (11), and it soon becomes clear that she, of all the children, is the "man of action." " 'I am Pargiter of Pargiter's Horse,' she said, flourishing her hand, 'riding to the rescue!' She was riding by night on a desperate mission to a besieged garrison, she told herself. She had a secret message—she clenched her fist on her purse—to deliver to the General in person. All their lives depended upon it" (27). Where Delia's vision of unity is shattered by false vision in the form of passive religion, Rose's devotion to action is threatened by the ugliest form of fact; for as she runs to the toy store, pretending she is a military hero, she suddenly encounters a sexual pervert who reaches for her out of the night. For a moment the game is over; but Rose is strong and even when grown up is still galloping to the aid of various political causes, being wounded by bricks or thrown into jail, but never abandoning her ideal. Perhaps because she, like Mary Datchet in *Night and Day*, has only one chance at vision and that snatched from her before she can profit from it, Rose sees most clearly the need to accept the factual world and fight against its limitations with ceaseless effort. Thinking back on her youth, the middle-aged Rose stands on a bridge and watches the water flow beneath her.

As she stood there, looking down at the water, some buried feeling began to arrange the stream into a pattern. The pattern was painful. She remembered how she had stood there on the night of a certain engagement, crying; her tears had fallen, her happiness, it seemed to her, had fallen. Then she had turned—here she turned—and had seen the churches, the masts and roofs of the city. There's *that,* she

had said to herself. . . . A queer expression, half frown; half
smile, formed on her face and she threw herself slightly
backwards, as if she were leading an army (161).

If one cannot find unity and freedom through love or one of
the other doors to vision, one must carve a tunnel of pattern
through the granite of fact using only the tools of effort and
action.

Edward, Morris, Martin, Milly, Delia, and Rose each tackle
the factual dragon in a different way. Edward and Morris
weave a net of abstraction to throw over it; Martin rides against
it with a fragile spear of rebellion; Milly gets out her milk pail
and leads it to the stable; Delia and Rose saddle it and charge
out against the world. And the Abel Pargiters are not alone in
this struggle to extract a pattern from life. Their cousins Kitty,
Maggie, and Sara each do their part in adding to the general
store of experience that may one day subdue deformity and
confusion by uniting in a common and endless rhythm.

Kitty, a professor's daughter who spends her girlhood pouring tea and entertaining scholarly dignitaries, longs for the
flow of natural life reflected in the seasons, looks for the difficult but satisfying existence that Susan embodied in *The
Waves*. The thought of being kissed by a young man who has
just come inside from repairing a chicken coop makes her
feel "as if she had given her nurse the slip and run off on her
own" (71). But before many years have passed, she finds herself the wife of a nobleman, frequenting the opera and riding
about in luxurious cars. Kitty, now Lady Lasswade, is as strong-
minded in her own way as Rose is in hers. So she "gives her
nurse the slip" (270) in her adulthood by flying to her northern
estate whenever she can and works her way into the heart of
nature by grubbing in the garden or walking with her dog
into the fields. There, "as she watched, light moved and dark
moved; light and shadow went travelling over the hills and
over the valleys. A deep murmur sang in her ears—the land
itself, singing to itself, a chorus, alone. She lay there listening.
She was happy, completely. Time had ceased" (278). By denying the limitations that surround her and insisting on her own

form of fulfillment, whatever the effort it may cost her, Kitty finds her own visionary pattern in the natural world.

Her cousin Maggie Pargiter approaches life with a question rather than a statement, trying to find a sequence in the flow of the years. "She had been thinking, Am I that, or am I this? Are we one, or are we separate . . ." (140). To her the solid elements of life are undeniably real. She cannot accept the idea that "The world's nothing but thought . . ." (140) because such a theory leaves out colors and trees. Her watchword is "And then?" She longs to extract the essence from each event and find some stability and order in fact alone. "She ran her eye from thing to thing. In and out it went, collecting, gathering, summing up into one whole . . ." (349); but each time the pattern nears completion, some new event leaps up and demands to be included, so that the search continues.

If most of the Pargiters choose fact as the key to open life, looking at events as items in a series, there is one who insists upon seeing the world as a visionary whole. That one is the crooked but keen-eyed Sara Pargiter who weaves a web of poetry around the facts and blurs their sharp edges together into vision. The city she lives in, however, is one that throws up ugliness in the face of anyone who shuns concrete reality, so Sara never appears as a prophet, or even as a poet proper. As if her body has absorbed the limitations that her soul denies, she always looks like "a somewhat dishevelled fowl . . ." (228) and her physical deformity sets her ironically in the ranks of people like her Uncle Abel with his clawed hand. Nevertheless, her sight and soul never lose their clarity. She can catch the rhythm of limited fact and make it comic in its emptiness, as when she mimics her father's "to—er—to—er—reform one's habits" (127), retaining the shell of sound while discarding the sense. If she can see so accurately the approach to reality that she rejects, she is also able to capture the fluidity of her mother's almost visionary beauty, in spite of her own angularity, thus showing her spiritual affinity with the less rigid side of life.

Like Bernard in *The Waves,* the poetic Sara borrows or coins for each member of her family a phrase that shows in miniature that person's way of life. But at the same time she herself diffuses her identity into every crook and cranny of the world and swathes the fragments of fact she sees in stories that transform the scattered shards to unified vision. So, as her parents and sister go off to a party, leaving her in bed to rest her sickly body, Sara can become "something; a root; lying sunk in the earth; veins seemed to thread the cold mass; the tree put forth branches; the branches had leaves. '—the sun shines through the leaves,' she said, waggling her finger" (133). Sara is the root and the tree, by now established symbols in Virginia Woolf's work of total vision, founded in fact. But in the purely factual world she inhabits, vision comes hard and trees "far from being dappled with sunlight . . . had no leaves at all" (133). So Sara must forge the vision out of words and dress each bare branch in intangible leaves. To create this vision she builds love around casual encounter as she looks out her bedroom window to a party next door and watches a couple standing talking outside. Imagining their conversation she lets the man say, "Behold, Miss Smith, what I have found on the grass—a fragment of my heart; of my broken heart . . ." (134). But as she grows older, her stories must metamorphose more than just the banal side of life; they must also face the task of making poverty and ugliness palatable to the vision. Sara is well aware of the extent of this misshapen aspect of the world. Living in a London slum, she sees many sights that make her say, "In time to come . . . people looking into this room—this cave, this little antre, scooped out of mud and dung, will hold their fingers to their noses . . . and say, 'Pah. They stink!' " (189). But even when confronted with the need to enter personally the limited world of business and society, Sara shrouds the fact in story, saying,

> So I put on my hat and coat and rushed out in a rage . . .
> and stood on the bridge, and said, "Am I a weed, carried this way, that way, on a tide that comes twice a day without a meaning?" . . .
> And there were people passing; the strutting; the tiptoeing; the pasty; the ferret-eyed; the bowler-hatted,

servile innumerable army of workers. And I said, "Must I
join your conspiracy? Stain the hand, the unstained hand
. . . and sign on, and serve a master . . .?" (341).

As an outsider to this bounded world, Sara has an objective
eye that allows her to see the pattern. She understands that
"people always say the same thing" (297) and that this repetition itself is part of the vision. Thus although Sara cannot experience the factual life of the world as others do, she can
recognize the hope of pattern and unity underlying its superficial formlessness and create for herself a life that hovers at
the threshold of concrete reality.

Sara is not entirely alone in her role as visionary outsider,
for there is another character in this novel who shares her
sudden insights into truth. Nicholas Pomjalovsky, called
"Brown" because no one can pronounce or remember his
real name, stands apart from the rest of English society, not
only because he is actually a foreigner, but because his approach to life is alien to those who grapple exclusively with
fact. Like Sara, he is also isolated by his own "deformity" for
he is a homosexual and thus does not fit into the ordinary
pattern of social existence. Because their ideas are so similar,
Nicholas and Sara join forces and pursue their own unusual
love affair. Eleanor Pargiter, whose life embraces the lives of
all the other characters in the novel, understands the depth
and importance of this relationship when she thinks: "And
if this love-making differs from the old, still it has its charm;
it was 'love,' different from the old love, perhaps, but worse,
was it? Anyhow, she thought, they are aware of each other; they
live in each other; what else is love . . ." (370). Where Sara
tries to articulate the vision in poetry, Nicholas expresses it
in concentrated conversation with those receptive to his ideas.
So, as he speaks with the perceptive Eleanor, he says, " 'I was
saying we do not know ourselves, ordinary people; and if we do
not know ourselves, how then can we make religions, laws,
that—' he used his hands as people do who find language
obdurate, 'that—' 'That fit—that fit,' she said . . ." (281). And
when she shows surprise that he should put in words her own

feelings about the limitations of factual truth, he answers,
" 'Why is that odd? . . . We all think the same things; only we
do not say them' " (282). Having thus revealed his belief in
underlying unity, Nicholas is almost ready for the summary
speech that leaps to his lips at moments of greatest communion,
a speech that would catch the vision and make it fast. When
interrupted, as Bernard was always interrupted on the brink
of finding the perfect phrase, Nicholas can only share his understanding of the difficulty of reconciling fact and vision by
saying privately to Eleanor:

> "The soul—the whole being." . . . He hollowed his
> hands as if to enclose a circle. "It wishes to expand; to
> adventure; to form—new combinations? . . . Whereas now,"
> —he drew himself together; put his feet together; he
> looked like an old lady who is afraid of mice—"this is how
> we live, screwed up into one hard little, tight little—
> knot?" (296).

In this world of insistent fact, vision cannot be disseminated
through speeches but must be fought for, struggled for, individually. Each character must find his own way of infusing life
with meaning and cannot be assisted by those directly in
touch with vision. So Sara and Nicholas remain eccentrics who
can share their insights only with those who already perceive
the vision dimly.

If the life of vision cannot be taught but must grow naturally
out of fact, it can be perceived as a whole by those whose lives
are large enough to encompass both fact and vision. Eleanor
Pargiter gradually assumes this comprehensive role in *The
Years*. Although her unifying function is similar to that of
Mrs. Ramsay or Bernard, and although all three characters
recognize the need for ceaseless effort to achieve the all-inclusive vision, Eleanor inhabits a world so bounded by actual fact
that her struggle takes on more realistic overtones than the
carefully expressed but seldom demonstrated exertions of the
other two. To begin with, as the eldest daughter of a large
motherless family, Eleanor is forced into domesticity and must
act as wife and mother without the compensation of love and

unity that would exist were the children her own and the father not her father but her husband. Her sister Milly thinks of Eleanor as "the soother, the maker-up of quarrels, the buffer between her and the intensities and strifes of family life" (14); and although this role as mediator will eventually strengthen her ability to reconcile the fact and the vision, Eleanor will find this duty burdensome for many years. Whenever she drifts off in dreams, watching the sun flicker among the leaves, for example, some child clatters in and shatters her peace. The cut-and-dried aspects of family life, the most limited of all factual tasks, are always hers. She must handle the finances, a chore that gives her pain whenever she undertakes it (19, 20, 91); she must discuss facts and careers with her brothers rather than share their hidden thoughts (35); she must stay at home for years to tend her crotchety and unimaginative father and so renounce the visionary possibilities of love and marriage. But Eleanor does not belittle this demanding life. Instead, she carries her will to tackle unpleasantness beyond the limits of Abercorn Terrace and out into the world. She realizes that the bounded world cannot be wished away but must serve as the battleground upon which the war against limitation must be fought. So she does not talk "about 'the poor' as if they were people in a book" (30–31), but sets about bringing a taste of vision to their lives, building an apartment house where rents are low and where a "sunflower on the terracotta plaque" stands over the door "to signify flowers, fields in the heart of London . . ." (101). Even this little symbol of vision cracks and fades as the building develops its own leaks and sour drains, but the effort was made and must continue to be made. Eleanor senses this pattern of effort, momentary success, and disappointment in the flux of life about her when she thinks: "This was her world; here she was in her element. The streets were crowded; women were swarming in and out of shops with their shopping baskets. There was something customary, rhythmical about it . . . like rooks swooping in a field, rising and falling" (94). In an essay entitled "Reading," Virginia Woolf writes, "Through the tremor and vibration of daily custom one discerns bone and form, endurance and permanence";[16] and it is this permanence that Eleanor will slowly grow to recognize as she works her way through life.

In order to perceive the pattern that gives life its infinite meaning, Eleanor must never accept passively the ebb and flow of her days but must, like Bernard, be always ready for the unexpected, be open to the flashes of understanding when they come. Her capacity for wonder, which gives her this necessary openness of being, is demonstrated by the fact that "For some reason she always felt that she was the youngest person in an omnibus . . ." (101). Like a child, she is always ready to welcome new experience, to run off to India or rejoice in the invention of the shower bath. As a result, she is able to absorb the visionary side of life while maintaining her activities on the factual plane. At a regularly scheduled social workers' meeting, for example, "She found that her pencil could take notes quite accurately while she herself thought of something else. She seemed able to divide herself into two. One person followed the argument—and he's putting it very well, she thought; while the other . . . walked down a green glade and stopped in front of a flowering tree" (176). So, because she never grows a hard shell of limited selfhood that is immune to change, she never becomes a single definable person, bound by fact. Even in her old age she thinks, "Oughtn't a life to be something you could handle and produce?—a life of seventy odd years. But I've only the present moment . . ." (366).

Because she has never limited herself to one life only, Eleanor is able to absorb both the concrete and the spiritual and see each world in the other. So, as she looks at an old ink-corroded walrus that has become a permanent fixture in Abercorn Terrace, she thinks, "That solid object might survive them all. If she threw it away it would still exist somewhere or other. But she never had thrown it away because it was a part of other things—her mother for example. . . . She drew on her blotting paper; a dot with strokes raying out round it" (91). This odd geometric symbol, like Ralph Denham's similar drawing in *Night and Day*, represents the visionary transcendence of fact in which solid objects seem to contain a limitless world. So, after doing valiant battle with limitation, Eleanor can now and again crack off the shell of the bounded world and find the infinite vision beneath. These moments of infinite awareness flicker up and die down throughout her life and often come at moments of greatest limitation. When she hears the news of Parnell's death, for example, "Suddenly the whole scene froze into immobility. A man was joined to a pillar; a lion was joined to a man; they seemed stilled, connected, as if they would never move again" (113); and at this moment she becomes conscious of the coexistence of "two worlds; one flowing in wide sweeps overhead, the other tip-tapping circumscribed upon the pavement" (114). Then again, in the midst of the war, she feels that "Things seemed to have lost their skins; to be freed from some surface hardness . . ." (287). Of course such moments always fade before they can be fully grasped. Just as she sees "the only point that was of any importance" (178) someone interrupts. Yet Eleanor never loses her resilience and always fights back against the interrupting force, be it poverty or the monumental bullying of a dictator (330).

As the fragments of understanding collect in her life, Eleanor tries more and more to find a pattern into which they may fit. She reads Renan because "She had always wanted to know about Christianity—how it began; what it meant, originally. God is love, The kingdom of Heaven is within us, sayings like that . . . what did they mean?" (154). Such sayings seem to support her growing sense that life has a rhythm that underlies the superficial, meaningless restrictions and confusions of daily living. "Things can't go on for ever, she thought. Things pass, things change, she thought, looking up at the ceiling. And where are we going? Where? Where? . . ." (213). As the novel draws to a close, Eleanor experiences her greatest revelation in which the growing pattern emerges clear and sharp for a moment and these questions are answered by others more perceptive:

Does everything then come over again a little differently? she thought. If so, is there a pattern; a theme, recurring, like music; half remembered, half foreseen? . . . a gigantic pattern, momentarily perceptible? The thought gave her extreme pleasure: that there was a pattern. But who makes it? Who thinks it? Her mind slipped. She could not finish her thought (369).

If, for the moment, the vision fades, it soon returns, and Eleanor holds "her hands hollowed; she felt that she wanted to enclose the present moment; to make it stay; to fill it fuller and fuller, with the past, the present and the future, until it shone, whole, bright, deep with understanding" (428). Virginia Woolf has prepared the way for this moment with great care. She has substantiated Eleanor's theory of pattern symbolically with leitmotifs that recur "like music" and that often *are* music. She has let her characters relive moments, repeat actions, reiterate conversations nearly word for word, until their lives have made a pattern linking past to present in an unchanging rhythm. Now all that remains is to suggest the continuation of this rhythm into the future. This she accomplishes within the story by showing us the minds of the younger generation, represented by Peggy and North Pargiter; and symbolically by ending the novel on a note of recurrence and renewal.

If the older generation consists of those who bow to facts and those who sense the vision, the younger generation carries on this same endless duality. Peggy Pargiter is one who cannot see beyond the ugliness and limitations of the moment, who looks at people as "sparks of life enclosed in . . . separate bodies" (334). She herself recognizes her limitation when she thinks, "I'm good . . . at fact-collecting. But what makes up a person—(she hollowed her hand), the circumference,—no, I'm not good at that" (353). She cannot see the stars as symbols of eternity and does not pretend to. To her they are "little bits of frosty steel. And the moon . . . is a polished dishcover" (360). Because she cannot sense a deeper reality below the world of action in which she plays her difficult part as doctor, life seems to her an endless succession of "Death; or worse— tyranny; brutality; torture; the fall of civilisation; the end of freedom" (388). Like Mr. Ramsay she refuses to "give up thinking, and drift and dream" (388); for she recognizes the need to do what one can to fight this horror. Nevertheless, life is summed up for her by the pessimistic thoughts of a man who writes, *"La médiocrité de l'univers m'étonne et me révolte . . . la pauvreté des êtres humains m'anéantit"* (383). Yet even she, by facing the misery squarely in the monsters that the party games create from composite drawings, gains respite from sorrow in laughter, and catches a glimpse of "a state of being, in which there was real laughter, real happiness, and this fractured world was whole; whole, vast, and free" (390).

If Peggy represents the new generation of those who see and are driven by the objective world around them and seldom recognize any pattern or meaning in their busy lives, her brother North is her spiritual opposite. Having spent most of his adulthood as a sheep rancher in Africa where he existed as an integral part of the natural world, he has gained a foundation of belief in unity with which he must tackle the hostile, divisive London world. As he enters the confusion, he recognizes the barriers of isolation that appear, not in the fields, but in a crowd of hard-shelled human beings, saying, "hills and trees accept one; human beings reject one" (403). He sees, too, that the world of the Pargiters is generally limited to a narrow social band and does not embrace universal man (404). Thus, as a seeker of unity among the divided, "He had a feeling that he was no one and nowhere in particular" (311). Not until he dines with Sara, to whom he can confide his sense of pattern and speak of Nicholas's theories of limitation that have been discussed so often (". . . how can we make laws, religions, that fit, that fit, when we don't know ourselves?" [315]) is North able to face the final reunion at Delia's. Taking up his hat and starting toward the party, he watches as his action becomes a symbol of his reconciling his African vision of unity with the unordered world of London society: "was there always, he thought, . . . something that came to the surface, inappropriately, unexpectedly, from the depths of people, and made ordinary actions, ordinary words, expressive of the whole being, so that he felt, as he turned to follow Renny to Delia's party, as if he were riding to the relief of a besieged garrison across a desert?" (349). Once there, he, like Eleanor, begins to see a pattern emerge, a pattern of being and action that includes Rose Pargiter's campaigns and Sara's poetry. "But a world, he thought, that was all one jelly, one mass, would be a rice pudding world, a white counterpane world. To keep the emblems and tokens of North Pargiter—the man Maggie laughs at; the Frenchman holding his hat; but at the same time spread out, make a new ripple in human consciousness, be the bubble and the stream, the stream and the bubble—myself and the world together . . ." (410).

Thus Peggy and North together demonstrate the validity of that pattern that Eleanor grasped for a moment, and when the vision that she holds in her cupped hands begins to fade, the dawning future carries that vision beyond the boundaries of the novel: "It's useless, she thought, opening her hands. It must drop. It must fall. And then? she thought. For her too there would be the endless night; the endless dark. She looked ahead of her as though she saw opening in front of her a very long dark tunnel. But, thinking of the dark, something baffled her; in fact it was growing light" (428). The vision never dies. Dawn always follows night. As this story, so full of disappointments and failures, draws to a conclusion, it seems not to end, but to begin again. Just as the first scene at Abercorn Terrace was marked by a cab driving up to the house next door, so in the final scene, as day begins to dawn and "the sky above the houses wore an air of extraordinary beauty, simplicity and peace" (435), a cab drives up again. "And now?" (435) asks Eleanor. For the pattern has begun again and life stretches new and full before her.

So *The Years,* like *The Waves,* ends on a note of vision, pattern, and renewal of effort. The world of fact has been accepted and then tamed by revelation and repetition. Yet it cannot be denied that the victory has been won at a great price; for the constant interruptions, the sudden, unexplained deaths, the war, the ugliness, each takes its toll on the sense of unity. The result is an uncomfortable tension between the intentional disorder and the symbolic order, a pull of fact against vision that robs the pattern of much of its impact. In *Between the Acts,* Virginia Woolf's last novel, the balance of the two worlds is achieved more successfully as the disruptive elements of life are deemphasized and are allowed to sink naturally into the larger pattern of effort and vision where they belong.

8

Between the Acts

BOTH because *Between the Acts* is Virginia Woolf's last novel and because it contains so many of her familiar themes and techniques, refined and polished through frequent use, it is difficult not to see in it a summary statement of all that has come before. Virginia Woolf herself thought the book "more quintessential than the others. More milk skimmed off. A richer pat, certainly a fresher than that misery *The Years*."[1] So although this novel may have been her finale only through circumstance, it makes a fitting and proper closing chapter to her work.

Although the setting of *Between the Acts* and the poetry with which its prose is saturated set this book among Virginia Woolf's visionary novels, the darkness of *The Years* still broods over it. Many critics have seen this note of pessimism in the light of her suicide, which followed close on the heels of this her final work, and have concluded that the "present," which comes "between the acts" of past and future, is the last glimmering of peace before the ultimate holocaust. C. Basham says that "the present of 1939 is precariously balanced—or hemmed in—between a trivial past and an ominous future";[2] and David Daiches, that "history flowering into the present is no story of happy fulfillment and heroic promise: the past has made the present fragmentary and the present has made the past petty."[3] Others who concentrate on the dark side of this novel are Bernard Blackstone,[4] J. K. Johnstone,[5] Jean Guiguet,[6] and Melvin Friedman.[7] But the more perceptive approaches to this novel are those that do not let the events surrounding it—the war, and Virginia Woolf's own suicide—engulf the theme of hope that lies at the heart of *Between the Acts*. A. D. Moody, for example, says that in this novel Virginia Woolf, "accepting that the human condition is unmitigably one of flux and process, had sought out and affirmed such positive powers as men have to control and construct their lives within nature."[8] Those critics who join him in examining *Between the Acts* from a purely literary point of view have illuminated many of the elusive themes and symbols that the novel contains.

In attempting to explain the meaning of the title, Joan Bennett has offered three equally valid suggestions: that "between the acts" refers to the human comedy played out between the acts of the pageant, that the interval in question is the lull between the two World Wars, or that the entire novel is an interlude in love between Giles and Isa Oliver.[9] John Graham has offered yet another interesting interpretation, saying that "the novel as a whole is a pageant occurring literally *between the acts* of the drama which the reader himself plays before and after reading it."[10] Mr. Graham also has some enlightening thoughts on the pageant itself, seeing in it the theme of return, and saying, "The play is as old as the swallows coming ages ago; and as new as the swallows swooping above them [the audience] in the present moment."[11] Because this play is so obviously central to the theme of the novel, a great deal of attention has been paid to its meaning, and the consensus agrees with Graham that the play links present inseparably to past. Ann Yanko Wilkerson and Marilyn Zorn[12] have shown the greatest perception in their studies of *Between the Acts,* especially in their analyses of the pageant, which may be summarized by Mrs. Wilkerson's statement that "drama becomes . . . not only a principle of unity in the novel, but a diagram for the process of unification by which Art, Life and History are created, both within the novel and without."[13]

In her own discussion of *Between the Acts,* Virginia Woolf sees the book in terms of " 'We' . . . the composed of many different things . . . we all life, all art, all waifs and strays—a rambling capricious but somehow unified whole" (suspension points are Virginia Woolf's).[14] In order to achieve this sense of totality, she turns again to the technique used in *Mrs. Dalloway* of presenting characters who symbolize the opposing factual and visionary sides of life. Because she is more practiced in this use of symbol, or perhaps because her theories on the dualistic world have become clear-cut through constant examination, the characters in *Between the Acts* are more easily recognizable as representatives of reason, faith, action, or vision than their earlier counterparts.[15] The net result of presenting a many-sided cast of characters is shown in miniature in this barn scene:

> The Barn was empty. Mice slid in and out of holes or stood upright, nibbling. Swallows were busy with straw in pockets of earth in the rafters. Countless beetles and insects of various sorts burrowed in the dry wood. A stray bitch had made the dark corner where the sacks stood a lying-in ground for her puppies. All these eyes, expanding and narrowing, some adapted to light, others to darkness, looked from different angles and edges.[16]

So the many eyes of the characters, focused together on the pageant that makes up the bulk of the book, add fact to vision, art to reality, mind to body, and so form a unified whole.

In *The Years* Virginia Woolf followed the lives of several successive generations of a single family in order to show how everything repeats itself a little differently as time passes. *Between the Acts* presents the same pattern of generations on a smaller scale, with Lucy Swithin and Bartholomew Oliver representing the late Victorian/early Edwardian past; Giles and Isa Oliver and their guests, Mrs. Manresa and William Dodge, portraying the generation of the present; and little George Oliver giving hints of what the future holds.

Bart and his sister Lucy represent those opposing aspects of fact and vision—reason and faith. From the very beginning Virginia Woolf makes it plain that although "Nothing changed their affection; no argument; no fact; no truth" (26), and although the two respect each other's attitudes toward life, "What she saw he didn't; what he saw she didn't—and so on, *ad infinitum"* (26). Like Mr. and Mrs. Ramsay in *To the Light-house,* this pair stands opposite but inseparable, combining the antipodal elements of reality. That their antithetical identities may be summarized as reason and faith is indicated early in the novel in this brief interchange of thoughts: " 'It's very unsettled. It'll rain, I'm afraid. We can only pray,' she added, and fingered her crucifix. 'And provide umbrellas,' said her brother" (23). Even though Lucy's life is centered in the Christian church, there is no doubt that her role includes all the nuances of Virginia Woolf's visionary, while Bart Oliver stands firm upon the rock of fact. He himself describes their differences by saying that "she belonged to the unifiers; he to the separatists" (118); while Lucy sees their lives this way: "He would carry the torch of reason till it went out in the darkness of the cave. For herself, every morning, kneeling, she protected her vision" (205–6).

All of Bart's thoughts and actions on the day that the novel describes combine to give the reader a picture of a man who has chosen the factual way to truth. " 'Are we really . . . a hundred miles from the sea?' " asks Isa. " 'Thirty-five only,' her father-in-law said, as if he had whipped a tape measure from his pocket and measured it exactly" (29). This precision of thought carries over into his enjoyment of the pageant, for his greatest applause goes to the personification of Reason in the scene presenting the eighteenth century. " 'Hear! Hear!' he cried. 'Bravo! Bravo!' Thus encouraged Reason spoke out" (123). Because he represents all factual truth for his generation, Bart Oliver includes in his admiration not only clarity of mind but also solidity of flesh, blessing "the power of the human body to make the earth fruitful" (119). His awareness of all aspects of the concrete external world gives him the insight to understand that once the pageant is over, all the author wants is "darkness in the mud; a whiskey and soda at the pub . . ." (203). Because his perception is limited to the physical world around him, however, he cannot understand the peace and joy his sister derives from contemplation of spiritual truth. " 'O sister swallow, O sister swallow,/ How can thy heart be full of the spring?' " (115) he asks, adapting Swinburne's poem to his own thoughts. Yet if he cannot share his sister's beliefs, he can sense that her God is not an old man in the sky. "It was, he supposed, more of a force or a radiance, controlling the thrush and the worm; the tulip and the hound; and himself, too, an old man with swollen veins" (25).

If Bart, then, symbolizes intellectual fact and appreciation of the fecundity of the body, Lucy Swithin embodies vision and the unifying power of the spirit. Most critics agree on this point, and Margaret Church even sees in the name Swithin ("S-within") an indication that "Mrs. Woolf saw her as a person whose inner recognition of reality was paramount."[17] One exception is Jean O. Love who allows the negative connotations of the church scene in *The Voyage Out* to flood over into this final novel, making Lucy, in her religious life, "a symbol of equivocation more than of unity, an expression of dialectic and not of synthesis."[18] But faith per se receives little criticism in Virginia Woolf's novels. Only the narrow-sighted, half-hearted, or self-centered interpretations of Christianity are subject to her censure. After all, Mrs. Ramsay did identify herself with the mysticism of Roman Catholicism in *To the Lighthouse,* and Eleanor studied Renan in *The Years.* So each new presentation of Christianity must be accepted on its own terms and analyzed in context. The opening description of Mrs. Swithin suggests one reason for Virginia Woolf's decision to make her a practicing Christian. "So she sat down to morning tea, like any other old lady with a high nose, thin cheeks, a ring on her finger and the usual trappings of rather shabby but gallant old age, which included in her case a cross gleaming gold on her breast" (10). Because she is a carry-over from an early age, Mrs. Swithin can validly incorporate her sense of unity into the formal structure of the Church. The very house she lives in, Pointz Hall, has seen the more solemn aspects of life undergo a "kitchen change" (32) in time: "For the house before the Reformation, like so many houses in that neighborhood, had a chapel; and the chapel had become a larder, changing . . . as religion changed" (32). So Mrs. Swithin represents the old approach to vision and works to keep her belief in unity alive by trotting off to church every morning. The younger generation, although they find her particular form of vision unsuited to their own lives, appreciate her attempts to bring the divided world together.

> She was off, they guessed, on a circular tour of the imagination—one-making. Sheep, cows, grass, trees, ourselves—all are one. If discordant, producing harmony— if not to us, to a gigantic ear attached to a gigantic head. And thus—she was smiling benignly—the agony of the particular sheep, cow, or human being is necessary; and so—she was beaming seraphically at the gilt vane in the distance—we reach the conclusion that *all* is harmony, could we hear it. And we shall. Her eyes now rested on the white summit of a cloud. Well, if the thought gave her comfort, William and Isa smiled across her, let her think it (175).

The fact that Lucy's religion is anything but passive gives added weight to her beliefs—not that she ever attempts conversion, but that she resists any threat to her vision, be it her brother's taunts or menacing clouds hovering over the site for the pageant.

Like Eleanor, the youngest on the omnibus; like Mrs. Ramsay, sensing herself a wanderer in distant worlds; like Rhoda, incorporeal; Lucy Swithin always approaches life full of expectation and never seems to be limited to a single space or time. "The door trembled and stood half open. That was Lucy's way of coming in—as if she did not know what she would find. Really! It was her brother! And his dog! She seemed to see them for the first time. Was it that she had no body? Up in the clouds, like an air ball, her mind touched ground now and then with a shock of surprise" (116). If she transcends space in her semitransparency, she also increases "the bounds of the moment by flights into past or future; or sidelong down corridors and alleys . . ." (9). So she can begin by wondering why stale bread is easier to cut than fresh, skip from yeast to alcohol to inebriation to Bacchus and end up lying "under purple lamps in a vineyard in Italy . . ." (34) centuries before the time she stands in the kitchen, cutting sandwiches. Because she can embrace infinity in a moment, she recognizes the limitations of speech as a means to express man's most important thoughts (55); she shares her vision, creates it in others who need it most, in actions as well as in words. For example, when she senses that William Dodge is feeling isolated among her other guests, she takes him away to see the house and soothes the pain of separation by suggesting that "we have other lives, I think, I hope. . . . We live in others. . . . We live in things" (70). This hint of a pattern extending beyond the single life expands as the two wander up the stairs and through the empty halls, until, when she says, simply, " 'The nursery' . . . words raised themselves and became symbolical. 'The cradle of our race,' she seemed to say" (71). Her suggestion that each generation continues the pattern begun by the one before has already been substantiated by the fact that little George Oliver, her grandnephew, has just that day begun to sense her vision as he watches a single flower blossom into an entire world (11).

As Virginia Woolf's novels have progressed, the importance of pattern in life and in history has grown to represent the concrete manifestation of vision. So when Lucy demonstrates her awareness of this endless design, her role as "one-maker" is no longer in doubt. In her first appearance in *Between the Acts,* and in her last, she is shown reading her favorite book—an Outline of History—that tells of

> rhododendron forests in Piccadilly; when the entire continent, not then, she understood, divided by a channel, was all one; populated, she understood, by elephant-bodied, seal-necked, heaving, surging, slowly writhing, and, she supposed, barking monsters; the iguanodon, the mammoth, and the mastodon; from whom presumably, she thought . . . we descend (8–9).

Because she recognizes that men have not changed in essence from their first appearance on the earth, she understands the symbolic meaning of the pageant. " 'The Victorians,' Mrs. Swithin mused. 'I don't believe,' she said with her odd little smile, 'that there ever were such people. Only you and me and William dressed differently' " (174–75). When someone asks,

" 'Was it an old play? Was it a new play?' " (109), she answers somewhat enigmatically, pointing at the swallows, " 'Look!' " (109); " 'They come every year,' she said, 'the same birds' " (101). " 'They come every year,' said Mrs. Swithin, ignoring the fact that she spoke to the empty air. 'From Africa.' As they had come, she supposed, when the Barn was a swamp" (103). Thus the swallows, the Outline of History, the pageant, and the people at Pointz Hall are all part of the pattern. By joining in the play, either as actors or audience, the characters in *Between the Acts* unconsciously reaffirm their unity with all other people and times. And Lucy understands. " 'What a small part I've had to play!' " she exclaims to the authoress of the pageant. " 'But you've made me feel I could have played . . . Cleopatra!' " (153). If the others are puzzled or despairing at the fragmentation of humanity displayed in the act entitled "The Present Time. Ourselves" (178) and need someone to interpret the scene for them, Lucy senses the pattern remaining firm below the surface (205).

If Bart and Lucy, in their roles as opposites living in the past, retain their affection for one another while maintaining their contrary ways of life, their nephew and niece do the same. Their relationship is a combination of love and hate (48), for the husband stands immovably for action and physicality while his wife represents contemplation and poetry. Because neither of them has faith in any established method of applying these theories to life, they both experience a greater sense of helplessness than do Bart and Lucy. Still these two, though having suffered a kitchen change from the reason and faith of their elders, continue to embody the opposing worlds of fact and vision.

Physically, Giles Oliver is the perfect specimen of a sturdy man of action. "His hair curled; far from running away, as many chins did, his was firm; the nose straight, if short; the eyes, of course, with that hair, blue; and finally to make the type complete, there was something fierce, untamed, in the expression . . ." (47). Because he believes in physical action as the solution to all problems, his position in life surrounds him with frustration. "Given his choice, he would have chosen to farm. But he was not given his choice. So one thing led to another; and the conglomeration of things pressed you flat; held you fast, like a fish in water" (47). Spending every day chained to a desk, he must come home and dress up in flannels and a blazer, play the host, while violent events on the continent work up to World War II and he is helpless to do anything about it. His pent-up desire to act bursts out in little abortive gestures, anger with his contemplative Aunt Lucy, for example. "At any moment guns would rake that land into furrows; planes splinter Bolney Minster into smithereens and blast the Folly. He, too, loved the view. And blamed Aunt Lucy, looking at views, instead of—doing what?" (53). Because she is his opposite, he often finds himself "taking sides with authority against his aunt" (161) and thereby easing his guilt, brought on by spiritual paralysis. Like Mr. Ramsay, he damns those who fly in the face of facts. Indeed, there is quite a resemblance between that irritable scholar and this young stockbroker. Giles remains "like a stake in the tide of the flowing company" (96) and quotes Cowper to himself (85), linking his approach to life with that of the uncompromising Mr. Ramsay. But while the earlier man tries to subdue the world by mental exercise, Giles Oliver resorts to kicking stones along the road and symbolically conquering lust, perversion, and cowardice by this child's game. Action or reason alone is never enough to bring the world to order, so that when Giles is actually faced with an example of the horrors of life, he is not equipped to handle it successfully. As he kicks his pebble toward its imaginary goal, thinking of the war and his own inaction, he is confronted with a chance to prove himself.

> There, couched in the grass, curled in an olive green ring, was a snake. Dead? No, choked with a toad in its mouth. The snake was unable to swallow; the toad was unable to die. A spasm made the ribs contract; blood oozed. It was birth the wrong way round—a monstrous inversion. So, raising his foot, he stamped on them. The mass crushed and

slithered. The white canvas on his tennis shoes was
bloodstained and sticky. But it was action. Action relieved
him (99).

Such destruction, as James Hafley has pointed out, "moves
away from consciousness and creative perception to material
action, in a path opposite to that of the vital impetus."[19] This
is the side of Giles that creates hatred in his visionary wife.
" 'No,' said Isa, as plainly as words could say it. 'I don't admire
you,' and looked, not at his face, but at his feet. 'Silly little
boy, with blood on his boots' " (111). Before the two can be
reconciled in love at the end of the novel, Giles must find a
means to purge away his sense of being merely an ineffectual
spectator of life.

Mrs. Manresa, the "wild child of nature" (41), is the
woman who brings Giles back into the ebb and flow of things.
Almost from the very moment she descends upon the family,
"a thread united them—visible, invisible, like those threads,
now seen, now not, that unite trembling grass blades in autumn
before the sun rises" (55–56). "And she was a thorough good
sort," thinks Giles, "making him feel less of an audience, more
of an actor, going round the Barn in her wake" (108). Who
is this woman who extracts the knot of frustration from Giles's
mind and leaves him free to rejoin his wife? She is the representative of the unashamed, natural body and brings a sense
of unchecked instinct to the refined life of Pointz Hall. "Vul-
gar she was in her gestures, in her whole person, over-sexed,
over-dressed for a picnic. But what a desirable, at least valuable, quality it was—for everybody felt, directly she spoke,
'She's said it, she's done it, not I,' and could take advantage of
the breach of decorum of the fresh air that blew in, to follow
like leaping dolphins in the wake of an ice-breaking vessel"
(41). Like Jinny in *The Waves,* she savors every sensation,
pours rich cream and brown sugar into her coffee, then looks
over the rim of her cup at Giles before she drinks. "Looking
was part of drinking. Why waste sensation, she seemed to
ask, why waste a single drop that can be pressed out of this
ripe, this melting, this adorable world?" (56). Mrs. Manresa's

love of sensual experience is not limited to Jinny's social world but shares in Susan's country life as well; for while enjoying all the civilized pleasures, she also claims to be a wild child of nature and loves to take off her stays and roll in the grass. "She had given up dealing with her figure and thus gained freedom" (42). Therefore she combines in herself all the physicality of life, without flowing over into child-bearing and so becoming one of those who foster life's perpetuity. Because she is all body, she of all the members of the audience is the only one to face herself unflinchingly in the mirrors of "Present Day. Ourselves." While others shrink back from a sudden fragmentary glimpse of themselves, "Alone she preserved unashamed her identity, and faced without blinking herself. Calmly she reddened her lips" (186).

If Giles Oliver is isolated in his paralyzed force and needs Mrs. Manresa to assure him that he is part of the active world, his wife Isa is even more divorced from those around her because she lives like Lucy Swithin in a spiritual world but without that sense of community felt by the older woman. When Isa first enters the scene of *Between the Acts,* she, like Lucy, appears to be awash in fluidity and to be startled by the presence of others. "She came in like a swan swimming its way; then was checked and stopped; was surprised to find people there; and lights burning" (4). Where her husband approaches the world through the body and is marked by a series of stillborn actions, she experiences life through her spirit and flounders about in directionless attempts at love and poetry. Only after the pageant and the day itself have taught them that there is order in life will they begin to be reconciled to each other and to the world around them.

Isa's initial dream of love is fruitlessly centered, not upon her husband, about whom her feelings are ambiguous, but upon Rupert Haines, a man who once "had handed her a cup and a racquet—that was all. But in his ravaged face she always felt mystery; and in his silence, passion" (5). Although their relationship never progresses beyond social gesture, Isa sees in him the poetic fulfillment she has been unable to achieve. At the same time she recognizes that her daydream will never approach reality; for when her father-in-law quotes several random lines of Byron she thinks: "The words made two rings, perfect rings, that floated them, herself and Haines, like two swans down stream. But his snow-white breast was circled with a tangle of dirty duckweed; and she too, in her webbed feet was entangled, by her husband, the stockbroker" (5). The complicated and divided feelings she has about the two men are brought to the surface when she sits at her dressing-table, looking into the mirror: " 'In love,' was in her eyes. But outside, on the washstand, on the dressing-table, among the silver boxes and tooth-brushes, was the other love; love for her husband, the stockbroker—'The father of my children...' " (14). She knows nothing of Mr. Haines and so can weave around him in her mind a love that is never tarnished by the limitations of reality. On the other hand, the love that is imprisoned by concrete places and people is also the productive love that brings continuity through children. "Love. Hate. Peace. Three emotions made the ply of human life" (92), thinks Isa. Her love for Rupert Haines, because it is totally detached from the external world, is the peaceful kind of love that requires no effort to maintain. Her husband's love, which confines her to the exacting physical world of active love and hatred, demands of her participation in actuality. Although this second love is often painful, it is the emotion of fulfillment; for by requiring constant effort on her part, it forces her to connect her world of vision to her husband's struggle for action and so leads toward that reconciliation that keeps the pattern of life alive.

Isa's visionary nature manifests itself not only in her search for love, but also in her efforts to catch the truth in poetry. "She used to stay when she was a child, when she had the whooping cough, with an uncle, a clergyman; who wore a skull cap; and never did anything; didn't even preach; but made up poems, walking in his garden, saying them aloud" (50–51). If Lucy finds her vision in Christianity, Isa senses it in poetry; and the old poetizing clergyman uncle bridges the gap between the two seekers of changeless truth. Isa's poetry, like the moments of understanding experienced by all of Virginia Woolf's earlier characters, is always interrupted by external reality. " 'Where we know not, where we go not, neither know nor care,' she hummed. 'Flying, rushing through the ambient, incandescent, summer silent . . .' The rhyme was 'air.' She put down her brush. She took up the telephone. . . . 'There to lose what binds us here,' she murmured. 'Soles. Filletted. In time for lunch please,' she said aloud" (15). So phrases about incorporeality combine with orders for lunch, bringing the two contrary worlds together. Because she feels her husband could never understand this urge to poetry, Isa keeps her half-written lines in a book "bound like an account book in case Giles suspected. 'Abortive,' was the word that expressed her" (15). Alone, she cannot complete her vision, but her fragmentary verses suggest that her search may lead her toward fulfillment: ". . . Isa hummed: 'What do I ask? To fly away, from night and day, and issue where—no partings are—but eye meets eye— and . . .'" (83). This half-seen world where "no partings are," where "unblowing, ungrowing are the roses" and "Change is not . . . nor furtive findings and feelings, where hand seeks hand . . ." (155), is the world of total vision. It may be achieved in part by poetry, in part by love, or by death, and only by constant striving. It demands a wide perspective a comprehensive view that the solitary individual usually perceives only dimly and in flashes of understanding. The pageant of *Beween the Acts* will provide this broad view of life, but Isa will not see it until she loses her sense of isolation. Like Rhoda in *The Waves,* Isa pictures the rest of humanity sporting and playing together while she is left behind. "I grieving stay," she thinks. "Alone I linger, I pluck the bitter herb by the ruined wall, the churchyard wall . . ." (112). Because she thinks herself the last little donkey in a long caravan crossing the desert, she often longs for death in her loneliness. Yet the beauty of life still holds her, the "may tree or nut tree," the thrush singing "on the trembling spray," and "dipping and diving as if he skimmed waves in the air, the yellow woodpecker" (104). So she, like her husband, needs someone to assure her that she is not alone in her thoughts of life, to prove the validity of her dreams as Mrs. Manresa substantiated Giles's hope for action.

The man who serves as Isa's double is William Dodge. "A poor specimen he was," Isa thinks at first; "afraid to stick up for his own beliefs—just as she was afraid, of her husband. Didn't she write her poetry in a book bound like an account book lest Giles might suspect?" (50). As the day proceeds, the spiritual kinship of these two becomes more evident. Like Isa, William lives in a world divorced from the body, and when he overhears her whispering poetry to herself, "He smiled. She smiled. They were conspirators; each murmuring some song my uncle taught me" (105). A woman who divorces herself from action in the world is more acceptable to society in general than the man who does the same, so that William's isolation is even greater than Isa's. Giles, for example, thinks the man "A toady; a lickspittle; not a down-right plain man of his senses; but a teaser and twitcher; a fingerer of sensations; picking and choosing; dillying and dallying; not a man to have straightforward love for a woman . . ." (60). The fact that William is one of Virginia Woolf's homosexuals makes him akin to Isa in his abortive approach to love, and she can sympathize with his trouble rather than condemn him as does Giles. "Isabella guessed the word that Giles had not spoken. Well, was it wrong if he was that word? Why judge each other? Do we know each other? Not here, not now. But somewhere . . . somewhere surely one sun would shine and all, without a doubt, would be clear" (61). But Isa's unspoken sympathy is not enough. It takes the powerful insight and active under-standing of Lucy Swithin to poultice William's wounds. " 'I took you,' " she apologizes to him as they tour the house, " 'away from your friends, William, because I felt wound tight here. . . .' She touched her bony forehead . . ." (73). Her kind-ness and half-spoken discernment make him wish to kneel to her, as Charles Tansley wished to kneel to Mrs. Ramsay:

> . . . her eyes in their caves of bone were still lambent. He
> saw her eyes only. And he wished to kneel before her, to

kiss her hand, and to say: "At school they held me under a bucket of dirty water, Mrs. Swithin; when I looked up, the world was dirty, Mrs. Swithin; so I married; but my child's not my child, Mrs. Swithin. I'm a half-man, Mrs. Swithin; a flickering, mind-divided little snake in the grass, Mrs. Swithin; as Giles saw; but you've healed me . . ." (73).

There is no need, however, to confess or explain, for "She had guessed his trouble" (71) and has shared her knowledge with him. After the pageant, which unites the entire audience, consciously or unconsciously, in this same knowledge of unity, William thanks Lucy Swithin for the gift that is borne out by the play. " 'And we musn't, my brother says, thank the author . . .' " says Lucy. " 'So I thank you,' he said. He took her hand and pressed it" (207).

The suggestion that human history is a repeated pattern, that Giles and Isa, Mrs. Manresa and William, are merely variations on the lives of Bart and Lucy, is supported by the world these characters live in. The novel opens: "It was a summer's night and they were talking, in the big room with the windows open to the garden, about the cesspool" (3). The fact that this modern convenience is only part of a continuous chain of marks upon the landscape is soon made clear, since, according to Bart Oliver, "the site they had chosen for the cesspool was, if he had heard aright, on the Roman road. From an aeroplane, he said, you could still see, plainly marked, the scars made by the Britons; by the Romans; by the Elizabethan manor house; and by the plough, when they ploughed the hill to grow wheat in the Napoleonic wars" (4). And Pointz Hall, the home of the Olivers, is still the same as it was many years before. "The Guide Book still told the truth. 1830 was true in 1939" (52). Of course small changes have been made, chapels become larders, cars replace carriages, but the variations are minor, and simply melt into the body of the whole just as in the pond outside. "Water, for hundreds of years, had silted down into the hollow, and lay there four or five feet deep over a black cushion of mud" (43).

It is soon made clear that without the presence of the people who live and work here, the pattern would fade, for visionary repetition depends on human effort. "The fire greyed, then glowed, and the tortoiseshell butterfly beat on the lower pane of the window; beat, beat, beat; repeating that if no human being ever came, never, never, never, the books would be mouldy, the fire out and the tortoiseshell butterfly dead on the pane" (17). But people do come and keep the great design in motion. Bond, the cowman, seems to have always been part of the landscape: "he was like a withered willow, bent over a stream, all its leaves shed, and in his eyes the whimsical flow of the waters" (28). Even the Olivers, relative newcomers to Pointz Hall, repeat the same seasonal actions year by year:

> "I've been nailing the placard on the Barn," she [Lucy] said, giving him [Bart] a little pat on the shoulder.
> The words were like the first peal of a chime of bells. As the first peals, you hear the second; as the second peals, you hear the third. So when Isa heard Mrs. Swithin say: "I've been nailing the placard on the Barn," she knew she would say next:
> "For the pageant."
> And he would say:
> "Today? By Jupiter! I'd forgotten!" (21-22).

Because of the activity of the inhabitants of Pointz Hall, butterflies will not beat themselves to death against the windowpanes, but will become part of the repeated pattern of life.

> In the summer there were always butterflies; fritillaries darting through; Red Admirals feasting and floating; cabbage whites, unambitiously fluttering round a bush, like muslin milkmaids, content to spend a life there. Butterfly catching, for generation after generation, began there; for Bartholomew and Lucy; for Giles; for George it had begun only the day before yesterday, when, in his little green net, he had caught a cabbage white (56–57).

In this setting of recurrent history where habits and beliefs are passed perpetually from generation to generation, a play is given—a play that will mirror in miniature the world and the ages that surround it.

In an essay entitled "The Moment; Summer's Night," Virginia Woolf wrote, "One becomes aware that we are spectators and also passive participants in a pageant. And as nothing can interfere with the order, we have nothing to do but accept, and watch."[20] The pageant in *Between the Acts* embodies this metaphor, containing in its half-dozen scenes the essence of the human pattern that is reflected more subtly in the Olivers and Pointz Hall itself. It must not be forgotten, after all, that the object of this entertainment is "the illumination of our dear old church" (193), in other words, the translating of Lucy Swithin's belief in mystical unity into modern terms, accessible to the less trusting younger generation.

Miss La Trobe, the mysterious author of this little play, is as determined to uncover the roots of life in her work as her own creator is to do the same in the novel as a whole. Approaching the vast tangle of life, "She splashed into the fine mesh like a great stone into the lily pool. The criss-cross was shattered. Only the roots beneath water were of use to her" (64). "She was not merely a twitcher of individual strings; she was one who seethes wandering bodies and floating voices in a cauldron, and makes rise up from its amorphous mass a re-created world" (153). This creative process is never easy, and Miss La Trobe suffers agonies each time the thread of her meaning threatens to break. But when each important scene is over she thinks, "Hadn't she, for twenty-five minutes, made them see? A vision imparted was relief from agony . . . for one moment . . . one moment" (98). Since her message is the message of Virginia Woolf, that life is an endless pattern of human effort to discover order and meaning in existence, Miss La Trobe cannot rest when the pageant is over. "For another play always lay behind the play she had just written" (63).

As the audience assembles on the lawn and looks out onto the still-empty clearing where the play will be presented, the natural stage itself seems to intimate that the pageant will have visionary implications. The trees that line the clearing are "not too regular; but regular enough to suggest columns in a church; in a church without a roof; in an open-air ca-thedral, a place where swallows darting seemed, by the regu-larity of the trees, to make a pattern" (64–65). And if the set-ting is to be part of the pageant, the audience, too, has its own role to play. " 'Our part,' " says Bart Oliver, " 'is to be the audience. And a very important part too' " (58). His words rise up symbolically (59) and seem to say that because the audience is full of representatives of the ancient families, both peasant and gentry, the afternoon's entertainment is to embrace all people in all times, to evoke essential and critical responses in all who watch.

So the play begins. It is to be a summary of English history, seen from a literary perspective. In the background, the chorus of villagers sings of the time when England was a land of ac-tion and primitive toil: *"Cutting the roads . . . up to the hill top . . . we climbed. Down in the valley . . . sow, wild boar, hog, rhinocerous, reindeer . . . Dug ourselves in to the hill top . . . Ground roots between stones . . . Ground corn . . . till we too . . . lay under g-r-o-u-n-d"* (78). Then, after this age of physical toil, comes the time of Chaucer when the Canterbury pilgrims sing of faith and love: *"To the shrine of the Saint . . . to the tomb . . . lovers . . . believers . . . we come . . ."* (81). As the phonograph ticks off the march of time, faith follows action and is followed in turn by another age of action, the age of Elizabeth. "Everyone was clapping and laughing. From be-hind the bushes issued Queen Elizabeth—Eliza Clark, licensed to sell tobacco" (83). As the present mixes thus with the past, on stage a play within a play appears. It is full of the multi-plicity of Elizabethan times, being "About a false Duke; and a Princess disguised as a boy; then the long lost heir turns out to be the beggar, because of a mole on his cheek . . ." (88). Yet beneath the diversity of action, as the visionary Isa recognizes, "There were only two emotions: love; and hate. There was no need to puzzle out the plot" (90). So when the Princess says to the Prince, " *'My love! My lord!'* 'It was enough. Enough. Enough,' Isa repeated. All else was verbiage, repetition" (91). Repetition. That is the key to the play and to life. As the Elizabethan age passes from the scene, little "England" comes on stage and says,

> Our act is done, our scene is over.
> Past is the day of crone and lover.
> The bud has flowered; the flower has fallen.
> But soon will rise another dawning . . . (95).

An interval follows and, for a time, the vision is shattered. "The music chanted: *Dispersed are we*. It moaned: *Dispersed are we*. It lamented: *Dispersed are we . . .*" (95).

But while the voices of the audience chatter, "The inner voice, the other voice was saying: How can we deny that this brave music, wafted from the bushes, is expressive of some inner harmony?" (119). The vision will always return, the pattern of effort repeat itself. After the audience has had a chance to digest the first part of the play, the music summons them again, making them "see the hidden, join the broken" (120). When they are seated, the repeated chorus begins again, "*Digging and delving, ploughing and sowing*" (124), while a new symbolic figure comes on stage. She is Reason, the representative of the eighteenth century's approach to truth. Her narrative of peace and prosperity is accompanied by the gramophone that plays

> For peace has come to England,
> And reason now holds sway.
> What pleasure lies in dreaming
> When blue and green's the day?
> Now cast your cares behind you.
> Night passes: here is Day (124).

In case the audience cannot perceive unaided the fact that this new age is essentially no different in its aims from those that came before, the chorus reinforces the message, singing, "*the earth is always the same, summer and winter and spring; and spring and winter again; ploughing and sowing, eating and growing . . .*" (125). And the gramophone takes up the theme.

> The view repeated in its own way what the tune was saying.
> The sun was sinking; the colours were merging; and the

view was saying how after toil men rest from their labours;
how coolness comes; reason prevails; and having
unharnessed the team from the plough, neighbours dig in
cottage gardens and lean over cottage gates.

The cows, making a step forward, then standing still,
were saying the same thing to perfection (134).

So when Mrs. Otter of the End House, who played the crone in
the first scene, reappears as Lady Harpy Harridan (126), the
pattern continues, and once again a flutter of interwoven action dresses the simple fact of love in a new disguise. " 'All that
fuss about nothing!' " (138) a voice exclaims as the stylized
eighteenth-century lovers wrap their emotion in wit and rhet-
oric. "People laughed. The voice stopped. But the voice had
seen; the voice had heard" (138). Again, to confirm the
meaning that the voice descried, the chorus chants, *"Summer
and winter, autumn and spring return . . . All passes but we,
all changes . . . but we remain forever the same"* (139). But
as they sing of the rise and fall of civilizations, suddenly because the words are blown away by the wind, the message
threatens to be lost. "Miss La Trobe leant against the tree,
paralyzed. Her power had left her. . . . Illusion had failed"
(140). Then, just as the vision that art portrays totters on
the brink of destruction, nature again steps in to affirm what
art suggests:

> . . . as the illusion petered out, the cows took up the burden.
> One had lost her calf. In the very nick of time she lifted
> her great moon-eyed head and bellowed. All the great
> moon-eyed heads laid themselves back. From cow after cow
> came the same yearning bellow. The whole world was
> filled with dumb yearning. It was the primeval voice
> sounding loud in the ear of the present moment. . . . The
> cows annihilated the gap; bridged the distance; filled the
> emptiness and continued the emotion (140–41).

So the pattern has been saved, and once again an interval in the
play arrives to let the audience ponder what they have seen.
"Presumably there was time then for a stroll round the gar-

dens, even for a look over the house. Yet somehow they felt
—how could one put it—a little not quite here or there. As
if the play had jerked the ball out of the cup; as if what I
call myself was still floating unattached, and didn't settle"
(149). The vision is beginning to penetrate the present. Exposed to concentrated repetition, seeing their fellow towns-
people reappear in separate ages, the audience senses the continuity and begins to feel it permeate even the seemingly disconnected, war-threatened days of 1939.

Again the wandering spectators of life are called together
by the music. "Once more a huge symbolical figure emerged
from the bushes. It was Budge the publican; but so disguised
that even cronies who drank with him nightly failed to recognize him . . ." (160). The closer one gets to the present, the
more difficult it is to gain enough perspective to recognize the
familiar, to see the order and pattern. But Budge soon reveals
himself by his voice, while maintaining his role as a Victorian
constable. For many of the older members of the audience, the
nineteenth century is as real as the twentieth, and several old
ladies reminisce about street cries and peddlars. " 'How lovely
the clothes were' " (150), someone had said longingly as the
eighteenth century slipped from view. Now others regret the
passing of the close-knit, religious family of Victorian times.
But the years cannot be stopped: ". . . change had to come, unless things were perfect; in which case . . . they resisted Time"
(174). If an age passes, however, it soon reappears in another
form. Fact and vision alternate as the central emphasis of life:
first come the fighting, toiling Britons; then the pilgrims of
love and faith; next the Elizabethans who combine both love
and action; then the reason-directed men of the eighteenth
century; now Victorian times return again to love and faith,
represented by Lucy Swithin; and so the pattern continues.
Always at the heart of each age lies love, which resists time
since it always reflects the unity that each age seeks. Thus in
the Victorian picnic scene, though prayer and missionary work
stand out to mark the age, love is at the root, as it was in the
scene of crone and disguised heir, or the playlet in the Restora-
tion manner.

It is all very well to watch the pattern grow through earlier ages, but it takes the visionary eye to grasp with ease the fact that Elizabethans or Victorians were only people like ourselves in different clothing. As the audience returns to the programme after the strains of "Home, Sweet Home" have died away, they become suddenly apprehensive; " 'Ourselves. . . .' But what could she know about ourselves? The Elizabethans, yes; the Victorians, perhaps; but ourselves; sitting here on a June day in 1939—it was ridiculous" (178–79). They wait, they fidget, but nothing happens. "Miss La Trobe stood there with her eye on her script. 'After Vic.,' she had written, 'try ten mins. of present time. Swallows, cows, etc.' She wanted to expose them, as it were, to douche them, with present-time reality. But something was going wrong with the experiment. 'Reality too strong,' she muttered" (179). Then, as though to give tangibility to the elusive present moment, nature again provides what art fails to give alone: ". . . the shower fell, sudden, profuse. No one had seen the cloud coming. There it was, black, swollen, on top of them. Down it poured like all the people in the world weeping. Tears. Tears. Tears. . . . The rain was sudden and universal. Then it stopped. From the grass rose a fresh earthy smell" (180). Each age springs fresh and green from the death of the one before, and so the present grows out of the past.

Having let the rain point out the fact that sorrow leads to joy, effort to vision, the play states the same message in symbol. " 'With the very limited means at her disposal,' " writes a reporter assigned to cover the fête, " 'Miss La Trobe conveyed to the audience Civilization (the wall) in ruins; rebuilt (witness man with hod) by human effort; witness also woman handing bricks' " (181). This, then, is the pattern, but it is not always recognizable amid the turmoil of present time. To make this threat of confusion clear, the music suddenly stops, changes, snaps, breaks, and seems to represent the young who "shiver into splinters the old vision; smash to atoms what was whole" (183). Then out of the bushes comes a flock of children, holding up bits of mirror and old tin cans, "Anything that's bright enough to reflect, presumably, ourselves" (183), while the rest of the characters appear and recite scraps and fragments of their earlier lines, creating an atmosphere of disorder and confusion. "The hands of the clock had stopped at the present moment. It was now. Ourselves" (186).

So the play proper ends; but before the audience can disperse, feeling disoriented and confused, "a megaphonic, anonymous, loud-speaking affirmation" (186) asserts itself—an unknown voice that presents the meaning of the present, saying, "*Look at ourselves, ladies and gentlemen! Then at the wall; and ask how's this wall, the great wall, which we call, perhaps miscall, civilization, to be built by* (here the mirrors flicked and flashed) *orts, scraps and fragments like ourselves?*" (188). Yet, says the voice, there is some hint of love, of kindness, of beauty, of refusal to give up the vision. "*There is such a thing—you can't deny it. What? You can't descry it? All you can see of yourselves is scraps, orts and fragments? Well then listen to the gramophone affirming . . .*" (188). The music speaks:

Like quicksilver sliding, filings magnetized, the distracted united. The tune began; the first note meant a second; the second a third. Then down beneath a force was born in opposition; then another. On different levels they diverged. On different levels ourselves went forward; flower gathering some on the surface; others descending to wrestle with the meaning; but all comprehending; all enlisted. The whole population of the mind's immeasurable profundity came flocking; from the unprotected, the unskinned; and dawn rose; and azure; from chaos and cacophony measure; but not the melody of surface sound alone controlled it; but also the warring battle-plumed warriors straining asunder: To part? No. Compelled from the ends of the horizon; recalled from the edge of appalling crevasses; they crashed; solved; united (189).

Here is Virginia Woolf's moment of greatest affirmation and unity, a moment when all efforts, factual and visionary, come together to create the infinite, indestructible pattern. The most fragmented, most threatened, most doubt-torn members of the audience have, for an instant, seen the thread that unites all time, all people. And the reader too, as part of the audience, has experienced the revelation.

To those in the audience for whom religion is no longer meaningful, the sight of the Reverend Streatfield "surreptitiously mounting a soap-box" (189), like the fluttering about of "Old Flimsy" Swithin before the pageant, may seem ridiculous. But he, as spokesman for Lucy's form of vision, is best equipped to summarize the message of the pageant, to put into words the subtle meaning of the music. After all, as has been noted before, this pageant was written for the illumination of the church. Humbly, recognizing that he can only constrict the significance of the play by putting it into words, the good man says,

> "We were shown, unless I mistake, the effort renewed.
> A few were chosen; the many passed in the background.
> That surely we were shown. But again, were we not
> given to understand—am I too presumptuous? Am I
> treading, like angels, where as a fool I should absent
> myself? To me at least it was indicated that we are members
> of one another. Each is part of the whole. Yes, that occurred
> to me, sitting among you in the audience. Did I not
> perceive Mr. Hardcastle here ... [one of the "Victorians"]
> at one time a Viking? And in Lady Harridan—excuse
> me, if I get the names wrong—a Canterbury pilgrim?
> We act different parts; but are the same" (191–92).

What he says is true. He notices accurately also that nature played a part in the pageant, and that the attention of the audience was sometimes distracted, just as people are often distracted from intensive pursuit of life. As he pauses to ask for donations for the church, such an interruption occurs as a formation of airplanes drones overhead and drowns out his speech with the sound of war, suggesting that though his vision may survive, the church in which it is embodied may be forced to take on another, more contemporary form. Then, as he fumbles for a proper ending to his speech, the music finally assists him and sings out: *"Dispersed are we; who have come together. But,* the gramophone asserted, *let us retain whatever made that harmony"* (196).

Now the audience scatters, each person resuming his own role in the repeated pattern of life. As they go their separate ways, they keep with them the question that the play has raised, while Miss La Trobe contemplates her next attempt at vision-making: " 'I should group them,' she murmured, 'here.' It would be midnight; there would be two figures, half concealed by a rock. The curtain would rise. What would the first words be? The words escaped her" (210). The cycle of life is ready to repeat itself. Evening comes; Lucy returns to her Outline of History; and Giles and Isa begin to thrash out their differences in order to achieve unity on their own small scale through love. "Left alone together for the first time that day, they were silent. Alone, enmity was bared; also love. Before they slept, they must fight; after they had fought, they would embrace. From that embrace another life might be born. . . . Then the curtain rose. They spoke" (219). So Giles and Isa, as representatives of modern fact and vision, achieve a moment of reconciliation that keeps the continuity alive. In their union, they become the two figures for Miss La Trobe's next play; for art must take its form from life, building and rebuilding the vision.

In many ways, Virginia Woolf's study of fact and vision culminates in *Between the Acts*. Pointz Hall, the pageant, and the Olivers themselves reflect on different scales the endless repeating pattern of man's search for unity throughout the whole of human history. Love, beauty, art, and faith have been revealed as the unchanging forces that reconcile men's differences and keep the vision alive in a world that is ever threatened by war, disease, and death.

In *The Voyage Out* Virginia Woolf showed the pattern at work in a single life as she followed Rachel Vinrace's awakening to selfhood, joining another in love, and finally finding complete unity with those around her in death. *Night and Day* was the first attempt at reconciling this sense of oneness with the chaotic fragmentation of society. Katharine and Ralph, both in their love and in their self-awareness, were meant to combine both worlds. In *Jacob's Room* Virginia Woolf made her last essay at bringing the opposing sides of life, the finite and infinite, into one person. The result was not entirely successful. So in *Mrs. Dalloway* she began to dissect her theories, assign each attitude toward life a separate character, and watch the interaction create its own subtle social pattern. *To the Lighthouse* continued this refining process, taking the polar worlds away from the distractions of society and testing the artistic and personal visions in the fires of death and time. Then in *The Waves,* another book divorced from the ordinary flow of life, Virginia Woolf completed her examination of the pattern, tracing six views of reality from childhood to old age, and showing how human existence comprises flashes of vision achieved through long periods of effort. *The Years* once again returned the theory to the practical world in which the bulk of life is disappointment and the underlying unity revealed only to those who have survived the winds of isolation and restriction. *Between the Acts,* Virginia Woolf's final effort, is shadowed by the doubtful future of war and pain and so includes the menacing reality of *The Years.* But in its repetition and constant suggestion of continuity, it intimates that the pattern will never be destroyed and that even the most disparate lives, the most ominous clouds of the future, will be absorbed into the infinite, the visionary whole.

Earlier Criticism of Virginia Woolf

THE body of Virginia Woolf's fiction, like a large country manor house with its many wings and gardens, balconies and terraces, presents a unified but complex view to any one approaching, canvas and brushes in hand, to paint a true and accurate portrait of the whole. Set one's easel where one will, one is sure to miss some important ell jutting out behind; or attempt to note everything in one room, and whole floors, whole formal gardens, cry out to be included. One may well sympathize with Mrs. Hilbery who grew confused, wandering through the rooms of *Mrs. Dalloway.* "There were so many doors, such unexpected places, she could not find her way."[1] Critics have long recognized the complexity of Mrs. Woolf's novels, and everyone who has approached her work has been forced to choose a door: no one can hope to "sum up" and include everything.

Trying to take in as much as possible of the outer structure, some critics have settled for an aerial view, placing her work in the larger landscape of her age or her country. R. L. Chambers, for example, looks at her as, par excellence, the novelist of the 1920s,[2] treating her work as representative of an age. J. K. Johnstone[3] and Irma Rantavaara[4] approach her through her inner circle, showing how the theories and philosophies of her family and friends are transferred to or transmuted in her novels. Biography is another outer gateway that Aileen Pippett uses widely in her criticism.[5] Of course such external approaches, valuable as they are, often exclude much of the delicate inner workings of her novels, but each attempt reveals some angle others are forced to neglect.

At the opposite pole from those who view Virginia Woolf's work in the light of her social setting are those who treat her purely aesthetically, concentrating on the architectural nuances of her novels, the style or structure, rather than on theme or social significance. These critics may be subdivided into two schools. The first, more common in the early years of Woolf criticism, tends to use terms such as "highbrow," "aesthete," or "impressionist" to describe her art; and more often than not these terms have negative connotations, implying a lack of theme, of social impact, of a realistic world view in her novels. Lord David Cecil, who sees Virginia Woolf's theme as "the fact of beauty on the one hand, the fact of mutability on the other,"[6] is one of the few early "aesthetic" critics who praises her. Wyndham Lewis's is a prime example of the more common negative criticism,[7] and Philip Henderson[8] and William C. Frierson[9] march to the same drummer. Arnold Kettle, too, criticizes Virginia Woolf for her "overriding concern with texture and form";[10] and Leon Edel, under her poetic prose, finds ideas that are "rather thin and unoriginal,"[11] but these men are not representative of the newer stylistic approach to Virginia Woolf that sees her style as the key to her theme, not as an end in itself. In this second school one finds such critics as N. C. Thakur[12] who gives microscopic but slightly myopic attention to Virginia Woolf's use of symbol, or Lotus A. Snow who concerns herself with "the contribution of imagery to the structure of Virginia Woolf's novels."[13] Robert Humphrey approaches Virginia Woolf's emphasis on "inner realization of truth"[14] through her stream of consciousness technique; and Erich Auerbach, studying one scene from *To the Lighthouse* in detail, finds the key to her presentation of reality in her style.[15]

There are those, then, who approach her work through her age or social environment and those who examine one representative aspect of its style; but the method most commonly used by the critics is to focus on some central theme and concentrate on her novels from that point of view. The most comprehensive of these critics is Jean Guiguet,[16] who attempts to include in his study a vast number of themes and stylistic techniques, covering in review all those who have come before him and leaving it to those who follow to elaborate on his work. One popular door to Virginia Woolf's novels, mentioned by Guiguet but used more extensively by others before and after him, is what one might term the "temporal" door. Floris Delattre, who was the first to take this approach,[17] treats her primarily as a Bergsonian, looking at other themes in the light of *durée*. J. W. Graham,[18] who is also interested in Virginia Woolf's sense of time, attacks those who give undue emphasis to the influence of Bergson and develops his own ideas of her approach to the temporal theme. And if there are those who enter Virginia Woolf's world through the door of time, there is at least one major critic who emphasizes the spatial aspect of her work. Dorothy Brewster, as the title of her book would suggest, is concerned with the importance of the outer world in Virginia Woolf's novels. For her, the central theme in all the novels is "the interaction of the organism with the environment,"[19] and the need "to bring inner and outer into harmony."[20]

Not surprisingly, considering Virginia Woolf's own interest in the feminine plight as expressed in *A Room of One's Own* and *Three Guineas,* several critics have approached her work from the feminist viewpoint. Ruth Gruber stresses her feminine style and notes "the implicit peculiar vision of her sex";[21] while Herbert Marder's intelligent *Feminism and Art* looks closely, primarily on a social level, at her view of the fragmentation of the modern world and the need to combine masculine intellect and feminine intuition in some form of reconciliation.[22]

Maxime Chastaing and Harvena Richter both focus on perception as the key to Virginia Woolf's novels. The former sees the gathering and communicating of perceptions[23] as Woolf's central concern, while the latter looks at the Woolfian world as "subsumed in the 'projections' of the viewer,"[24] a subjective world that defines reality as the emotional life.

Joan Bennett, too, sees emotional experience as important in the novels. As she puts it: "It is clear that it is not the width and variety of the human comedy, nor the idiosyncrasies of human character, that most interest her. Rather it is the deep and simple human experiences, love, happiness, beauty, loneliness, death."[25] Another critic who approaches Virginia Woolf through the various aspects of perception is Ralph Freedman who sees a gradual growth in her work toward a "formal rendering of consciousness."[26]

If these critics enter Virginia Woolf's novels through the perception or consciousness of her characters, others concentrate on the problems that these characters must face both in themselves and in the world around them. David Daiches defines Virginia Woolf's major theme as "the theme of time, death, and personality and the relations of these three to each other and to some ultimate which includes them all."[27] A. A. Mendilow looks at "temporal aspects of theme, form, and medium of the novel,"[28] and Margaret Church, in a similar approach, sees time and flux, or the search for permanence in change[29] as Virginia Woolf's theme.

To enter these novels through a double door such as flux versus permanence, or masculine versus feminine, is often an effective way to present a unified picture of her work; and many other critics have used a similar approach. Bernard Blackstone, for example, finds a series of counterpoints in her novels: life and death, the solitary mind and society, individual insight as opposed to predisposed patterns of ideas.[30] Jean O. Love discusses a dialectic between subjective thought and objective reality;[31] and James Hafley, among others, sees Virginia Woolf's main theme as the need for a blending of the social and inner worlds.[32] Virginia Woolf's novels lend themselves naturally to a dualistic approach, as the many polar problems I have noted would indicate, and a number of important insights into her work as a whole have been gained through this use of the double door. Yet, because of the complexity of her novels and in spite of the many inspired studies of her themes and style, much in her total volume of work is yet unstudied; and hidden rooms or less accessible views await the eyes of the diligent critic.

Notes

INTRODUCTION

1. *A Writer's Diary*, p. 179. For editions of Virginia Woolf's
books utilized as well as full references to other books and journals
mentioned see Bibliography of Works Consulted, pp. 263–74.
2. See Appendix for discussion of earlier criticism of Virginia
Woolf's fiction.
3. *Principia Ethica*, p. 110.
4. Ibid., pp. 206–7.
5. Ibid., p. 116.
6. Ibid., p. 188.
7. *The Common Reader*, p. 343.
8. *A Writer's Diary*, p. 137.
9. *A Room of One's Own*, pp. 113–14.
10. *Collected Essays*, 1:346.
11. Because Virginia Woolf herself looked upon *Orlando* as "too
long for a joke, and too frivolous for a serious book" (*A Writer's
Diary*, p. 123), and because the work is formally so unlike her other
fiction, I am not treating it as a novel and shall not include a discussion of it here.

CHAPTER 1. THE VOYAGE OUT

1. *Virginia Woolf and her Works*, p. 195.
2. Ibid., pp. 199–200.
3. *The Voyage Out*, p. 150. All other references to the novel in
this chapter will be found in parentheses at the end of each quotation.
4. *The Glass Roof: Virginia Woolf as Novelist*, p. 16.
5. Ibid., p. 17.
6. Ibid.

7. *The Free Spirit: A Study of Humanism in the Novels of George Eliot, Henry James, E. M. Forster, Virginia Woolf, Angus Wilson*, p. 103.

8. *The Novel and the World's Dilemma*, p. 7.

9. Guiguet, p. 202.

10. *Le roman psychologique de Virginia Woolf*, p. 81.

11. *Stream of Consciousness: A Study in Literary Method*, p. 188.

12. Ibid.

13. Guiguet, pp. 200–201.

14. P. 12.

15. *The Common Reader*, p. 60.

16. *Virginia Woolf: A Commentary*, pp. 24–25.

17. *Virginia Woolf and Lytton Strachey: Letters*, p. 84.

CHAPTER 2. NIGHT AND DAY

1. *The Novel and the Modern World*, p. 19.

2. *Virginia Woolf and Bloomsbury*, p. 90.

3. *Virginia Woolf's London*, p. 30.

4. *The Free Sprit: A Study of Humanism in the Novels of George Eliot, Henry James, E. M. Forster, Virginia Woolf, Angus Wilson*, p. 104.

5. *The Glass Roof: Virginia Woolf as Novelist*, p. 28.

6. *Virginia Woolf and Her Works*, p. 208.

7. *Virginia Woolf: A Commentary*, p. 43.

8. Ibid., p. 44.

9. *The Bloomsbury Group: A Study of E. M. Forster, Lytton Strachey, Virginia Woolf, and Their Circle*, p. 146.

10. *Virginia Woolf: The Inward Voyage*, p. 122.

11. Hafley, p. 33.

12. Charles G. Hoffman, "From Lunch to Dinner: Virginia Woolf's Apprenticeship," pp. 609–27.

13. *Feminism and Art: A Study of Virginia Woolf*, p. 35.

14. Ibid.

15. *Night and Day*, p. 39. All other references to the novel in this chapter will be found in parentheses at the end of each quotation.

16. Marder, p. 131.

17. Ibid., p. 35.

CHAPTER 3. JACOB'S ROOM

1. *Virginia Woolf*, p. 106.

2. "From Lunch to Dinner: Virginia Woolf's Apprenticeship," pp. 609–27.

3. *Virginia Woolf*, p. 17.

4. *The Glass Roof: Virginia Woolf as Novelist*, p. 54.

5. *The Novel and the Modern World*, p. 262.

6. "Virginia Woolf: The Poetic Method," pp. 53–63.

7. *Le roman psychologique de Virginia Woolf*, p. 95.

8. *The Lyrical Novel: Studies in Hermann Hesse, André Gide, and Virginia Woolf*, p. 208.

9. *Virginia Woolf and Her Works*, p. 223.

10. *Virginia Woolf*, p. 135.

11. Moody, p. 16.

12. *Stream of Consciousness: A Study in Literary Method*, p. 190.

13. *The Bloomsbury Group: A Study of E. M. Forster, Lytton Strachey, Virginia Woolf, and Their Circle*, p. 334.

14. *Jacob's Room*, p. 95. All other references to the novel in this chapter will be found in parentheses at the end of each quotation.

15. *Virginia Woolf: A Commentary*, p. 67.

CHAPTER 4. MRS. DALLOWAY

1. *A Writer's Diary*, p. 63.

2. *The Twentieth Century Novel: Studies in Technique*, p. 131.

3. D. S. Savage, *The Withered Branch: Six Studies in the Modern Novel*, p. 82.

4. A. D. Moody, *Virginia Woolf*, p. 26.

5. David Garnett, "Virginia Woolf," pp. 371–86.

6. *Virginia Woolf: The Inward Voyage*, p. 112.

7. *The Lyrical Novel: Studies in Hermann Hesse, André Gide, and Virginia Woolf*, p. 216.

8. *Virginia Woolf: A Commentary*, pp. 74–76.

9. *Virginia Woolf*.

10. *Virginia Woolf and Her Works*, p. 235.

11. *A Writer's Diary*, p. 20.

12. *Mrs. Dalloway*, p. 150. All other references to the novel in this chapter will be found in parentheses at the end of each quotation.

13. *The Novel and the Modern World*, p. 209.

14. *The Symbolic Rose*, p. 127.

15. Reuben Arthur Brower, *The Fields of Light: An Experiment in Critical Reading*, p. 130.

16. James Hafley, *The Glass Roof: Virginia Woolf as Novelist,* p. 66.

17. Garnett, p. 382.

18. P. 110.

19. P. 61.

20. Guiguet, p. 236.

CHAPTER 5. TO THE LIGHTHOUSE

1. *A Writer's Diary,* p. 80.

2. Ibid., p. 83.

3. One of the most thorough studies of *To the Lighthouse,* emphasizing Virginia Woolf's use of point-of-view as a tool to explore "the quality and complexity of human relationships" (p. 63) is Mitchell A. Leaska's *Virginia Woolf's Lighthouse: A Study in Critical Method.* Another recent study, showing great insight into Virginia Woolf's presentation of perception as well as into her philosophical interests, is S. P. Rosenbaum's "The Philosophical Realism of Virginia Woolf."

4. *Feminism and Art: A Study of Virginia Woolf,* p. 53.

5. *The Glass Roof: Virginia Woolf as Novelist,* p. 81.

6. Ibid., p. 82.

7. "The Waters of Annihilation: Double Vision in *To the Lighthouse,"* pp. 61–79.

8. "Time in the Novels of Virginia Woolf," pp. 186–201.

9. *To the Lighthouse,* p. 10. All other references to the novel in this chapter will be found in parentheses at the end of each quotation.

10. "Vision in *To the Lighthouse,"* pp. 585–600.

11. "The Lighthouse, Face to Face," pp. 107–23.

12. A. D. Moody recognizes the importance of this admission when he says, "Mrs. Ramsey's final triumph in life had been to acknowledge the truth of her husband's facts, and to make the acknowledgement an expression of love, so that their differences were resolved" (*Virginia Woolf,* p. 40).

13. *Collected Essays,* 2:33.

14. John M. Warner sees Mr. Carmichael as an example of someone who "lives in subjective reality, so we never see inside him" (Symbolic Patterns of Retreat and Reconciliation in *To the Lighthouse,"* pp. 376–92).

15. Herbert Marder also comments on this power of the home (*Feminism and Art: A Study of Virginia Woolf,* p. 45).

16. Several critics have assigned symbolic meanings to colors in Virginia Woolf's novels. Green is interpreted by David Daiches as impersonality (*Virginia Woolf*, p. 88) and by Maxime Chastaing as generosity *(La philosophie de Virginia Woolf,* p. 18).

17. *Virginia Woolf and Her Works,* p. 252.

18. *Virginia Woolf: Her Art as a Novelist,* p. 105.

19. Ibid.

20. Hafley, p. 85.

21. Peter Burra, "Virginia Woolf," pp. 112–35.

22. Bennett, p. 103.

23. Two critics in particular take this stand (Joseph L. Blotner, "Mythic Patterns in *To the Lighthouse,*" pp. 547-62, and Lotus A. Snow, "Imagery in Virginia Woolf's Novels," p. 65).

24. *The Literary Symbol,* p. 160.

25. *Time and Reality: Studies in Contemporary Fiction,* pp. 85–86.

26. "*To the Lighthouse:* Symbol and Vision," pp. 328–46.

27. *The Free Spirit: A Study of Humanism in the Novels of George Eliot, Henry James, E. M. Forster, Virginia Woolf, Angus Wilson,* p. 112.

28. Daiches, p. 86.

29. A. D. Moody confines the artist's achievement to the preserving of the visionary rather than the creation of vision (p. 9).

30. "*To the Lighthouse:* Symbol and Vision."

CHAPTER 6. THE WAVES

1. *A Writer's Diary,* p. 134.

2. Ibid., p. 105.

3. Ibid., p. 136.

4. *The Novel and the Modern World,* p. 215.

5. *The Glass Roof: Virginia Woolf as Novelist,* p. 108.

6. *Virginia Woolf,* p. 187.

7. *Virginia Woolf,* p. 54.

8. *Worlds in Consciousness: Mythopoetic Thought in the Novels of Virginia Woolf,* p. 209.

9. *Virginia Woolf: A Commentary,* p. 166.

10. *Virginia Woolf: The Inward Voyage,* p. 120.

11. *Virginia Woolf,* p. 126.

12. *The Moth and the Star,* p. 292.

13. *Virginia Woolf and Her Works,* pp. 286–87.

14. "Time in the Novels of Virginia Woolf," pp. 186–201.

15. "The Eclipse of Order: The Ironic Structure of *The Waves*," pp. 209–18.

16. *Virginia Woolf: Her Art as a Novelist*, p. 90.

17. "Notes on the Style of Mrs. Woolf," pp. 33–39.

18. "Bateau-Ivre: The Symbol of the Sea in Virginia Woolf's *The Waves*," pp. 9–17.

19. Hafley, p. 112.

20. *The Waves*, p. 179. All other references to the novel in this chapter will be found in parentheses at the end of each quotation.

21. Richter, p. 121.

22. Pippett, p. 292.

23. *La philosophie de Virginia Woolf*, p. 168.

24. Hafley, p. 107.

25. *The Lyrical Novel: Studies in Hermann Hesse, André Gide, and Virginia Woolf*, p. 246.

26. *Le roman psychologique de Virginia Woolf*, p. 195.

27. "Imagery in Virginia Woolf's Novels," p. 85.

28. Blackstone, p. 172.

29. Alice Fox Kornbluth also points out that this poem reflects Louis's anonymity ("A Suicidal Ending in Virginia Woolf," p. 82).

Chapter 7. The Years

1. *A Writer's Diary*, p. 179.

2. Ibid., p. 186.

3. *Virginia Woolf*, p. 71.

4. *Virginia Woolf*, p. 17.

5. *The Glass Roof: Virginia Woolf as Novelist*, p. 132.

6. Ibid., p. 133.

7. *Feminism and Art: A Study of Virginia Woolf*, p. 27.

8. *Virginia Woolf*, p. 146.

9. *Virginia Woolf*, p. 34.

10. *Time and Reality: Studies in Contemporary Fiction*, p. 75.

11. *Virginia Woolf*, p. 112.

12. *Virginia Woolf and Her Works*, p. 311.

13. Marder, p. 172.

14. *Virginia Woolf: A Commentary*, p. 205.

15. *The Years*, p. 7. All other references to the novel in this chapter will be found in parentheses at the end of each quotation.

16. *Collected Essays*, 2:25.

Chapter 8. Between the Acts

1. *A Writer's Diary,* p. 331.
2. "Between the Acts," pp. 87–94.
3. *Virginia Woolf,* p. 123.
4. *Virginia Woolf: A Commentary,* p. 235.
5. *The Bloomsbury Group,* p. 372.
6. *Virginia Woolf and Her Works,* p. 326.
7. *Stream of Consciousness: A Study in Literary Method,* p. 190.
8. *Virginia Woolf,* p. 84.
9. *Virginia Woolf: Her Art as a Novelist,* p. 113.
10. "Time in the Novels of Virginia Woolf," p. 186–201.
11. Ibid.
12. "The Pageant in *Between the Acts,*" pp. 31–35.
13. "A Principle of Unity in *Between the Acts,*" pp. 53–63.
14. *A Writer's Diary,* pp. 268–69.
15. John Graham recognizes these symbolic roles of the Olivers when he sees Bart as reason, Lucy as faith, Giles as creative action, and Isa as creative vision ("Time in the Novels of Virginia Woolf," pp. 186–201).
16. *Between the Acts,* p. 100. All other references to the novel in this chapter will be found in parentheses at the end of each quotation.
17. *Time and Reality: Studies in Contemporary Fiction,* p. 72.
18. *Worlds in Consciousness: Mythopoetic Thought in the Novels of Virginia Woolf,* p. 237.
19. *The Glass Roof: Virginia Woolf as Novelist,* p. 182.
20. *Collected Essays,* 2:293.

Appendix: Earlier Criticism of Virginia Woolf

1. *Mrs. Dalloway,* p. 291.
2. *The Novels of Virginia Woolf.*
3. *The Bloomsbury Group.*
4. *Virginia Woolf and Bloomsbury.*
5. *The Moth and the Star.*
6. *Poets and Storytellers,* p. 165.
7. *Men without Art.*
8. *The Novel Today: Studies in Contemporary Attitudes.*
9. *The English Novel in Transition.*

10. *An Introduction to the English Novel,* 2:102.

11. *The Modern Psychological Novel,* p. 129.

12. *The Symbolism of Virginia Woolf.*

13. "Imagery in Virginia Woolf's Novels," p. 7.

14. *Stream of Consciousness in the Modern Novel,* p. 12.

15. *Mimesis: The Representation of Reality in Western Literature.*

16. *Virginia Woolf and Her Works.*

17. *Le roman psychologique de Virginia Woolf.*

18. "Time in the Novels of Virginia Woolf," pp. 186–201.

19. *Virginia Woolf's London,* p. 80.

20. *Virginia Woolf,* p. 30.

21. *Virginia Woolf: A Study,* p. 3.

22. *Feminism and Art: A Study of Virginia Woolf.*

23. *La philosophie de Virginia Woolf.*

24. *Virginia Woolf: The Inward Voyage,* p. viii.

25. *Virginia Woolf: Her Art as a Novelist,* p. 3.

26. *The Lyrical Novel: Studies in Hermann Hesse, André Gide, and Virginia Woolf,* p. 290.

27. *The Novel and the Modern World,* p. 195.

28. *Time and the Novel,* p. 200.

29. *Time and Reality: Studies in Contemporary Fiction.*

30. *Virginia Woolf: A Commentary.*

31. *Worlds in Consciousness: Mythopoetic Thought in the Novels of Virginia Woolf.*

32. *The Glass Roof: Virginia Woolf as Novelist.*

Bibliography of Works Consulted

1. Books by Virginia Woolf

Between the Acts. New York: Harcourt, Brace, 1941.

Collected Essays. 4 vols. London: Hogarth Press, 1966–67.

The Common Reader. New York: Harcourt, Brace, Harvest Book, 1953.

A Haunted House and Other Short Stories. New York: Harcourt, Brace, Harvest Book, 1949.

Jacob's Room. In *Jacob's Room* and *The Waves.* New York: Harcourt, Brace, Harvest Book, 1959.

Mrs. Dalloway. New York: Harcourt, Brace, Harvest Book, 1953.

Night and Day. London: Hogarth Press, 1966.

Orlando. New York: Harcourt, Brace, 1928.

A Room of One's Own. New York: Harcourt, Brace, 1957.

The Second Common Reader. New York: Harcourt, Brace, 1932.

Three Guineas. London: Hogarth Press, 1938.

To the Lighthouse. New York: Harcourt, Brace, Harvest Book, 1955.

Virginia Woolf and Lytton Strachey: Letters, ed. Leonard Woolf and James Strachey. New York: Harcourt, Brace, 1956.

The Voyage Out. London: Hogarth Press, 1966.

The Waves. In *Jacob's Room* and *The Waves.* New York: Harcourt, Brace, Harvest Book, 1959.

A Writer's Diary, ed. Leonard Woolf. New York: Harcourt, Brace, 1954.

The Years. New York: Harcourt, Brace, 1937.

2. OTHER WORKS CONSULTED: BOOKS

Auerbach, Erich. *Mimesis: The Representation of Reality in Western Literature.* Garden City, N.Y.: Doubleday, Anchor Book, 1957.

Beach, Joseph Warren. *The Twentieth Century Novel: Studies in Technique.* New York: Appleton-Century-Crofts, 1932.

Bell, Quentin. *Virginia Woolf: A Biography.* New York: Harcourt, Brace, 1972.

Bennett, Joan. *Virginia Woolf: Her Art as a Novelist.* Cambridge: Cambridge University Press, 1964.

Blackstone, Bernard. *Virginia Woolf: A Commentary.* London: Hogarth Press, 1949.

Brewster, Dorothy. *Virginia Woolf.* New York: New York University Press, 1962.

———. *Virginia Woolf's London.* London: Allen & Unwin, 1959.

Brower, Reuben Arthur. *The Fields of Light: An Experiment in Critical Reading.* New York: Oxford University Press, 1951.

Burgum, Edwin Berry. *The Novel and the World's Dilemma.* New York: Russell & Russell, 1963.

Cecil, David. *Poets and Storytellers.* New York: Macmillan, 1949.

Chambers, R. L. *The Novels of Virginia Woolf.* Edinburgh: Oliver and Boyd, 1947.

Chastaing, Maxime. *La philosophie de Virginia Woolf.* Paris: Presses universitaires de France, 1951.

Church, Margaret. *Time and Reality: Studies in Contemporary Fiction.* Chapel Hill: University of North Carolina Press, 1963.

Cox, C. B. *The Free Spirit: A Study of Humanism in the Novels of George Eliot, Henry James, E. M. Forster, Virginia Woolf, Angus Wilson.* London: Oxford University Press, 1963.

Daiches, David. *The Novel and the Modern World.* Rev. ed. Chicago: University of Chicago Press, 1960.

————. *Virginia Woolf*. New York: New Directions, 1963.

Delattre, Floris. *Le roman psychologique de Virginia Woolf*. Paris: J. Vrin, 1932.

Edel, Leon. *The Modern Psychological Novel*. New York: Grosset & Dunlap, 1964.

Edgar, Pelham. *The Art of the Novel from 1700 to the Present Time*. New York: Macmillan, 1933.

Forster, E. M. *Virginia Woolf*. New York: Harcourt, Brace, 1942.

Freedman, Ralph. *The Lyrical Novel: Studies in Hermann Hesse, André Gide, and Virginia Woolf*. Princeton: Princeton University Press, 1963.

Friedman, Melvin. *Stream of Consciousness: A Study in Literary Method*. New Haven: Yale University Press, 1955.

Frierson, William C. *The English Novel in Transition*. Norman: University of Oklahoma Press, 1942.

Gruber, Ruth. *Virginia Woolf: A Study*. Bochum-Langendreer: Druck H. Pöppinghaus, 1934.

Guiguet, Jean. *Virginia Woolf and Her Works*, trans. Jean Stewart. New York: Harcourt, Brace, 1966.

Hafley, James. *The Glass Roof: Virginia Woolf as Novelist*. Berkeley: University of California Press, 1954.

Henderson, Philip. *The Novel Today: Studies in Contemporary Attitudes*. London: John Lane, 1936.

Holtby, Winifred. *Virginia Woolf*. London: Wishart & Co., 1932.

Johnstone, J. K. *The Bloomsbury Group: A Study of E. M. Forster, Lytton Strachey, Virginia Woolf, and Their Circle*. New York: Noonday Press, 1954.

Kettle, Arnold. *An Introduction to the English Novel*. 2 vols. London: Hutchinson's University Library, 1953.

Kornbluth, Alice Fox. "A Suicidal Ending in Virginia Woolf." Master's thesis, University of Tennessee, 1957.

Latham, Jacqueline E. M. *Critics on Virginia Woolf*. London: Allen and Unwin, 1970.

Leaska, Mitchell A. *Virginia Woolf's Lighthouse: A Study in Critical Method*. London: Columbia University Press, 1970.

Lewis, Wyndham. *Men without Art*. London: Cassell, 1934.

Love, Jean O. *Worlds in Consciousness: Mythopoetic Thought in the Novels of Virginia Woolf.* Berkeley: University of California Press, 1970.

Mansfield, Katherine. *Novels and Novelists.* New York: Knopf, 1930.

Marder, Herbert. *Feminism and Art: A Study of Virginia Woolf.* Chicago: University of Chicago Press, 1968.

Mendilow, A. A. *Time and the Novel.* New York: Humanities Press, 1965.

Moody, A. D. *Virginia Woolf.* Edinburgh: Oliver and Boyd, 1963.

Moore, George Edward. *Principia Ethica.* Cambridge: Cambridge University Press, 1922.

Muir, Edwin. *Transition: Essays in Contemporary Literature.* New York: Viking Press, 1926.

Muller, Herbert J. *Modern Fiction: A Study of Values.* New York: Funk & Wagnalls, 1937.

O'Faolain, Sean. *The Vanishing Hero: Studies in Novelists of the Twenties.* London: Eyre & Spottiswoode, 1956.

Pippett, Aileen. *The Moth and the Star: A Biography of Virginia Woolf.* Boston: Little, Brown, 1953.

Rantavaara, Irma. *Virginia Woolf and Bloomsbury.* Helsinki, 1953.

———. *Virginia Woolf's "The Waves."* Helsinki, 1960.

Richter, Harvena. *Virginia Woolf: The Inward Voyage.* Princeton: Princeton University Press, 1970.

Savage, D. S. *The Withered Branch: Six Studies in the Modern Novel.* London: Eyre & Spottiswoode, 1950.

Schaefer, Josephine O'Brien. *The Three-fold Nature of Reality in the Novels of Virginia Woolf.* The Hague: Mouton, 1965.

Seward, Barbara. *The Symbolic Rose.* New York: Columbia University Press, 1960.

Snow, Lotus A. "Imagery in Virginia Woolf's Novels." Ph.D. dissertation, University of Chicago, 1948.

Sprague, Claire, comp. *Virginia Woolf: A Collection of Critical Essays.* Englewood Cliffs: Prentice-Hall, 1971.

Thakur, N. C. *The Symbolism of Virginia Woolf*. London: Oxford University Press, 1965.

Tindall, William York. *The Literary Symbol*. New York: Columbia University Press, 1955.

Woodring, Carl. *Virginia Woolf*. New York: Columbia University Press, 1966.

Woolf, Leonard. *Beginning Again: An Autobiography of the Years 1911–1918*. London: Hogarth Press, 1964.

———. *Downhill All the Way: An Autobiography of the Years 1919–1939*. London: Hogarth Press, 1963.

———. *Growing: An Autobiography of the Years 1904–1911*. London: Hogarth Press, 1961.

———. *The Journey Not the Arrival Matters: An Autobiography of the Years 1939–1969*. New York: Harcourt, Brace, 1969.

———. *Sowing: An Autobiography of the Years 1880–1904*. New York: Harcourt, Brace, 1960.

3. Other Works Consulted: Articles

Aiken, Conrad. "The Novel as a Work of Art," *Dial* 83 (July 1927) : 41–44.

Baldanza, Frank. "Clarissa Dalloway's 'Party Consciousness,' " *Modern Fiction Studies* 2 (February 1956) : 24–30.

———. "*Orlando* and the Sackvilles," *PMLA* 70 (1955) : 274–79.

———. "*To the Lighthouse* Again," *PMLA* 70 (1955) : 548–52.

———. "Virginia Woolf's 'Moments of Being,' " *Modern Fiction Studies* 2 (February 1956) : 78.

Basham, C. "*Between the Acts*," *Durham University Journal* 21 (December 1959) : 87–94.

Batchelor, J. B. "Feminism in Virginia Woolf," *English* 17 (1968) : 1–7.

Beach, Joseph Warren. "Virginia Woolf," *English Journal* 26 (October 1937) : 603–12.

Beja, Morris. "Matches Struck in the Dark: Virginia Woolf's

Moments of Vision," *Critical Quarterly* 6 (Summer 1964): 137–52.

Benjamin, Anna S. "Towards an Understanding of the Meaning of Virginia Woolf's *Mrs. Dalloway*," *Wisconsin Studies in Contemporary Literature* 6 (1965): 214–27.

Berman, Ronald. "L'univers Woolfien," *Sewanee Review* 72 (1964): 157–66.

Bevis, Dorothy. "*The Waves:* A Fusion of Symbol, Style, and Thought in Virginia Woolf," *Twentieth Century Literature* 2 (April 1956): 5–20.

Blotner, Joseph L. "Mythic Patterns in *To the Lighthouse*," *PMLA* 71 (1956): 547–62.

Borgal, Clément. "Virginia Woolf ou le point de vue de Sirius," *Critique* 158 (July 1960): 609–14.

Bowen, Elizabeth. "*Between the Acts*," *New Statesman and Nation* (19 July 1941): 63–64.

Boyd, Elizabeth F. "Luriana, Lurilie," *Notes and Queries,* n.s. 10 (October 1963): 380–81.

Bradbrook, M. C. "Notes on the Style of Mrs. Woolf," *Scrutiny* 1 (May 1932): 33–39.

Brogan, Howard O. "Science and Narrative Structure in Austen, Hardy, and Woolf," *Nineteenth Century Fiction* 11 (March 1957): 276–87.

Brooks, Benjamin G. "Virginia Woolf," *Nineteenth Century and After* 130 (December 1941): 334–40.

Brown, Robert Curtis. "Laurence Sterne and Virginia Woolf," *University of Kansas City Review* 26 (Winter 1959): 153–59.

Burra, Peter. "Virginia Woolf," *Nineteenth Century and After* 115 (January 1934): 112–25.

Church, Margaret. "Concepts of Time in Novels of Virginia Woolf and Aldous Huxley," *Modern Fiction Studies* 1 (May 1955): 19–24.

Cohn, Ruby. "Art in *To the Lighthouse*," *Modern Fiction Studies* 8 (1962): 127–36.

Cox, C. B. "The Solitude of Virginia Woolf," *Critical Quarterly* 1 (1959): 329–34.

Craven, Thomas Jervell. "Mr. Roger Fry and the Artistic Vision," *Dial* 71 (July 1921) : 101–6.

Delattre, Floris. "La durée bergsonienne dans le roman de Virginia Woolf," *Revue Anglo-Américaine* 2 (December 1931) : 97–108.

Derbyshire, S. H. "An Analysis of Mrs. Woolf's *To the Lighthouse*," *College English* 3 (January 1942) : 353–60.

Doner, Dean. "Virginia Woolf: The Service of Style," *Modern Fiction Studies* 2 (February 1956) : 1–12.

Eliot, T. S. "Virginia Woolf," *Horizon* 3 (May 1941) : 313–16.

Fairley, Margaret. "Symbols of Life," *Canadian Forum* 12 (January 1932) : 150–51.

Fishman, Solomon. "Virginia Woolf on the Novel," *Sewanee Review* 51 (1943) : 321–40.

Fortin, René E. "Sacramental Imagery in *Mrs. Dalloway*," *Renascence* 18 (Autumn 1965) : 23–31.

Francis, Herbert E., Jr. "Virginia Woolf and 'The Moment,'" *Emory University Quarterly* 16 (1960) : 139–51.

Franks, Gabriel. "Virginia Woolf and the Philosophy of G. E. Moore," *Personalist* 50 (1969) : 222–40.

Friedman, Norman. "The Waters of Annihilation: Double Vision in *To the Lighthouse*," *ELH* 22 (1955) : 61–79.

Fromm, Harold. "*To the Lighthouse:* Music and Sympathy," *English Miscellany* 19 (1968) : 181–95.

Gamble, Isabel. "The Secret Sharer in *Mrs. Dalloway*," *Accent* 16 (1956) : 235–51.

Garnett, David. "Virginia Woolf," *American Scholar* 34 (Summer 1965) : 371–86.

Gelfant, Blanche. "Love and Conversion in *Mrs. Dalloway*," *Criticism* 8 (Summer 1966) : 229–45.

German, Howard, and Sharon Kaehale. "The Dialectic of Time in *Orlando*," *College English* 24 (1962) : 35–41.

Goldman, Mark. "Virginia Woolf and the Critic as Reader," *PMLA* 80 (1965) : 275–84.

Graham, J. W. "A Negative Note on Bergson and Virginia Woolf," *Essays in Criticism* 6 (1956) : 70–74.

Graham, John. "Time in the Novels of Virginia Woolf,"

University of Toronto Quarterly 18 (January 1949) : 186–201.

Green, David Bonnell. "*Orlando* and the Sackvilles: Addendum," *PMLA* 71 (1956) : 268–69.

Hartley, Lodwick. "Of Time and Mrs. Woolf," *Sewanee Review* 47 (1939) : 235–41.

Hartman, Geoffrey H. "Virginia's Web," *Chicago Review* 14 (Spring 1961) : 20–32.

Havard-Williams, Peter and Margaret. "Bateau-Ivre: The Symbol of the Sea in Virginia Woolf's *The Waves*," *English Studies* 34 (1953): 9–17.

———. "Mystical Experience in Virginia Woolf's *The Waves*," *Essays in Criticism* 4 (1954) : 71–84.

———. "Perceptive Contemplation in the Work of Virginia Woolf," *English Studies* 35 (1954) : 97–116.

Herrick, Robert. "The Works of Mrs. Woolf," *Saturday Review of Literature* 8 (December 1931) : 346.

Hildick, Wallace. "In That Solitary Room," *Kenyon Review* 27 (Spring 1965) : 302–17.

Hoffman, Charles G. "From Lunch to Dinner: Virginia Woolf's Apprenticeship," *Texas Studies in Language and Literature* 10 (Winter 1969) : 609–27.

———. "From Short Story to Novel: The Manuscript Revisions of Virginia Woolf's *Mrs. Dalloway*," *Modern Fiction Studies* 14 (1968) : 171–86.

———. "The 'Real' Mrs. Dalloway," *University of Kansas City Review* 22 (Spring 1956) : 204–8.

———. "Virginia Woolf's Manuscript Revisions of *The Years*," *PMLA* 84 (1969) : 79–89.

———. "Woolf's *To the Lighthouse*," *Explicator* 10 (1951) : item 13.

Hollingsworth, Keith. "Freud and the Riddle of *Mrs. Dalloway*," *Studies in Honor of John Wilcox*, ed. A. Dayle (Detroit: Wayne State University Press, 1958) , pp. 239–50.

Hungerford, Edward A. " 'My Tunnelling Process': The Method of *Mrs. Dalloway*," *Modern Fiction Studies* 3 (Summer 1957) : 164–67.

Jones, E. B. C. "E. M. Forster and Virginia Woolf," *The English Novelists: A Survey of the Novels by Twenty Contemporary Novelists,* ed. Derek Verschoyle (London, 1936), pp. 259–76.

Kaehale, Sharon, and Howard German. "*To the Lighthouse:* Symbol and Vision," *Bucknell Review* 10 (1962) : 328–46.

Kelsey, Mary E. "Virginia Woolf and the She-Condition," *Sewanee Review* 39 (1931) : 425–44.

King, Merton P. "The Androgynous Mind and *The Waves,*" *University Review* 30 (Spring 1964) : 221–24.

————. "*The Waves* and the Androgynous Mind," *University Review* 30 (Winter 1963) : 128–34.

Kohler, Dayton. "Time in the Modern Novel," *College English* 10 (October 1948) : 15–24.

Kumar, Shiv K. "Memory in Virginia Woolf and Bergson," *University of Kansas City Review* 26 (Spring 1960) : 235–39.

————. "Virginia Woolf and Bergson's 'Mémoire Par Excellence,' " *English Studies* 41 (1960) : 313–18.

Latham, Jacqueline F. "The Model for Clarissa Dalloway—Kitty Maxse," *Notes and Queries* 16 (19 July 1969) : 262–63.

Leavis, F. R. "After *To the Lighthouse,*" *Scrutiny* 10 (January 1942) : 295–98.

Le Breton, Maurice. "Problème du moi et technique du roman chez Virginia Woolf," *Journal de Psychologie* (January-March 1947) , pp. 20–34.

Lehmann, John. "Working with Virginia Woolf," *Listener* 53 (January 1955) : 60–62.

Lorberg, Aileen D. "Virginia Woolf, Benevolent Satirist," *Personalist* 33 (1952) : 148–58.

Lund, Mary Graham. "The Androgynous Moment: Woolf and Eliot," *Renascence* 12 (Winter 1960) : 74–78.

McConnell, Frank D. " 'Death among the Apple Trees': *The Waves* and the World of Things," *Bucknell Review* 16 (1968) : 23–39.

McIntyre, Clara F. "Is Virginia Woolf a Feminist?" *Personalist* 41 (1960) : 176–84.

Marder, Herbert. "Beyond the Lighthouse: *The Years,*" *Bucknell Review* 15 (1967) : 61–70.

————. "Virginia Woolf's 'System That Did Not Shut Out,'" *Papers on Language and Literature* 4 (1968) : 106–11.

May, Keith M. "The Symbol of Painting in Virginia Woolf's *To the Lighthouse*," *Review of English Literature* 8 (1967) : 91–98.

Mayoux, J. J. "A propos d'*Orlando* de Virginia Woolf," *Europe* 22 (1930) : 117–22.

Mellers, W. H. "Virginia Woolf: The Last Phase," *Kenyon Review* 4 (Autumn 1942) : 381–87.

Mollach, Francis L. "Thematic and Structural Unity in *Mrs. Dalloway*," *Thoth* 5 (1964) : 62–73.

Moloney, Michael T. "The Enigma of Time: Proust, Virginia Woolf, and Faulkner," *Thought* 32 (1957) : 69–85.

Monroe, H. Elizabeth. "The Inception of Mrs. Woolf's Art," *College English* 2 (1940) : 217–30.

Muller, Herbert J. "Virginia Woolf and Feminine Fiction," *Saturday Review of Literature* 15 (6 February 1937) : 14, 16.

Overcarsh, F. L. "The Lighthouse, Face to Face," *Accent* 10 (Winter 1959) : 107–23.

Page, Alex. "A Dangerous Day: Mrs. Dalloway Discovers Her Double," *Modern Fiction Studies* 7 (Summer 1961) : 115–24.

Payne, Michael. "The Eclipse of Order: The Ironic Structure of *The Waves*," *Modern Fiction Studies* 15 (Summer 1969) : 585–600.

Pederson, Glenn. "Vision in *To the Lighthouse*," *PMLA* 73 (1958) : 585–600.

Plomer, William. "Virginia Woolf," *Horizon* 3 (May 1941) : 323–27.

Ramsay, Warren. "The Claims of Language: Virginia Woolf as Symbolist," *English Fiction in Transition* 4 (1961) : 12–17.

Rantavaara, Irma. " 'Ing'-forms in the Service of Rhythm and Style in Virginia Woolf's *The Waves*," *Neuphilologische Mitteilungen* 61 (1960) : 79–97.

————. "On Romantic Imagery in Virginia Woolf's *The Waves*, with Special Reference to Antithesis," *Neuphilologische Mitteilungen* 60 (1959) : 72–89.

Roberts, John H. "Toward Virginia Woolf," *Virginia Quarterly Review* 10 (October 1934) : 587–602.

———. "'Vision and Design' in Virginia Woolf," *PMLA* 61 (1946) : 835–47.

Roll-Hansen, Diderik. "Peter Walsh's Seven-League Boots: A Note on *Mrs. Dalloway*," *English Studies* 50 (1969) : 301–4.

Rosenbaum, S. P. "The Philosophical Realism of Virginia Woolf," in *English Literature and British Philosophy*, ed. S. P. Rosenbaum (Chicago: University of Chicago Press, 1971), pp. 316–56.

Rosenberg, Stuart. "The Match in the Crocus: Obstrusive Art in Virginia Woolf's *Mrs. Dalloway*," *Modern Fiction Studies* 23 (Summer 1967) : 211–20.

Russell, H. K. "Virginia Woolf's *To the Lighthouse*," *Explicator* 8 (March 1950) : item 38.

Sackville-West, Victoria. "Virginia Woolf and *Orlando*," *Listener* 53 (1955) : 157–58.

Samuelson, Ralph. "More Than One Room of Her Own: Virginia Woolf's Critical Dilemmas," *Western Humanities Review* 19 (Summer 1965) : 249–56.

Simon, Irene. "Some Aspects of Virginia Woolf's Imagery," *English Studies* 41 (1960) : 180–96.

Smart, J. A. E. "Virginia Woolf," *Dalhousie Review* 21 (April 1941) : 37–50.

Smith, J. Oates. "Henry James and Virginia Woolf: The Art of Relationships," *Twentieth Century Literature* 10 (October 1964) : 119–29.

Steinberg, Erwin R. "Freudian Symbolism and Communication," *Literature and Psychology* 3 (1953) : 2–5.

Summerhayes, Don. "Society, Morality, Analogy: Virginia Woolf's World Between the Acts," *Modern Fiction Studies* 9 (1963) : 329–37.

Tindall, William York. "Many-leveled Fiction: Virginia Woolf to Ross Lockridge," *College English* 10 (November 1948) : 65–71.

Toynbee, Philip. "Virginia Woolf: A Study of Three Experimental Novels," *Horizon* 14 (November 1946) : 290–304.

Troy, William. "Virginia Woolf: The Poetic Style," *Symposium* 3 (April 1932) : 153–66.

————. "Virginia Woolf: The Poetic Method," *Symposium* 3 (January 1932) : 53–63.

Turnell, Martin. "Virginia Woolf," *Horizon* 6 (July 1942) : 44–57.

Warner, John M. "Symbolic Patterns of Retreat and Reconciliation in *To the Lighthouse,*" *Discourse* 12 (Spring 1969) : 376–92.

Wilkerson, Ann Yanko. "A Principle of Unity in *Between the Acts,*" *Criticism* 8 (Winter 1966) : 53–63.

Wilson, James S. "Time and Virginia Woolf," *Virginia Quarterly Review* 18 (Spring 1942) : 267–76.

Wright, Nathalie. "*Mrs. Dalloway:* A Study in Composition," *College English* 5

Zorn, Marilyn. "The Pageant in *Between the Acts,*" *Modern Fiction Studies* 2 (February 1956) : 31–35.

Note: The following books are not mentioned in my text since they were issued while my book was in press.

Bazin, Nancy T. *Virginia Woolf and the Androgynous Vision.* New Brunswick, N.J.: Rutgers University Press, 1973.

Heilbrun, Carolyn G. *Toward a Recognition of Androgyny.* New York: Knopf, 1973.

McLaurin, Allen. *Virginia Woolf: The Echoes Enslaved.* Cambridge: Cambridge University Press, 1973.

Naremore, James. *The World Without a Self: Virginia Woolf and the Novel.* New Haven: Yale University Press, 1973.

Index

275